South Asian Buddhism

South Asian Buddhism presents a comprehensive historical survey of the full range of Buddhist traditions throughout South Asia from the beginnings of the religion up to the present. Starting with narratives on the Buddha's life and foundational teachings from ancient India, the book proceeds to discuss the rise of Buddhist monastic organizations and texts among the early Mainstream Buddhist schools. It considers the origins and development of Mahāyāna Buddhism in South Asia, surveys the development of Buddhist Tantra in South Asia and outlines developments in Buddhism as found in Sri Lanka and Nepal following the decline of the religion in India. Berkwitz also importantly considers the effects of colonialism and modernity on the revivals of Buddhism across South Asia in the nineteenth and twentieth centuries.

South Asian Buddhism offers a broad, yet detailed perspective on the history, culture, and thought of the various Buddhist traditions that developed in South Asia. Incorporating findings from the latest research on Buddhist texts and culture, this work provides a critical, historically based survey of South Asian Buddhism that will be useful for students, scholars, and general readers.

Stephen C. Berkwitz is Associate Professor of Religious Studies at Missouri State University, USA, and Editor of the Routledge Critical Studies in Buddhism Series. His publications include *The History of the Buddha's Relic Shrine: A Translation of the* Sinhala Thūpavaṃsa (2007).

South Asian Buddhism

A Survey

Stephen C. Berkwitz

Routledge
Taylor & Francis Group
LONDON AND NEW YORK

First published 2010
by Routledge
2 Park Square, Milton Park, Abingdon, Oxon OX14 4RN

Simultaneously published in the USA and Canada
by Routledge
270 Madison Ave, New York, NY 100016

Routledge is an imprint of the Taylor & Francis Group, an informa business

Typeset in Sabon by
HWA Text and Data Management, London
Printed and bound in Great Britain by
TJ International, Padstow, Cornwall

British Library Cataloguing in Publication Data
A catalogue record for this book is available from the British Library

Library of Congress Cataloging-in-Publication Data
Berkwitz, Stephen C., 1969-
South Asian Buddhism : a survey / Stephen C. Berkwitz.
p. cm.
Includes bibliographical references and index.
1. Buddhism--South Asia. I. Title.
BQ322.B47 2009
294.30954--dc22
2009000384

ISBN10: 0-415–45249–X (hbk)
ISBN10: 0-415–45248–1 (pbk)

ISBN13: 978-0-415–45249–6 (hbk)
ISBN13: 978-0-415–45248–9 (pbk)

Dedicated with love to my
precious daughter, Rashmi

Contents

Illustrations

Abbreviations

BCE Before the Common Era
CE Common Era
P Pāli
Skt. Sanskrit

Acknowledgments

Writing a one-volume survey of the history of South Asian Buddhism is an ambitious, perhaps even foolhardy, task. But I saw a need for such a text when I taught the Religions of India course as a visiting lecturer at the University of California, Riverside in 1997. I discovered then that there were no books that take a comprehensive view of Buddhism in South Asia. Other texts either focused primarily on Indian Buddhist philosophy, ended their surveys of Buddhism in India with its "disappearance" around the twelfth and thirteenth centuries, or squeezed a more limited treatment of South Asian traditions into a textbook on Buddhism as a whole. I could not find a book on the cultural history of Buddhism in South Asia in particular.

Ten years later, when I noted the enduring absence of such a text, I proposed the idea of writing a regional survey of South Asian Buddhism to Lesley Riddle of Routledge Press. She had already contracted a text on East Asian Buddhism, and thus she received my idea with enthusiasm. As it stands, *South Asian Buddhism: A Survey* presents a historically and regionally inclusive view of the various Buddhist traditions found in South Asia—including India, Sri Lanka, Nepal, Bhutan, Bangladesh and the ancient region of Gandhāra in parts of modern-day Pakistan and Afghanistan. The book is organized chronologically into six chapters. It begins with the historical Buddha, who lived around the fifth century BCE, and ends in the early twenty-first century CE. Given such a vast historical timeline, it has been necessary to make difficult choices on what to include and how much space can be given to any particular subject. It is inevitable that readers will disagree with some of my decisions. A glossary of selected terms and names follows the chapters. Finally, there is an appendix of numerical lists containing some Pāli and Sanskrit terms for easy reference. In the appendix and in the book as a whole, I have chosen to use both Pāli and Sanskrit terms since I believe that it would be useful for students to become familiar with the terminology from both languages.

My interest in writing a historical survey of South Asian Buddhism that could be useful to a broad audience of scholars, students, and general readers also pushed me to limit my critical reflections on the source materials. I have endeavored to make use of the latest scholarship in South Asian Buddhism. Nevertheless, there are sections wherein I had little choice but to rely on traditional Buddhist accounts. Adopting a tradition's own account of its origins is problematic but perhaps unavoidable until more critical scholarly research is completed. There is a difference of course between the normative ideals of scriptures and the historical realities they purport to represent. In some cases, however, we have few other options than to base our histories of Buddhism on material taken from Buddhist texts. In such cases, I believe we can employ such historical narratives as long as we remain skeptical of their actual facticity. To paraphrase Keith Jenkins, history is what we write about the past, but should never be confused with the past itself.

I am obliged to many people for their generous assistance in my efforts to write a survey that I hope will be interesting and useful. I am grateful to Lesley Riddle, Amy Grant, and everyone else at Routledge for their support in publishing this book. A number of colleagues agreed to read through various chapters of the manuscript and offered valuable advice and encouragement. I wish to thank these esteemed readers, namely Christoph Emmrich, Natalie Gummer, David McMahan, Susanne Mrozik, John S. Strong, Kevin Trainor, and Vesna Wallace. Several other people made helpful suggestions and offered more general advice and assistance. In this regard, I owe thanks to Dan Arnold, Daniel Boucher, Kate Crosby, Ronald Davidson, David Gray, Chris Haskett, Todd Lewis, and Vanessa Sasson. Needless to say, I alone should be held responsible for the errors or other shortcomings in the present text. I wish to thank the students in my Buddhism course at Missouri State University for offering helpful suggestions to improve selected chapters. Additionally, I am grateful to Gerald J. Larson for shaping how I think about teaching South Asian Buddhism. I must also thank Ivan Strenski for hiring me to teach the Religions of India course at UC-Riverside, where I first had the idea for this book.

I also wish to acknowledge the various sources from which the illustrations used in this book were obtained without charge. Jane Terry produced the map and charts with her impressive skills. Jens Braarvig and Hermes Academic Publishing kindly granted me permission to reproduce two images from *Buddhist Manuscripts in the Schøyen Collection*, vols. I and II (Oslo: 2000, 2002). Prince Roy allowed me to use his photo of the ruins at Nālandā. Imali Berkwitz took the photo of the Buddha image at Buduruwayaya in Northwest Sri Lanka. Dina Bangdel provided the photo of the Svayambhu Stūpa in Kathmandu. ABC-CLIO kindly allowed me to reproduce my photo of newly ordained Buddhist nuns in Sri Lanka, which appears in Stephen C. Berkwitz, ed., *Buddhism in World Cultures: Comparative Perspectives* (Santa Barbara, CA: 2006).

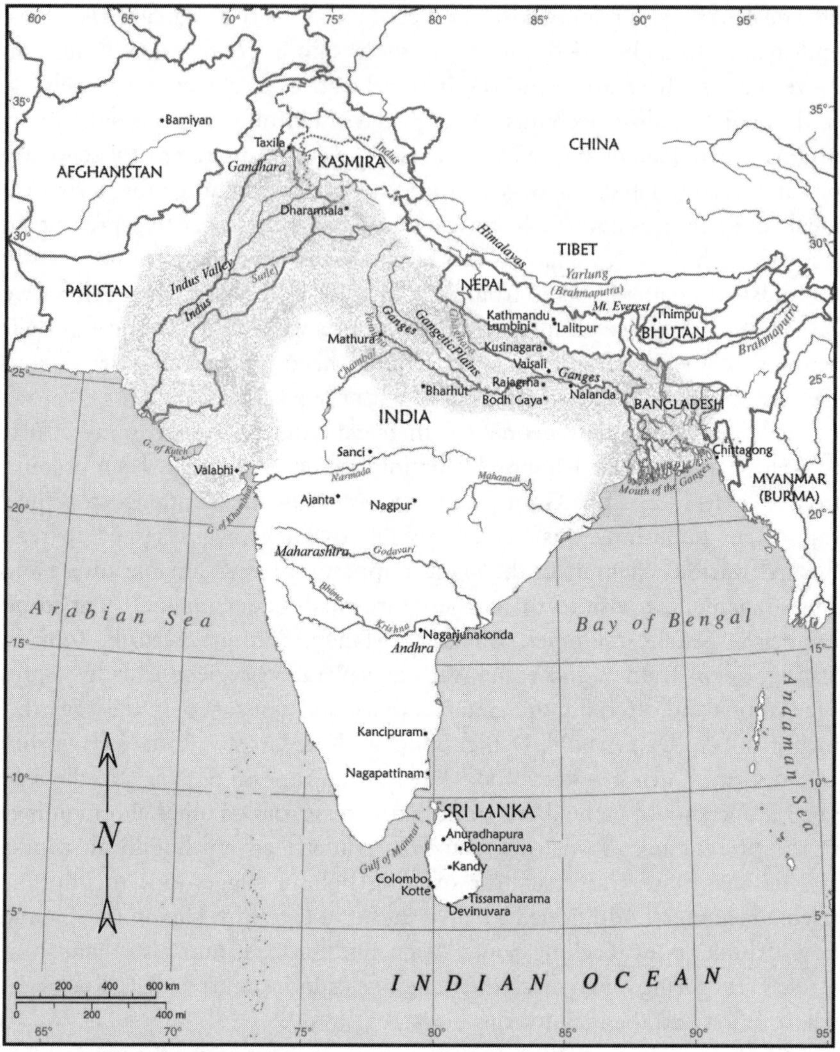

Map of South Asian Buddhist sites (created by Jane Terry)

1

Formations:

The Buddha and his Dharma

The world of the Buddha

The ancient Indic world in which Gautama Buddha lived and established the Buddhist path was characterized by dramatic social change. While various Buddhist traditions and scholars give different estimates about when the Buddha lived, recent scholarly opinion suggests he lived some time between the fifth and the fourth centuries BCE (Bechert 2004: 82). Some Buddhist traditions on the other hand have typically dated the Buddha around one to two hundred years earlier. Regardless of the uncertainty surrounding the dates of the Buddha's life, the historical context in which he lived appears clearer. Historians commonly speak of the era beginning around the sixth century BCE as a second wave of urbanization and the expansion of settlements around the Gangetic Plains in Northern India (Thapar 2002: 137–9). The first wave of urbanization in the Indian subcontinent is thought to have occurred much earlier when the ancient urban centers of Harappa and Mohenjo-daro arose in the Punjab and Sind regions in what scholars often call the Indus Valley Civilization around 2600 BCE. Archaeological evidence of fortified walls and urban planning in these sites speak to an ancient form of city living prior to the first recitations and compilations of

Vedic texts by (Indo-)Aryans. The decline of these prehistoric cities occurred around 1800 BCE for reasons not adequately understood.

The period roughly corresponding with between 1800 BCE and 600 BCE is often called the Vedic period of ancient Indian history. It is a period marked by the development of royal and priestly institutions based on the orally transmitted Sanskrit texts of the Hindu Veda. The Aryans who migrated into Northwest and Northern India during the second millennium BCE were nomads who traveled with livestock. Along with cattle, they brought with them certain cultural and religious forms that would prove to be determinative for the development of ancient Indian civilization. These forms included an archaic form of the Sanskrit language as exemplified in the oral scriptural collection called the Veda; a patrilineal, tripartite system of social organization organized around the roles performed by priests, warriors, and food-producers; an elaborate ritual system of sacrifices; and the worship of a pantheon of invisible deities (Larson 1995: 58). The priests, or *brāhmaṇa*s (anglicized as "Brahmins"), occupied an elite position in this early, village-based society, as they were the ones who recited and preserved the Sanskrit hymns that were uttered during the performance of sacrifices to the gods.

The Brahmins' ritual role was largely an exclusive one. Other members of this ancient Aryan society were deemed unqualified to perform the liturgical roles of the priests. The Brahmins were the ones who claimed the ability to consecrate kings with divine power. They conducted the ritual transactions between the gods in heaven and the humans on earth. And they placed themselves at the top of a social hierarchy that was endowed with the scriptural authority of Vedic creation myths, essentially claiming that the *varṇa* system of social classes in ancient India naturally evolved with the creation of the physical world (Smith 1994: 58–60). This system of social classification grew and became more complex over time. But by the middle of the first millennium BCE, the *varṇa* system comprised the Brahmin priests at the top, the *kṣatriya* class of kings and nobles second, the *vaiṣya* class consisting of providers of food and goods third, and the lowest *śūdra* class of those who were servants to the higher classes. This religious system placed a premium on social status and stability. The Vedic texts first used to promulgate and support this worldview depict a village-based society that subsisted on pastoral and agricultural activities.

At the center of this ancient Indic world was a Brahmanical theology that emphasized the potency of priestly rites and sacred *mantra*s, or chants. Rites and chants were performed together by priests during sacrifices made to a sacred fire believed capable of consuming the offering and transporting its subtle essence up to the heavenly realm where the gods would partake of it. Sacrificial rites were held on a small scale at the domestic household level, but over time larger and more complex sacrifices were performed by groups of priests in public ceremonies wherein only the higher social classes could participate (Thapar 2002: 128). Brahmin priests maintained that the ritual Vedic sacrifice, or *yajña*, replicated the primordial cosmic principle behind the creation of the world. The details for this ritual—whereby offerings of milk, honey, clarified butter (ghee), and animals were made into an open-air fire altar while Sanskrit *mantra*s were recited and a sacred, hallucinogenic drink called *soma* was drunk—were the exclusive privilege of the Brahmins. The cost of the items and personnel needed for its performance could be borne only by the upper classes. Therefore, the performance of the sacrifice tended to increase the status and importance of the priests who performed them and the nobles who sponsored them.

As long as ancient Aryan society was culturally uniform and rurally based, the sacrificial theology and ritual system of the Brahmin priests held sway. The search for better pastures, arable land, and goods, however, led groups of Aryans to migrate towards the east and settle in the fertile Gangetic Plains. This cultural shift that occurred sometime around the eighth and seventh centuries BCE brought Aryans into greater contact with other non-Aryan peoples. At the same time, the development of iron tools and techniques of wet-rice cultivation yielded larger surpluses of food, which in turn spurred trade and other occupations that supported the increased agricultural activity (Thapar 2002: 116–17). The rise of markets, trade, and coins began to take place in the sixth century BCE, setting into motion the second wave of urbanization in ancient India. The political and economic expansions in this region set the stage for rapid and dramatic changes in religious life. In contrast to many Brahmanical texts that appear to be set in village environments with tribal economies, early Buddhist texts depict large cities with diverse economies that illustrate early methods of urban trade and production (Bailey and Mabbett 2003: 58–61).

The relationship between urbanization and the rise of Buddhism in the Gangetic Plains is far from clear. Various theories abound on whether the Buddha's teachings gained popularity because they supported the values of new urban groups or because they rejected the materialist values of these new surroundings (Bailey and Mabbett 2003: 15–20). Clearly, the economic growth in this era may have facilitated the patronage of a new mendicant group of Buddhist monks. And the new urban settings may have diminished the influence of Brahmanical rites and traditions, providing a space for heterodox movements to emerge and flourish. Urban living, moreover, generated new economies that contributed to the rise of a greater level of individualism in this ancient period. Accordingly, an ascetic group like the Buddhists was a voluntary religious organization that needed to recruit its members from those who rejected the ascribed religious and cultural identities that they would have otherwise been expected to uphold (Olivelle 1992: 32–3). It is significant and not surprising then that early texts seem to indicate that a large proportion of those who joined the monkhood led by the Buddha did so in cities (Gokhale 1980: 74).

Urban areas were thus fertile grounds for the growth of new religious movements like Buddhism that departed from the Brahmanical traditions of sacrificial rites and a social hierarchy determined by birth. The Brahmanical religion was primarily a religion of householders, and it addressed the conditions of village life governed chiefly by agricultural cycles and family relationships. There is even evidence that Hindu Brahmins in the late Vedic period had a distaste for city life. Aside from the fact that late-Vedic texts rarely give mention to cities and the particular occupations that sprang up in them, it appears that urbanization and its concomitant political institutions were a development wholly independent of Vedic culture and were thus seen as a source of impurity to be avoided (Bronkhorst 2007: 251–5). Cities provided new avenues for earning wealth and a greater degree of social interaction across social classes, both of which undermined the stable social hierarchy implied in the Brahmanical ideology. Thus with Brahmins slow to embrace the urban centers of the Gangetic Plains, the Buddhists and other heterodox ascetic groups were attracted to cities where they received the interest and support of merchants, craftsmen, prostitutes, and other city-dwellers.

The renunciants of Ancient India

Early Indian Buddhists appeared along with other ascetic movements that sprang up in the middle of the first millennium BCE. In contrast to the priestly Brahmins who were concerned with the performance of sacrificial rites and the maintenance of a harmonious social order in the world of householders, the ascetic *śramaṇa*s renounced the householder life to adopt a mendicant, celibate lifestyle deemed conducive to gaining knowledge for liberation from the cycle of repeated births and deaths in the world (*saṃsāra*). The rejection of Brahmanical norms and rites placed many of these recluses outside of the dominant cultural system in ancient India. Generally speaking, the *śramaṇa*s refused to recognize the legitimacy of the sacrifices performed by the Brahmins in order to regenerate and sustain the cosmic order, as well as to ensure divine blessings and benefits for their patrons. Such recluses had no interest in the maintenance of the world, a world seen to be less real and more insufferable than whatever form of existence may lie outside of it. Instead, these recluses renounced the social world that under the influence of Brahmins valued power, prosperity, and procreation. They pursued paths designed to free themselves of social attachments and worldly existence.

Many of the Śramaṇic groups that existed around the middle of the first millennium BCE disappeared from history and are unknown to us today. It does appear, however, that during this period in the Gangetic Plains a number of new ideas about *karma*, rebirth (*saṃsāra*), and liberation (*mokṣa*) had taken root without the prior influence of the Vedic religion of the Aryans. Whereas the Brahmanical religion of the early Vedic period remarked on an afterlife whereby one travels either to be rewarded in a heavenly "World of the Fathers" or to be punished in a "House of Clay," the expansion of the Aryans eastwards appears to have led to some intermingling of social groups and the gradual adoption of a spiritual ideology that emphasized attaining liberation from *saṃsāra*. This soteriological stance became accepted into the Brahmanical religion through the medium of the *Upaniṣad*s, a collection of texts composed and edited over several centuries beginning around the seventh or sixth century BCE. The *Upaniṣad*s were incorporated in the Hindu Veda as the section wherein knowledge is the means to salvation (*jñānakaṇḍa*), in contrast to the older section on ritual performance (*karmakaṇḍa*).

What the renunciants had in common was a conviction that a path of ascetic and celibate living away from the usual family ties and social obligations held the key to liberation from a nearly interminable cycle of rebirth. A higher state of knowledge and bliss was thought to await all those who could transcend the path of repeated existence in the world. However, these same *śramaṇa*s were distinguished by different views on the reasons for the predicament of bondage and suffering in *saṃsāra*, as well as the means to attain liberation from this condition. One view, represented by some Upaniṣadic authors, held that the human bondage in *saṃsāra* was due to a lack of understanding, but this woeful state could be overcome by the development of knowledge (Olivelle 1992: 39). Another view, exemplified by the Jains, held that mental and physical activity was the primary cause for continued rebirth (Bronkhorst 2007: 24). Yet another view, one that would be later articulated by the Buddhists, identified mental intentions in the form of desire as responsible for rebirth and the suffering that goes along with it. To be sure, other mendicant groups came up with their own particular views on the causes and solutions for the problem of rebirth. All of these *śramaṇa*s, however, challenged the traditional Brahmanical orthodoxy, which held that priestly rites and the life of a householder were supremely valuable and meaningful.

Those renunciants who remained within the Brahmanical fold by acknowledging the authority of Vedic scriptures did not reject the traditional sacrificial rites entirely. They instead chose to reinterpret its significance by utilizing the image of the sacrificial fire to develop a theology of renunciation whereby yoga was reinterpreted as an internal sacrifice and the perfection of the ritual itself (Olivelle 1992: 68–9). In essence, Hindu renunciants retained the symbolism and categories of sacrifice to invest their ascetic practices with relevance and authority. And the larger Brahmanical tradition sought to lessen the threats they posed to itself by incorporating the ascetic's quest into the final stage of life (*āśrama*), whereby the pursuit of individual liberation is postponed until after one has performed the duties of domestic sacrifices, raising a family, and contributing to the welfare of society. Other renunciants, however, refused to accept the Brahmanical ideology as normative. These groups, to which the Buddhists should be added, distanced themselves from the ritualized sacrifices of Brahmins, protesting both the violence inherent in sacrificing animals and the social dominance of an elite priestly class.

The development of groups of wandering recluses who begged for food and sought liberation from the mundane and often disagreeable world of repeated births constituted a direct challenge to the religion purveyed by most Brahmins. It may have represented a distinctly new era of religious expression in post-Vedic India. Or it may have been the result of encounters and disputes among different religious groups in the more heterogeneous culture east of the confluence of the Ganges and Yamuna rivers—what Johannes Bronkhorst calls "Greater Magadha" (Bronkhorst 2007: 2–4). Regardless, after the sixth century BCE, the Gangetic Plains would become the center of new religious movements that repudiated much of what the Brahmanical religion deemed necessary and normative. The historical Buddha was certainly one of the leaders in this regard.

The Buddha and his Dharma

Numerous surveys of Buddhism begin their accounts with the birth of Siddhārtha Gautama, the Indian noble who at the age of 35 attained his Awakening (or "Enlightenment") and became known as the Buddha (or the "Awakened One"). While it is true that the narrative of the Buddha's life story would come to occupy a central place in the devotional expressions and literary recollections of Buddhists in ancient India, these biographic accounts appear somewhat later after older discursive texts that focus on the Buddha's teaching career. Indeed, the construction of a complete biography of the Buddha's life first took place at least two to three hundred years after his death with the composition of the *Mahāvastu*. Brief episodes and anecdotes from his youth appear in some older canonical texts, which can be combined and arranged to produce a fairly coherent life story of the Buddha (cf. Ñāṇamoli 1992). But since this story gains significance due to the condition of Buddhahood that Siddhārtha Gautama attained and then expounded upon to others, it makes sense to begin with the Buddha's Awakening. The Mahāvagga (Great Chapter) in the Pāli *Vinaya*, or book of monastic regulations, adopts this same formula when it opens its narrative account with the Buddha sitting under the Bodhi Tree, having just attained his Awakening. It is here too that we shall begin to recount how the story of the Buddha influenced the development of Buddhism in South Asia and beyond.

The newly awakened Buddha is said to have spent one week in meditation under the Bodhi Tree—a species of fig tree (*ficus religiosa*) with heart-shaped leaves that has apparently long been associated with religious worship in South Asia. It is during this time that he reflected on Dependent Co-Arising (Skt: *pratītyasamutpāda*/P: *paṭiccasamuppāda*)—a notion concerning the mutually conditioned rise and fall of all forms of existence that directly led to his Awakening. This doctrine, distinctive to Buddhism, affirms that (1) ignorance gives rise to certain karmic dispositions; (2) those same karmic dispositions give rise to consciousness; (3) consciousness gives rise to "name and form," or the combined mental and physical basis for existence; (4) name and form give rise to the six sense fields of seeing, hearing, smelling, tasting, touching, and discursive thinking; (5) the six sense-fields give rise to contact with particular mental and physical stimuli; (6) contact then gives rise to feelings that are positive, negative, or neutral; (7) feeling gives rise to craving or desire for sensory pleasure, the avoidance of pain, and continued existence; (8) craving thus gives rise to clinging or the attachment to what one desires out of pleasure and comfort; (9) clinging gives rise to becoming, which is roughly comparable to the will to live that leads to rebirth; (10) becoming therefore gives rise to conception and birth in a new form; (11) birth gives rise eventually to old age and death; and lastly (12) old age and

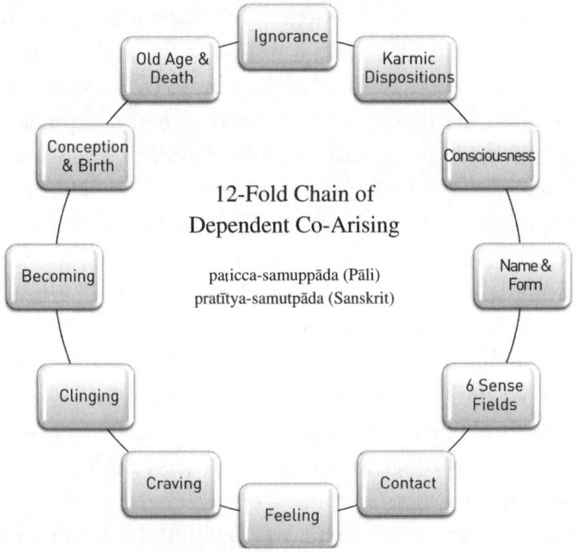

Figure 1.1 Dependent Co-Arising chart (created by Jane Terry)

death give rise to ignorance since when being reborn one generally forgets all that he or she had learned in the previous life.

While meditating on this system of causation that underlies all existence, the Buddha is said to have realized that all forms of life are conditioned by numerous events and phenomena. Thus, whatever exists is neither autonomous nor unchanging, but it rather arises and falls away due to its dependence on other factors or conditions that determine its course. This insight of the Buddha is depicted as a revolutionary discovery. It is from this recognition that existence is dependent on various conditions that led the Buddha to figure out the cause for "this whole mass of suffering" that characterizes life in *saṃsāra* (Davids and Oldenberg 1990: 77). And yet since all existence with its continual series of rebirths and its proclivity towards grief, sorrow, and despair is said to arise through a system of conditions, it is equally true that rebirth and life's inevitable suffering may be brought to an end through the destruction of ignorance and desire, which in turn destroys the other links in the chain of dependent co-arising. The textual tradition represents the Buddha's teaching on the causal connectedness of life as encapsulating the Dharma as a whole and as holding the secret of the cessation of suffering (Gethin 1998: 141).

After the Buddha's Awakening

The Mahavagga account of the newly Awakened Buddha continues by describing how over the next four weeks he meditated and enjoyed the bliss of *nirvāṇa*, or the liberation from all causes of suffering and rebirth that is obtained through the complete destruction of ignorance and desire. During this period of time he also instructs a Brahmin about the characteristics that make one a Brahmin, stays motionless as a large cobra shields him from the rain, receives offerings of food from the merchants Tapussa and Bhallika who then take refuge in the Buddha and his Dharma, and finally consents to the god Brahmā Sahampati's request that he preach the Dharma to others. A later tradition, seen for example in the fifth-century CE commentary to the *Jātaka* text, expands upon this account by adding three more weeks to the time the Buddha spent enjoying his awakened state. Therein he is said to have stood gazing at the Bodhi Tree with unblinking eyes out of appreciation for its assistance in his attainment of *nirvāṇa*, to have walked to and fro along a jeweled walking path in meditation, and to have sat in a jeweled house wherein he cogitated upon the contents of the Abhidharma—a collection of philosophical and psychological treatises that were added later to the canon of Buddhist scriptures (Jayawickrama 1990: 103–4).

The narration of the time spent by the Buddha immediately after his Awakening likely reflects attempts by later Buddhists to derive even more significance out of this highly significant event. It is in this manner that the life story of the Buddha appears as a hagiography wherein details were added over time to stress the saintly nature of the Buddha and to express the religious interests of the Buddhist community (Williams 2000: 26–7). The Mahāvagga account goes on to depict the Buddha seeking to find someone to whom he may teach the content of his realization. Upon deciding to seek out five mendicants with whom he once pursued the goal of liberation, the Buddha uses the extraordinary power of the Divine Eye, by which he is able to perceive that the five mendicants are staying miles away in a deer park near the city of Benares. On the way to the park, the Buddha meets an Ājīvika named Upaka who inquires into the reason for the Buddha's bright and serene appearance. The Ājīvikas were another group of *śramaṇa*s in the Gangetic Plains, but distinctive for their fatalistic doctrine holding that human destiny was fixed and unalterable by any effort on one's part. Instead, one simply had to live out one's appointed time in *saṃsāra* and abstain from further activity that might prolong one's stay in the cycle of birth and death (Bronkhorst 2007: 49–50). In the Mahāvagga, the Ājīvika is not convinced by the Buddha's claim to have attained liberation, and he walks away on a different path. This apparent failure to convert Upaka is more likely to be a commentary on the obtuseness to be found among this group of religious competitors than any acknowledged shortcoming on the Buddha's part.

When the Buddha arrived in the deer park outside of Benares, he approached his former colleagues who were unable to remain aloof to him despite the fact he had given up the ascetic exertions that they continued to observe. The five welcome and honor him by taking his bowl and robe from his hands, offering him a seat, and washing his feet. When they address him by his name and as "Friend," the Buddha corrects them and explains that he is the "Tathāgata" (Thus-Gone-One) who has traversed the path leading to Full Awakening and liberation from repeated births and deaths. He then preaches what is traditionally regarded as his first sermon—the Dhammacakkappavattana Sutta, or the "Discourse on the Setting in Motion of the Wheel of the Dharma." This first sermon outlines the Buddha's analysis of the human condition and offers a path to alleviate the suffering or *dukkha* that all conditioned beings experience in *saṃsāra*. The Buddha begins by defining the middle way of the Buddhist path that is said to lead to liberation or *nirvāṇa* (P: *nibbāna*).

> Monks, these two extremes should not be followed by one who has gone forth into homelessness. What two? The pursuit of sensual happiness in sensual pleasures, which is low, vulgar, the way of worldlings, ignoble, unbeneficial; and the pursuit of self-mortification, which is painful, ignoble, unbeneficial. Without veering toward either of the extremes, the

> Tathāgata has awakened to the middle way, which gives rise to vision, which gives rise to knowledge, and leads to peace, to direct knowledge, to enlightenment, to Nibbāna.
>
> (Bodhi 2005: 75)

The Buddha, in other words, admonishes the five ascetics not to embrace lives of sensual indulgence or severe asceticism. Following the middle way between both extremes sets the stage for progress toward reducing and ultimately eliminating suffering in one's life. Herein the Buddha appears to be inventing a new kind of recluse, one who splits the difference between the married life of a householder and the ascetic life of *śramaṇa*s like the Jains. Implicit in this critique is a claim that the desire to deny and punish oneself to undo the karmic effects of past actions and to suppress the karmic effects of future actions may become just as strong as the desire to please one's senses.

The Noble Eightfold Path

Instead, in his first sermon, the Buddha maps out a new path, equivalent to the middle way, called the Noble Eightfold Path. The Noble Eightfold Path consists of eight factors that are traditionally divided into three subgroups: wisdom (*paññā*), morality (*sīla*), and concentration (*samādhi*). The factors themselves are not taken up in sequence but should in theory all be developed concurrently. In the Dhammacakkappavattana Sutta, the Buddha only mentions the eight factors comprising the Noble Eightfold Path: right view, right intention, right speech, right action, right livelihood, right effort, right mindfulness, and right concentration. This path is said to be the way leading to the cessation of suffering. On other occasions, of course, the Buddha and his disciples explained these eight factors in more detail. (1) Right view does not entail adhering to a particular dogma, but rather it means viewing things as they really are and not merely as they appear to be (Piyadassi 1974: 89). The development of a correct understanding of reality is gained by hearing the Dharma and by directing one's mind to discern the basis for the Buddha's teaching on the cause and extinction of suffering. (2) Right intention comprises thoughts of selfless detachment, goodwill, and nonviolence that collectively prevent one from harming oneself or others.

Because words can have real effects in the world, the Buddha taught that (3) right speech or the abstention from harmful and unprofitable speech is the first factor in the development of morality. The second of three factors associated with morality is (4) right action. Right action involves developing the moral restraint necessary to abstain from immoral deeds such as taking the life of a sentient being, stealing from another, and engaging in sexual misconduct. The practice of moral restraints is thought to be crucial for building a good character and strengthening the mind (Piyadassi 1974: 143). The last moral factor in the Noble Eightfold Path is (5) right livelihood, which entails refraining from harmful professions such as trading in weapons, human trafficking, slaughtering animals, and selling intoxicants or poisons.

The final three factors of the Noble Eightfold Path are associated with meditative practice, an activity held to rest on moral restraint and to lead to the development of wisdom. The factor of (6) right effort involves, on the one hand, endeavoring to remove negative thoughts that have arisen and to prevent new negative thoughts from arising, and on the other hand, endeavoring to develop good thoughts and to maintain a favorable object of concentration when meditating (Piyadassi 1974: 168–9). Right effort then prepares a person for achieving success in the other aspects of meditative practice. The next factor, (7) right mindfulness, consists of developing a clear and steady awareness of how one speaks, acts, and thinks. Mindfulness thus involves efforts to develop a presence of mind that allows for exerting greater control over one's thoughts and acquiring both calm and insight. Lastly, (8) right concentration involves cultivating an unbroken attentiveness to the object chosen to focus the mind and the subsequent development of mental tranquility free from distractions (Bodhi 1984: 94). The development of higher levels of trance-states is held to complement the development of mental awareness in mindfulness, leading to the penetrating vision of reality that underlies wisdom.

The Four Noble Truths

While the Dhammacakkappavattana Sutta as preserved in the Pāli Mahāvagga lists the factors comprising the Noble Eightfold Path, it gives more attention to the Four Noble Truths, which together summarize the Buddha's analysis of and solution to the problems of the human condition. The First Noble Truth, according to the Buddha, relates to the reality of *dukkha* (Skt: *duḥkha*) or suffering, dissatisfaction, and discomfort as an inescapable part of life in this world. Most commonly translated as "suffering," *dukkha* actually refers to a broader range of unpleasant mental and physical experiences than that word implies. Critics of the Buddhist religion have frequently charged it with a pessimistic outlook given the fact that the First Noble Truth has often been translated as "Life is suffering." In fact, the Buddha did not deny the possibility of happiness in ordinary life. The point of the First Noble Truth is rather that given the conditioned and changeable nature of existence in *saṃsāra*, any experience of happiness based on what is conditioned and subject to change will inevitably disappear. It is thus impossible to sustain without end the happiness and pleasure that arise from things that do not last. *Dukkha* connotes the inability of persons always to get what they want or to keep what they have and enjoy. Aside from the inescapable reality that all living beings will at times experience physical pain and mental anguish, the idea of *dukkha* recognizes that life as something impermanent and conditioned inevitably gives rise to disappointment and dissatisfaction.

The Buddha's first sermon describes the Second Noble Truth in terms of the origin or cause of *dukkha*—the experience of suffering and dissatisfaction while in *saṃsāra*. The Buddha told the five ascetics that the cause of *dukkha* is one's craving or desire for sensual pleasures, objects of delight, and continued existence in the world so that one may continue to pursue one's cravings. In some cases, it may even include the desire to put an end to one's existence due to the mistaken conviction that death will bring an end to one's present suffering. In a world where everything is always changing, the desire to experience or possess that which one desires can never be fully satisfied, and this thus becomes the cause of suffering (Gethin 1998: 70).

The Buddha goes on to affirm that although living beings typically suffer from unquenchable cravings for manifold experiences and objects of delight, there exists the possibility of putting an end to *dukkha*. The Third Noble Truth of the cessation of suffering suggests that by abandoning and destroying one's cravings, one may become freed from their influence and attain a state of nonattachment. In other words, to destroy the desire to obtain what one cannot obtain—the continuous fulfillment of all of one's wishes—is to destroy the primary cause for the *dukkha* that one experiences throughout one's lifetime. While this is not an easy feat, other Buddhist texts describe various ways for lessening one's cravings or thirst that cause suffering and rebirth in *saṃsāra*. Among other things, one must recognize the Three Marks of existence in the phenomenal world—(1) impermanence (Skt: *anitya*/P: *anicca)*, (2) dissatisfaction (P: *dukkha*), and (3) the lack of a permanent Self (Skt: *anātman*/P: *anattā*), or less accurately a "soul" that could survive death intact and without change. Wisdom involves the perception that all of one's mundane desires are misplaced because one's desired objects and experiences cannot last indefinitely, are thereby linked with dissatisfaction, and mislead one into thinking that because I desire something, then this notion of "I" must refer to something concrete, lasting, and real. To put an end to the craving for permanence, satisfaction, and a selfhood that is discrete and eternal is to put an end to the very conditions that give rise to *dukkha* and continued rebirth in *saṃsāra*.

The Fourth Noble Truth cited by the Buddha is that the Noble Eightfold Path represents the way leading to the cessation of *dukkha*. The Buddha then asserts that he has fully understood the noble truth of suffering, has abandoned the cause of suffering, has realized the cessation of suffering, and has developed the path leading to the cessation of suffering (Bodhi

2005: 76–7). He makes these claims in the Dhammacakkappavattana Sutta to proclaim to the five ascetics that he has attained the unsurpassed, perfect Awakening and has achieved liberation or *nirvāṇa* from all factors leading to rebirth. He has become a Buddha. And although he had to live out the rest of his worldly existence and could still be subject to bodily pain, he was guaranteed not to experience mental anguish or to engage in any act that is productive of *karma* and would otherwise prolong his existence in *saṃsāra*.

The establishment of the Saṅgha

At the close of the Buddha's first sermon, the ascetic Koṇḍañña is said to have obtained a clear, penetrating vision of the truth of the Dharma, which the text summarizes, "All that is subject to origination is also subject to cessation" (Oldenberg 1997: 11). Koṇḍañña's realization of the Dharma leads to his attainment of liberation, in which he is said to have dispelled all doubts and to have gained for himself a complete understanding of the nature of existence. At this point the Dhammacakkappavattana Sutta, wherein the Buddha preached his first sermon on the Dharma and helped his first follower attain *nirvāṇa*, comes to a close. The Mahāvagga account, however, goes on to describe how the ascetic Koṇḍañña requests the Buddha to ordain him as a monk. The Buddha complies and ordains him by saying, "Come, monk. The Dharma has been well taught. Live the life of purity in order to bring an end to all *dukkha*" (Oldenberg 1997: 12). The Buddha continued to preach the Dharma, and two more ascetics perceived the truth of conditioned existence. They, too, were ordained by the Buddha, followed by the last two ascetics from his former group. Another account taken from the *Mahāvastu*, a lengthy text attributed to the early Mahāsāṃghika School and composed between the second century BCE and the fourth century CE, depicts the five ascetics as having first been ordained and provided with monastic requisites before the Buddha preached his sermon (Seth 1992: 166). Leaving aside the discrepancies in the sequence of these events, the ordination of the first five disciples is significant because it marks the initial establishment of the Saṅgha, or the monastic Buddhist order.

The five ascetics including Koṇḍañña had thus become *bhikkhu*s, the Pāli term that signifies "alms-recipients" or monks who renounce the world and follow the middle way as taught by the Buddha. As the account in the Mahāvagga continues, the Buddha preaches a second sermon to the five *bhikkhu*s about the doctrine of "No-Self" (*anattā*). Contrary to most other contemporary doctrines that affirmed the existence of a unique and permanent Self that survives death, transmigrates from one life to the next, and may ultimately win liberation from *saṃsāra*, the Buddha laid out a teaching that rejects the belief in a permanent substratum or core to one's individuality. In lieu of the Self (termed "*ātman*" by the teachers of the *Upaniṣads* and "*jīva*" by the Jains), the Buddha preached about the existence of "Five Aggregates" (*skandhas*) of physical and psychological components that collectively make up one's existence. The aggregates or "heaps" of material and mental events are divided into five categories. First, there is form (*rūpa*), which refers to the body or the totality of gross physical existence. Second, there are feelings (*vedanā*), which include all physical and mental sensations that may be pleasant, unpleasant, or neutral. Third, there are perceptions (*saṃjñā*), which refer to acts of recognizing, conceiving, and appraising particular things and ideas in the course of one's lived experience. Fourth, there are dispositions (*saṃskāra*), which comprise certain inclinations and impulses that are formed due to one's previous acts and experiences. Lastly, there is consciousness (*vijñāna*) or the unreflective awareness of oneself as a subject of experience and of things as objects of experience.

Taken together, the Five Aggregates constitute the entirety of life. And as physical and psychological phenomena that arise subject to various conditions, they are said by the Buddha to be impermanent and without substance or "Self." The Buddha questions the five *bhikkhus*, who are led to understand that their bodies, feelings, sensations, dispositions, and consciousness are all impermanent and unsatisfactory. The monks and later audiences learned from the Buddha that they lack complete control over their bodies, feelings, etc., that all parts of their physical and psychological experience are impermanent and unsatisfactory, and that it was pointless to speak of a Self apart from one's experience (Collins 1982: 97–9). If one can find no evidence of a permanent substratum that exists apart from the Five Aggregates, and the Buddha said he could not, there is no reason to affirm its existence. Moreover, the belief in a Self is also said to be harmful due to the feelings of desire, greed, and envy that this notion tends to produce. Along with the notion of a permanent Self come the ideas of "me" and "mine," which reinforce desire and greed. The doctrine of No-Self is thus meant to strip away all conceits of one's own unique and eternal existence.

Early accounts depict the Buddha as continuing to travel, preach, and acquire increasing numbers of monastic and lay followers. The number of *bhikkhus* who had abandoned permanent shelters and who wandered to receive alms grew. When the monks met people who wished to adopt the religious life as they had done, they initially had to bring these new converts back to where the Buddha was staying at that time for ordination. However, to lessen the burden of travel, the Buddha eventually granted the *bhikkhus* the authority to confer the novice ordination (*pabbajjā*) and higher ordination (*upasampadā*) upon those seeking to become a monk. They were instructed to cut off the hair and beard of the candidate, dress him in yellow robes, have him salute the feet of the *bhikkhus*, and make him recite the following lines three times: "I go to the Buddha for refuge, I go to the Dharma for refuge, I go to the Saṅgha for refuge" (Oldenberg 1997: 22). From this point on, *bhikkhu*s were entrusted with the authority to ordain new novices and monks into the monastic order, and the formula of taking the "Three Refuges" of the Buddha, Dharma, and Saṅgha became standardized as the method of joining the Buddhist community and indicating one's adherence to its ideals.

At this point in the history of the Saṅgha, it appears that the Buddha and monks wandered frequently without fixed abodes. Early texts make reference to the Buddha and various numbers of his followers residing in halls, forests, parks, and other places for shelter. Wandering was made necessary by the requirement of seeking food and other alms freely given by laypersons. The Buddha also encouraged travel as a means by which the monks could disseminate the Dharma and help people attain greater comfort and happiness in their current and future lifetimes.

> Monks, travel on a journey for the welfare of many people, for the happiness of many people, out of compassion for the world, for the benefit, welfare, and happiness of the gods and humans. May not two of you go in any one way. Monks, preach the Dharma that is good in the beginning, good in the middle, and good in the end in meaning and in letter. Proclaim the complete, perfect life of purity.
>
> (Oldenberg 1997: 21)

In speaking this way to the *bhikkhu*s, the Buddha displayed the aim to make his discovery of a path leading to the cessation of suffering and dissatisfaction as widely known as possible. The Buddha traveled around the Ganges basin, visiting and teaching those who would listen in towns and cities throughout the region. Early texts represent him as winning adherents through the power of his appearance and personality, through the miraculous display of his psychic powers gained through meditative practice, and through appealing to persons who were already seeking liberation from the difficulties of the world. Some adherents renounced their lives as laypersons and adopted the life of a Buddhist monk. Others remained in the world, but sought out opportunities to see and to listen to the Buddha, as well as to make offerings of alms to the *bhikkhu*s.

The establishment of the Saṅgha also entailed setting up some basic rules by which the *bhikkhu*s could subsist and practice the Dharma as preached by the Buddha. Some of the earliest customs and rules of conduct were connected with what the *bhikkhu*s could possess and where they could reside. Their lodgings varied and included locations in the open air, under trees, in caves, and in temporary huts of made wood and leaves (Lamotte 1988: 58). These *bhikkhus* sometimes stayed alone or in small groups. The Mahāvagga explains how a group of monks in Rājagaha once brought disrepute upon themselves by continuing to wander throughout the year, even during the rainy season when most ascetics observed a retreat to avoid harming living creatures sheltering under the quickly growing grass and plants. It seems likely that people would have disliked making offerings to recluses when rain and poor roads made it difficult to travel. At this point, the Buddha is said to have ordered the monks to observe a three-month retreat during the rainy season, whereupon they dwelt in temporary structures near villages and towns. This development in monastic life meant that despite the nomadic lifestyle of the *bhikkhu*, he typically engaged in periods of sedentary existence (Wijayaratna 1990: 21). Another contributing factor to the use of more fixed dwellings was the fact that wealthy lay donors began to make offerings of monasteries as temporary places of residence for the monks. The Buddha is said to have permitted such donations as long as they were located outside of towns and as long as they were given to the Saṅgha as a corporate body rather than to any individual monk.

The Buddha's early rivals

If the Buddha's efforts to teach gave rise to the dissemination of the Dharma and the expansion of the Saṅgha throughout the Gangetic Plains in the centuries before the Common Era, they also brought him and his followers into conflict and competition with other religious groups. These groups included orthodox Brahmins, Brahmanical renouncers, Jains, Ājīvikas (fatalists), Cārvākas (materialists), and others who espoused different teachings and practices. In many early discourses one finds the Buddha not only teaching the Dharma but also engaging and refuting his opponents. For example, the Buddha rejected the Vedic rites and teachings of orthodox Brahmins. Their teachings on caste, sacrifice, and the infallibility of the Vedas are singled out for being erroneous and immoral. In the Assalāyana Sutta from the *Majjhima Nikāya*, for instance, the Buddha is portrayed as convincing a Brahmin that traditional assertions about the primacy of Brahmins are unsustainable given that Brahmins are likewise susceptible to suffer for wicked deeds like everyone else, and that it is impossible for them to claim with certainty that their ancestors never married a non-Brahmin (Ñāṇamoli and Bodhi 1995: 763–70). In other words, the Buddha evidently denied Brahmanical claims to superiority and purity based on birth. The measure of one's greatness is located instead in morality, as the quality of one's personal conduct comes to substitute for genealogy in determining social status.

This emphasis on ethical behavior and reflection enabled the Buddha to chart a new religious path that differed from those of Brahmins and other *śramaṇa*s. It has been argued that the Buddha's move to redefine the notion of *karma* ("action") in terms of intention served to undermine the Brahmanical ideology by shifting the focus from ritual action to the psychological states held to exist behind the act and to condition its performance (Gombrich 2006: 50–1). In the Buddha's view, the correct performance of traditional Brahmanical rites would not suffice to purify a person and to spare them from *dukkha*. One must instead work to purify one's mind so that one's actions (i.e., *karma*) do not lead to hardship and further bondage to the cycle of rebirth. Fruitful actions—that is, acts that generate useful and positive results—may thus be done by anyone who has learned to control one's mind and to discipline one's senses. There is no real need for a Brahmin to act as a ritual specialist and to perform the correct ceremony to bring about desired effects in life. The Vedic sacrifices are unnecessary and even immoral when they involve taking the life of an animal. They are represented in the texts as little more than acts through which Brahmins may obtain more wealth and food for themselves.

An example of the supposedly mistaken nature of the theories of orthodox Brahmins is cited with reference to the Brahmanical myth of creation. The Buddha critiques the view wherein the god Brahmā is seen as the creator of the universe. He explains in the Brahmajāla Sutta of the *Dīgha Nikāya* how the Brahmins have completely misunderstood the nature of the origin of the world. Since, unlike the Buddhists, Brahmins fail to recognize that the world goes through endless, lengthy cycles of destruction and re-creation, and they have mistakenly accepted the view that Brahmā created the universe. Instead, according to the Buddha, the being that was reborn first into the world after it began its cycle of re-creation and growth was led to believe that he was the first in existence. After longing for company, when other beings began to be reborn in the world, the Brahmā deity mistakenly concluded that he brought them into being, when in fact they were simply reborn in the world from a formless realm when the time was right for them to be reborn (Walshe 1995: 75–6). As a result, the Brahmā who was reborn first in a new world cycle mistakenly thought he was an all-powerful creator deity. The orthodox Brahmins who view Vedic texts as true continue to affirm that Brahmā is the god of creation. The Buddha, however, deduced and taught that creation is a natural and cyclical process that occurs without any divine intervention.

During the course of his teaching career, the Buddha also refuted various doctrines espoused by Brahmanical renunciants who embraced ideas found in the *Upaniṣads*. These renunciants extolled the homeless life and the search for knowledge leading to liberation. Although they renounced the ritual sacrifices and childrearing that were otherwise central to Brahmanical life, these renouncers employed the imagery of traditional rites to portray their renunciation as the internalization and perfection of the sacrificial ritual

(Olivelle 1992: 71). The external sacrifice whereby various substances are burned in the sacred fire became mirrored by an internal sacrifice revolving around the generation of internal body heat (*tapas*) in the context of meditation. These Brahmanical renunciants also accepted notions of *karma* and *saṃsāra*, but they stressed efforts toward attaining knowledge of the true Self (*ātman*) as the means to liberation. The *Bṛhadāraṇyaka Upaniṣad* describes the *ātman* as "radiant and immortal," and as identifiable with the all-encompassing reality of Brahman (Olivelle 1996: 30). Similarly, the *Chāndogya Upaniṣad* includes numerous examples—the nectar used to make honey, rivers that flow into the ocean, salt dissolved in water, and so forth—to illustrate how the individual *ātman* is indistinguishable from the Self, or Brahman, of the whole world (Olivelle 1996: 153–5).

The idea of Brahman as found in several *Upaniṣads* is said to represent a single, formless universal reality that permeates the world and exists eternally beneath the superficial level of change and differentiation. The Brahmanical sages who subscribed to this monistic view of the world concluded that this eternal reality also incorporates the essential nature of one's individuality. By positing an eternal Self (*ātman*) that is different from the body and the mind, a core principle that does not act and thereby does not create *karma*, these renunciants maintained that developing knowledge of the true Self could effect liberation (Bronkhorst 2007: 28–31). One comes to realize that the core principle of one's individuality never acts and is thus not bound to the cycle of birth and death. The Buddha, for his part, disputed the validity of this notion of an eternal Self that exists apart from body and mind. He rejected the grounds for seeing the Self as eternal, as such a view he claims is borne of a lack of knowledge, worry and vacillation, and a craving for permanence (Walshe 1995: 73–4, 87–8). In a world of constantly changing factors and experiences, the notion of a permanent Self that is unaffected by change becomes counterintuitive. In the Mahānidāna Sutta, all views of the Self—whether material or immaterial, limited or unlimited—appear contradictory since if one attributes the Self to what is felt or what is imperceptible, one must either associate the Self with that which is impermanent like feeling or with something wholly unconnected with lived experience (Walshe 1995: 226–7).

Early Buddhist texts also portray the Buddha refuting the doctrines and practices of the Jains, a heterodox group of renunciants, who like the Buddhists rejected the claims of the Brahmins over the truth of the Vedas, the significance of caste distinctions, and the efficacy of Brahmanical rites. The Jains traditionally adhered to a strict code of asceticism, believing that bodily and mental inactivity would annihilate the karmic effects of former actions and prevent new actions from taking place (Bronkhorst 2007: 45). Although it is only with difficulty that one can begin to identify the earliest

Jain teachings, it nevertheless appears that Jains maintained that the world is characterized by ignorance, suffering, and pain caused by beings who are unaware that they are surrounded by life-forms and perform acts that cause fear and harm (Dundas 1992: 36–7). Therefore by refraining from action and embodying a non-violent stance towards all forms of life, a Jain ascetic may theoretically help reduce suffering in the world and put an end to his (or, in some cases, her) own rebirth. Self-mortification and severe asceticism were thus thought to effect the liberation of the soul and the attainment of an eternal state of perfect awareness and bliss. Accordingly, given their presence in the time and place wherein the Buddha taught his Dharma, Jain renunciants are frequently mentioned in early Buddhist texts. Not surprisingly, the Buddha, who taught the middle way between self-mortification and sensual indulgence, evidently denounced the strict form of asceticism embraced by the Jains.

Early Pāli texts usually refer to Jains as *nigaṇṭha*s, or customarily "those without ties" in the sense of depriving themselves of basic possessions including even clothing. The Buddha and his followers reproached Jain efforts to expend the effects of *karma* by subjecting themselves to extreme discomfort. In the Devadaha Sutta of the *Majjhima Nikāya*, the Buddha explains to his followers the folly of Jain ideas about the exhaustion of suffering through the destruction of action. If, as they claimed, that suffering in the present is caused solely by what was done in the past, then the "painful, racking, piercing feelings" Jain ascetics feel due to their severe austerities would be experienced even when they were not performing those austerities (Ñāṇamoli and Bodhi 1995: 830–1). Instead, says the Buddha, the "painful, racking, piercing feelings" that Jain ascetics experience are simply the products of their excessive self-mortification, and these self-imposed acts will not exhaust past actions but can only be described as fruitless deeds. Also in the *Majjhima Nikāya*, the Upāli Sutta describes how the Buddha convinced a follower of Nigaṇṭha Nātaputta (a figure customarily associated with Mahāvīra, the founder of the Jain tradition) to leave that community and become a supporter of the Buddhists. When the layman Upāli approached the Buddha to convince him of his error in holding mental acts as more responsible for wicked deeds than bodily acts, he was instead convinced by the Buddha about the primacy of the mind and declared his refuge in the Three Jewels of the Buddha, Dharma, and Saṅgha.

In addition to refuting the teachings of Brahmins and Jains, the Buddha also appears to have addressed the alleged errors found in the views of Ājīvikas and Cārvākas, groups of fatalists and materialists respectively, who were also competing with the Buddhists to win followers and material support. Although the Buddhists echoed these groups' rejections of many of the premises of the Brahmanical religion, there is evidence that the Buddha saw the Ājīvikas and Cārvākas as particularly harmful. The Ājīvikas appear to have split off from the Jains, maintaining unlike the latter that deliberate inactivity could not extinguish past *karma* (Bronkhorst 2007: 44–5). Their leader, called Makkhali Gosāla in Pāli Buddhist texts, taught a fatalistic philosophy whereby *karma* exists but is unchanged by any virtuous deed one performs. One's journey through *saṃsāra* is therefore not affected by what one does, and the Ājīvikas maintained that each soul must run its course through 8,400,000 *mahākalpas*—an inconceivably long period of time. The Buddha's problem with this position is not hard to discern. The Ājīvikas rejected human agency and moral causation, reducing life to a destiny (*niyati*) made up of a series of events wholly beyond one's control. The Buddha is quoted in the *Aṅguttara Nikāya* as repudiating this group in strong terms: "Monks, I have not perceived another individual who has thus followed a path leading to the harm of many people, to the unhappiness of many people, to the misfortune of many people, and to the harm and suffering of gods and persons like this fool Makkhali" (Morris 1961: 33). Despite such criticism, the Ājīvikas existed as a movement up to the second millennium of the Common Era.

The materialist doctrine of the Cārvākas, which likely derived from an older Lokāyata School, was also refuted by the Buddha as a teaching that undermined moral responsibility for one's actions. Their view, wherein matter is the only reality, presented a challenge to nearly every religious movement in ancient India. Buddhist texts identify Ajita Kesakambalin as the organizer of a materialist school that denied the reality of the soul, transmigration, and the fruits of good and evil deeds (Warder 1956: 53). There is essentially nothing worth knowing or striving for beyond the immediate sensory world. The Sāmaññaphala Sutta in *Dīgha Nikāya* describes the teachings of Ajita Kesakambalin as including, "[T]here are in the world no ascetics or Brahmins who have attained, who have perfectly practiced, who proclaim this world and the next, having realized them by their own super-knowledge" (Walshe 1995: 96). And further, he purportedly claimed, "This human being is composed of the four great elements, and when one dies the earth part reverts to the earth, the water part to the water, the fire part to the fire, the air part to the air, and the faculties pass away into space" (Walshe 1995: 96). Such views were seen as pernicious since the materialist view of the annihilation of existence after death meant that morality and the consequences of action were meaningless (Chakravarti 1987: 48).

As a teacher committed to helping others put an end to *dukkha*, the Buddha apparently found himself obliged to address the views of other religious teachers in ancient India. Not surprisingly, Buddhist texts unfailingly show the Buddha as triumphing over those who come to debate with him and to challenge his claim to have achieved complete wisdom. Although the objectivity of such accounts remains in doubt, they still demonstrate that the Buddha's teachings developed in terms of debates with other religious teachers of his day (Gombrich 2006: 3). Continually called upon to explain his ideas to those who were interested and to defend his ideas to those who were skeptical or hostile, the Buddha maintained the importance of moral restraint and mental development in laying out a path to *nirvāṇa*. The answer to the problems associated with existence in the world entail eliminating craving and ignorance, which was termed *kleśa-nirvāṇa* (P: *kilesa-nibbāna*) or the extinction of all mental defilements such as greed, ill-will, and delusion that condition karmic acts, which entangle one further in rebirth. And although one might continue to live out one's years with a pure mental state motivated by selfless generosity, universal friendliness, and wisdom, one who has attained *nirvāṇa* in terms of one's Awakening and severing the defilements will assuredly eventually attain *skandha-nirvāṇa* (P: *khandha-nibbāna*), or the extinction of the Five Aggregates that sustain worldly existence (Gethin 1998: 76). What follows the death of an Awakened One is not clear from the texts, but it seems to involve the attainment of an unconditioned state that transcends one's ordinary feelings, perceptions, and consciousness. It is the blissful, deathless *parinirvāṇa* (or "final" *nirvāṇa*) beyond all worldly conditions and experiences. Simply put, the Buddha is believed to have attained the highest goal, a goal about which he spent forty-five years teaching others.

Remembering and representing the Buddha

If, for his followers, the death of the Buddha served to confirm his attainment of a wholly transcendent condition beyond *saṃsāra*, it also presented some problems to the community of monastics and lay supporters that he founded. After all, Gautama Buddha was the individual who realized perfect wisdom and the way to end suffering. He was revered by many for his attainments and for his willingness to teach others how to attain the same goal. His disappearance from the world, however, meant that the monks and others could no longer rely on his guidance and his direct example. If the accounts of the Buddha's charisma and his skill in speaking are anywhere close to being accurate, one could easily imagine how his passing would have triggered efforts to recall his life and his presence in the world. Indeed, it appears that Buddhists quickly began remembering and representing the Buddha through narrative accounts, the cult of relics, and the formation of aniconic and iconic depictions of the Buddha in stone and other materials.

Biographies of the Buddha

Older accounts of what the Buddha did when he was alive typically provide only incidental details about his life. As a teacher the Buddha appears to have been focused primarily on showing others the way to put an end to *dukkha*. He may well have drawn upon stories and other anecdotes from his own life when teaching others, but no complete biography of his life appeared until several generations passed. If Heinz Bechert is correct in estimating that the Buddha passed away some time between 420–350 BCE, then the earliest attempt to compose a life-story of the Buddha did not occur for at least 150 years or so after his death (Bechert 2004: 82). Scholars agree that the *Mahāvastu* (Great Story), a text written between the second century BCE and the fourth century CE in Buddhist Hybrid Sanskrit, presents the oldest extant account of the Buddha's life as a whole. Attributed to a sect within the ancient Mahāsāṃghika School, the *Mahāvastu* compiled various accounts and legends associated with the Buddha into a single work. Subsequently, the ancient poet Aśvaghoṣa compiled a biography of the Buddha called *Buddhacarita* (Life-story of the Buddha) in ornate Sanskrit verse around the second century CE. Another work called *Lalitavistara* (Exposition of [the Buddha's] Amusements) contains a narrative on the Buddha's life in Buddhist Hybrid Sanskrit from roughly the third and fourth centuries CE. The famous monk Buddhaghosa composed the *Nidānakathā* (Account of the Origins) in Pāli as a prelude to his commentary on the *Jātaka* during the fifth century CE.

The different biographical sources generally share the same basic narrative outline of the Buddha's life. The important characters of Siddhārtha, his father Śuddhodana, his mother Mahāmāyā, his wife Yaśodharā, the donor of milk-rice Sujātā, and many others all appear in the different narrative accounts. The differences in these biographies lie more in their interpretations and elaborations of the various events said to have taken place during the Buddha's life. Two different theories exist on the development of biographical texts about the Buddha. One theory, advanced by the Indologist Erich Frauwallner in 1956, holds that the above-mentioned biographical accounts were based on an older, complete biographical work now lost to the world. Another view, advocated by scholars such as Étienne Lamotte (1958), Alfred Foucher (1963), and André Bareau (1963–71), holds that the biography of the Buddha took shape gradually over time when authors began to synthesize earlier episodes into longer, more coherent narratives (Reynolds and Hallisey 2005: 1063). Although the latter view is more likely correct, both positions recognize that early Buddhist communities displayed an interest in biographical accounts of the Buddha within a few centuries of his passing.

Narratives recalling the Buddha's life could serve several purposes. Such sacred biographies were used to entertain audiences and to instruct them in the forms of religious practice that he exhibited while alive (Schober 1997: 2). In this sense, these accounts provided more context to what the Buddha taught and more significance to what he accomplished. Whereas earlier references to the Buddha's life often appear as short preludes that are secondary to the discourse preached by the Buddha, the composition of complete biographies directed more attention to his life-story and the virtues he came to possess. In other words, the life he lived provided early Buddhist communities with a model of exemplary moral behavior and illustrated his great accomplishments to spur devotion and awe. The conventional view of the development of the Buddha's biography holds that over time a once fairly ordinary human Buddha became transformed into a superhuman figure. In spite of the fact that the Buddha's life-story was almost certainly embellished and expanded over time, it is reasonable to conclude that human and superhuman qualities were attributed to the Buddha at the very beginnings of Buddhist literature and possibly even while he was alive (Xing 2005: 7). And given the early Indian worldview, as seen for example in the early *Upaniṣad*s, it is unwise to assume that the Buddha and his early audiences favored solely rational explanations and doctrines over elements associated with myth, magic, and mysticism (Gethin 1992: 11).

The expansion of the Buddha's biography involved adding details to embellish and fill out his life story. Whereas older *sutta*s and Vinaya versions present fairly abbreviated accounts focusing mainly on the Buddha's teaching career, later narratives were composed to convey information about the Bodhisattva Siddhārtha's birth, upbringing, passing away, and even his previous lives. Around the beginning of the Common Era, Buddhist authors started to compose autonomous biographical works containing coherent albeit incomplete narratives about the Buddha's life story. For example, the *Mahāvastu* and the *Lalitavistara* both include miraculous accounts of the conception and birth of the future Buddha. The former text portrays the Bodhisattva in his penultimate lifetime as a deity in the Tuṣita Heaven specifically choosing the faultless Māyā to be his mother and then entering her womb under the watchful eyes of deities venerating both son and mother (Jones 1952, vol. 2: 4–14). The *Lalitavistara* presents an account wherein the Bodhisattva is born from the side of his mother without impurity and received in a piece of heavenly silk by the deities Brahmā and Śakra. Then the text depicts the newborn Bodhisattva as standing up, observing with his unlimited knowledge that no one in the world was his equal, and walking seven steps toward the east as lotus blooms miraculously sprung up under each step before finally declaring, "I am the foremost on earth, I am the supreme on earth. This is my last birth. I will put an end to birth, old age, death and sorrow" (Goswami 2001: 84–5). The birth story in many accounts is highlighted by the occurrence of numerous marvels such as earthquakes, the sudden growth and flowering of trees, and the temporary allaying of disease and other forms of suffering among all beings.

Older *sutta*s depict the young Siddhārtha as having reflected on the reality of aging, disease, and death, before deciding to renounce the comfortable household life in the ward of his father, a tribal chief in the Śākya clan. Later biographical works, however, portray the Bodhisattva as having encountered four divinely arranged signs—an old man, a diseased man, a dead man, and a recluse—that shocked him into wishing to abandon the luxurious household in which he lived. Another scene in this well-crafted story, the transformation of the beautiful harem women into grotesque and disfigured females who drooled and ground their teeth while asleep in his chamber, is said to have convinced the young man (who now appears as a "prince") to renounce the world without delay (Goswami 2001: 195). The *Buddhacarita* contains a dialogue wherein the young prince explains his distaste for the pleasures of lust.

> I show no contempt for pleasures of sense,
> I know that people are obsessed with them;
> But knowing that the world is transient,
> my heart finds no delight in them at all.
> For if old age, sickness, and death,
> these three things were not to exist,
> I would also have found delight
> in delightful pleasures of sense.
>
> (Olivelle 2008: 115)

Here and elsewhere in this early example of Sanskrit poetry, the Bodhisattva appears as a dispassionate person moved by his higher inclinations to seek his Awakening. In all of these biographies the Bodhisattva Siddhārtha appears headed towards his predestined goal of becoming a Buddha.

It is worth noting that aside from the *Buddhacarita*, the other biographies mentioned above end their narratives well before the Buddha passes away at age 80 in the grove at Kuśinagara. The *Mahāvastu* comes to a close after the Buddha converts the three Kaśyapa brothers and preaches to King Bimbisāra. The *Lalitavistara* ends with the Buddha preaching his first sermon to the five ascetics and setting into motion the Wheel of Dharma. The last event narrated in the *Nidānakathā* concerns the gifting of a monastery to the Saṅgha by the lay donor Anāthapiṇḍika. This may be in part due to the fact that these works seek to exalt the figure of the Buddha by constructing a life story that confirms his greatness and the greatness of his accomplishments. The narratives composed about the Buddha's life typically emphasize his extraordinary qualities, such as being endowed with the Thirty-Two Marks of a Great Man, which are said to include physical attributes such as golden skin, perfect teeth, the graceful gait of a swan, a divine voice, and a tuft of hair between his eyebrows (Jones 1952: 26; Lamotte 1988: 645). They also typically celebrate the Buddha by demonstrating how nearly all other humans, deities—and in the case of the *Lalitavistara*, the other Buddhas and *bodhisattva*s from the many Buddha-fields throughout the universe—approach and offer their reverence to Gautama Buddha (Goswami 2001: 270–7). The Buddha thus appears in these accounts as the one most worthy of veneration.

The development of the Buddha legend in later works not only embellished the life of Siddhārtha; such biographies began to incorporate and highlight stories of the Buddha's previous lives as well. Jātaka stories were rare in early *sutta*s and the Pāli Vinaya but became prominent features in later biographies such as the *Mahāvastu* and *Lalitavistara*, as well as the biographical sections of large *Vinaya* collections (Lamotte 1988: 684). Jātaka stories are typically structured by a narrative told by the Buddha concerning an event that occurred long ago. They concern the Bodhisattva, or the being who had resolved to become a Buddha. Appearing in various forms such as a human, an animal, or a deity, the Bodhisattva consistently finds himself confronting a difficult problem in which he inevitably decides to display and increase his virtue by performing good deeds that result in his further development of a moral perfection (Skt: *pāramitā*/P: *pārami*). In the Sasa (Skt: Śaśa) Jātaka, the Bodhisattva appears as a hare who jumps into a fire in order to offer himself to a hungry Brahmin. In the Nigrodhamiga Jātaka, the Bodhisattva appears as a deer who volunteers his life in place of a pregnant deer about to be killed to feed a king who craves venison. As a scholar in the Vyāghrī Jātaka, he throws himself off a cliff to feed a hungry tigress who is about to kill and eat her own cubs. As King Śibi in the Śibi Jātaka, the Bodhisattva gives up his eyes to a blind man. As King Kusa in the Kusa Jātaka, he appears as an ugly king who saves his recalcitrant wife from the leaders of seven armies and is rewarded with a beautiful appearance for his bravery and his bloodless victory. In the Sutasoma Jātaka, he appears as a prince who converts a cannibal to the Dharma by valuing true speech over his own life.

Perhaps the best-known Jātaka story is the Vessantara Jātaka. As a prince called Vessantara (Skt: Viśvantara), the Bodhisattva resolves to perfect the virtue of generosity. His willingness to give away whatever one asks of him leads the subjects of his father's kingdom to demand that he be sent away before he gives away more of the kingdom's wealth. In exile with his wife Maddī and two small children, Vessantara takes up the life of a hermit. Subsequently, when a cruel, old Brahmin comes to ask Vessantara for his two children as servants, the Bodhisattva complies. His young son and young daughter are then tied up and dragged off in tears by the Brahmin. Vessantara was not without affection and sadness, but his resolution to be generous remained unbroken. Later a deity seeking to test the Bodhisattva convinces Vessantara to give over his wife, and the Bodhisattva is left all alone. But the timely intervention of the deity leads to the reuniting of Vessantara and his family, and the heart-wrenching story comes to a happy end. In this story, as with all the Jātakas, the main characters are said to have been the Buddha and other family members and disciples close to him. The Jātakas also demonstrate how the Bodhisattva gradually developed the virtues that eventually led to his attainment of Buddhahood, such as the Ten Perfections in the Pāli tradition: (1) generosity, (2) morality, (3) renunciation, (4) wisdom, (5) effort, (6) patience, (7) truthfulness, (8) resolution, (9) loving-kindness, and (10) equanimity. The popularity of the Jātaka stories in ancient South Asia is seen in the eventual compilation of works devoted to this genre, such as the Pāli *Jātaka* text containing 547 stories of the Buddha's previous lives and the fourth-century Sanskrit work called the *Jātakamālā*. Scenes from these stories were also carved in reliefs that became common features on early Buddhist monuments.

As narrative representations of the Buddha's life expanded with new details and descriptions spanning his final and his previous lives, his life began to be seen as remarkably consistent with the lives of other Buddhas. Scattered references to the existence of other Buddhas are found in some canonical texts. A list of seven Buddhas preceding Gautama appears to have circulated at an early date and is found in a variety of early canonical sources from different sects. In the Pāli tradition, the late canonical work called the *Buddhavaṃsa* lists Gotama (Gautama) Buddha as the twenty-fifth Buddha to have appeared in the world. The previous Buddhas, starting here with the Buddha named Dīpaṅkara, are important chiefly for confirming that the Bodhisattva in some of his previous lifetimes would one day become a Buddha named Gotama. Although they have different names and different lifespans, the previous Buddhas and Gotama Buddha share many structural similarities as beings who obtained Awakening on their own under a *bodhi* tree and who taught the same Dharma as the way to attain *nirvāṇa* before eventually passing away. Furthermore, these lists of seven and twenty-five both presume the sequential appearance of Buddhas, wherein no more than one may appear in the world at the same time. Around the beginning of the Common Era, this sequence was extended into the future with the recognition of Maitreya (P: Metteya) as a *bodhisattva* who is destined to be the next Buddha to appear in the world. It is said that like Gautama once did, Maitreya is now waiting in heaven for the right time to take his rebirth as a person and eventually rediscover and teach the Dharma to all beings.

Symbols and images of the Buddha

While narrative accounts of the Buddha's life have been influential in shaping how devotees and scholars have understood him, representations of the Buddha in art and architecture also affected how he was perceived. In fact, there is ample evidence that Buddhist monuments, bas-reliefs, and sculpted images appeared widely throughout ancient Buddhist communities in India, and these were at least as influential, if not more so, than literary accounts in shaping people's understandings of the Buddha. It seems likely that funerary mounds called *stūpa*s were among the earliest monuments built by Buddhists to store relics associated with the Buddha or his disciples, as well as to commemorate his appearance and his attainments in the world. Based on pre-Buddhist monuments—including those built by Jains and the supporters of *yakṣa*-cults—Buddhist *stūpa*s originally appeared as solid mounds built of soil, brick, or earth over the Buddha's crematory remains (Coningham 2001: 72). These first monuments were fairly limited in size, but were soon expanded into large hemispherical domes of brick and stone that lay upon a terrace which was surrounded by a processional circular path to facilitate the veneration of devotees who would walk around the *stūpa* while engaging in worship (Lamotte 1988: 311). Smaller reliquaries containing bits of bone, ash, nail clippings, or hair from the Buddha or one of his disciples (*śarīra-dhātu*) would sometimes be enshrined within relic chambers that were sealed up inside the domed structure. Sometimes a relic in the form of an object used by the Buddha or one of his disciples (*pāribhogika-dhātu*)—such as a robe or an alms bowl—would be enshrined in these *stūpa*s and worshipped. Other *stūpa*s were built especially to mark important places and incidents from the Buddha's life.

Buddhist *stūpa*s were built during the Mauryan dynasty (ca. 323–185 BCE) by King Aśoka and possibly others. Later texts assert that Aśoka, the powerful emperor who ruled over much of the subcontinent and patronized Buddhism, arranged to have 84,000 *stūpa*s built throughout the vast empire he controlled over much of the Indian subcontinent. This number, however, is almost certainly an exaggeration. There is clearer evidence, partly circumstantial, that Aśoka built a number of *stūpa*s during his reign, including taking steps to enlarge a *stūpa* that had been built earlier for a previous Buddha named Konāgamana. Two more recent excavations at Vaiśālī and Piprāhwā in India have uncovered tentative evidence of *stūpa*s built before the Mauryan period in around the fifth or fourth centuries BCE (Trainor 1997: 43–4). If these archaeological findings are accurate, their dates would place the *stūpa*s at around the same era in which scholars now believe the Buddha passed away.

It is worth noting that these ancient Buddhist monuments served to recall what the Buddha attained by means of the Dharma. An account from the

Mahāparinibbāna Sutta depicts the Buddha instructing his disciple Ānanda on what to do with his remains. He tells Ānanda to have his body cremated and his remains interned in a *stūpa*, where those who lay offerings with a devout heart can receive good fruits such as auspicious rebirths by performing those deeds (Walshe 1995: 264–5). The tradition holds that after the death of the Buddha, his body was cremated and the remains were removed from the funeral pyre, divided into eight portions, and subsequently enshrined in *stūpa*s located in different kingdoms around the region. As such, *stūpa*s represent a fairly durable sign of the Buddha's *parinirvāṇa* and final transcendence from the cycle of birth and death. Some scholars, most notably Paul Mus, have argued that Buddhist *stūpa*s function to mediate between the human realm and the realm of *nirvāṇa*, simultaneously representing the Buddha's absence from the world after his *nirvāṇa* and his enduring presence in the form of his bodily relics interned within the *stūpa* (Mus 1978: 76–80). Buddhist literary accounts from Sri Lanka similarly attest to the desire of a monk from the third century BCE to "see" the Buddha in the form of his relics in order that he might venerate them while residing in Laṅkā (Geiger 2001: 116; Berkwitz 2007: 150). A *stūpa* may thus come to represent the Buddha in terms of his ultimate attainment of liberation, as well as contain relics that remain in the world for others to venerate and with which to attain fortunate rebirths.

The *stūpa* may serve as an abstract symbol of the Buddha, but it is not the only such symbol in ancient South Asian Buddhism. Scholars have noted that early on a variety of aniconic symbols were used to recall the Buddha without actually depicting his physical, human form. Images of a footprint decorated with auspicious marks, an empty throne, an empty seat beneath the Bodhi Tree, and a *dharmacakra* or Dharma-Wheel are among those aniconic symbols found at early Buddhist sites such as *stūpa*s in the centuries before the Common Era. It has long been thought that the absence of the Buddha from such images must have been due to a prohibition against depicting the Buddha in his human form or due to the doctrinal inconsistency of portraying him in such a manner after he attained *parinirvāṇa*. More recent views, however, challenge such theories. Evidence of sculpted Buddha images appearing around the first century CE suggests that iconic images began to appear while aniconic images continued to be made (Huntington 1990: 402). It has also been argued that the early use of aniconic images to recall the Buddha was simply an outgrowth of an ancient Indian visual culture that employed auspicious signs such as lotus flowers, wheels, trees, animals, and other objects that were later borrowed by Buddhists to represent the Buddha in symbolic form (Karlsson 2006: 73–4).

Aniconic symbols of the Buddha appear on some of the oldest, extant Buddhist sites in India. The Great Stūpa at Sāñcī has several such signs that scholars have traditionally taken to represent key events in the Buddha's life story. For example, the birth of the Buddha is commonly thought to have been depicted aniconically by a lotus—the multi-petal flower that is said to have blossomed under each step that the newborn Bodhisattva took after emerging from his mother's womb (Karlsson 2006: 88). Other symbols found on ancient Buddhist sites include the Bodhi Tree, which is associated with the Buddha's Awakening; the wheel, which is associated with the Buddha's first sermon; and the *stūpa*, which represents his *parinirvāṇa*. The Mahāparinibbāṇa Sutta in the *Dīgha Nikāya* depicts the Buddha instructing his followers to make pilgrimages to the sites of his birth, his Awakening, his first sermon, and his final passing away so that they may continue to arouse faith and confidence in the Buddha even after his death (Walshe 1995: 263–4). At the same time, some scholars have raised questions about the alleged connection between aniconic, auspicious symbols and events in the Buddha's life story. It has been suggested that the aniconic symbols at sites such as the Bhārhut Stūpa were instead meant to represent sacred locations of Buddhist pilgrimage where devotees were depicted as worshipping the Buddha in his absence (Huntington 1990: 403–4). And elsewhere, one scholar has suggested that the auspicious symbols actually served to influence the Buddha's life-story, wherein an ancient Buddhist visual culture led to particular elaborations on the narrative itself (Karlsson 2006: 88–92).

Despite the different theories about aniconism in early South Asian Buddhism, it does appear that the development of iconic representations of the Buddha as a human figure followed the earlier use of auspicious symbols, mythological creatures, and local deities adopted from the broader visual culture of ancient India. Whereas the oldest remaining Buddhist monuments contain traces of such sacred imagery, they also lack anthropomorphic images of the Buddha. However, in the first century of the Common Era, Buddha images began to be sculpted and presumably worshipped by devotees. Scholars have identified the locations of Mathurā (located some sixty miles south of modern Delhi) and Gandhāra (a region centered around Taxila in modern Pakistan) as the places where the oldest Buddha images were produced in South Asia. Their respective styles are distinct, and their appearance around the same period has given rise to considerable scholarly debate over which school is older. Alfred Foucher argued in 1913 that the origin of the Buddha image is found in Gandhāran works that displayed a Hellenistic style adopted from Greek Bactrian influence in the northwest originating with Alexander the Great. Such images were typically carved from grey schist wherein the figures have both shoulders covered and are enveloped in beautiful drapery with deep folds (Lohuizen-de Leeuw 1979: 383). Foucher's claim to assign the first Buddha images to Greek influence may have been meant to elevate the standing of a Greco-Buddhist art by associating it with the Greeks, but it also reiterated the common (and problematic) colonial-era bias which held that native Indian culture was, in contrast to the progress characteristic of Western civilization, marred by stagnation (Abe 1995: 80–3).

Contrary views about the origin of the Buddha image were advanced by Victor Goloubew in 1924 and then, more persuasively, by Ananda Coomaraswamy in 1927. These scholars argued that the creation of iconic forms of the Buddha were indigenous developments that possibly occurred first around the Mathurā region. Coomaraswamy challenged Foucher's view of Greek influence as being behind the creation of the first images of the Buddha. Instead, he cited native iconography associated with ancient *yakṣa* cults as the probable antecedent to the first Buddha images (Coomaraswamy 1927: 298–301). Spirit-deities in the forms of *yakṣa*s and *nāga*s were depicted in iconic stone forms from an early date. These same images were eventually adopted into Buddhist monastic complexes, wherein their very presence demonstrated to the laity the monks' abilities to tame local spirit-deities and to provide relief to the deceased (DeCaroli 2004: 186–7). The evidence for the assimilation of local spirit cults and shrines into early Buddhism may therefore point to a possible source from which Buddhist devotees began to form icons of the Buddha.

Another possible influence for the Mathurā Buddha images were the early Jain figures of Jinas, or liberated beings, that are seated in meditation (Lohuizen-de Leeuw 1979: 385–6). While making a claim for the specifically Indian origins of the Buddha image, Coomaraswamy argued that the first Buddha images in Mathurā were likely made in the latter half of the first century CE (Coomaraswamy 1927: 323–4). More recent research, however, suggests that the first iconic Buddha images were fashioned earlier in Mathurā. The influences of Jain iconography around Mathurā appears to have led Buddhists in the region to imitate their rivals and fashion images of the Buddha as early as 15 CE (Quintanilla 2007: 249–50). Modeled after images fashioned by a heterodox Jain sect that obtained considerable support and prosperity, Mathurā Buddhists apparently followed suit and formed their own images to win more patronage (Quintanilla 2007: 252). The evidence of an abundance of iconic figures made in Mathurā before the Common Era, and the dating of the earliest Buddha images to the second decade of the first century suggests that iconic images of the Buddha were first made in Mathurā and were patterned after Indian rather than Greek prototypes.

The debate over the origins of Buddhist iconography notwithstanding, it is clear that images of the Buddha were employed to represent and to worship the founder of the religion by the first century CE. The image cult thus started a few centuries after the cult of relics organized around *stūpa*s, but it appears to have spread quickly through the sponsorship of certain monks such as

Figure 1.2 Standing Buddha, 5th century, Mathura, India (reproduced courtesy of The Metropolitan Museum of Art, Purchase, Enid A Haupt Gift, 1979 (1979.6) Image © The Metropolitan Museum of Art).

Bala, who is known from inscriptions to have established several images for worship around northern India (Brown 2004: 81). Indeed, contrary to older views that associated the image cult with the devotional needs of the laity, there is considerable evidence to suggest that much of the early interest in Buddha images and the sponsorship needed to craft them was found among monks and nuns. Such a conclusion undercuts the common "two-tiered model" that divides the early Buddhist community into monastics and laypersons, and then attributes much of the development of cultic activities to the spiritual needs of the latter (Schopen 1997: 238–40). Furthermore, Gregory Schopen has argued that inscriptional evidence suggests that it was various monks from the early, so-called "Mainstream" Buddhist sects rather than from the so-called "Mahāyāna" school who displayed the earliest and greatest interest in fashioning and worshipping Buddha images (Schopen 2005: 132–8). Buddhists expressing adherence to the Mahāyāna ideology would later fashion countless images, but the initial efforts made to establish the Buddhist image cult began with other monks.

The actual forms of Buddha images were fashioned and replicated according to particular aesthetic conventions. Buddha images in ancient South Asia could be made in positions of sitting, standing, or reclining on their right side. Sitting images are positioned with crossed legs and an upright torso, and they typically feature one of five different hand gestures (*mudrā*). Images where the Buddha is depicted with both hands held in front of his chest with the right thumb and forefinger making a circle forms the *dharmacakra mudrā*, which represents him preaching the Dharma. When he is seated with both hands resting palms up on his lap signifies the *dhyāna mudrā* of meditative repose. When an image is shown with the right hand pointed towards the ground, it represents the *bhūmisparśa mudrā* recalling when, facing the hostile advances of Māra, the God of Death, he allegedly called upon the earth as a witness to the fact he had developed all the perfections and was ready to attain his Awakening. The *varada mudrā* is made with an open palm pointing downward to signify the giving of blessings. This gesture is often combined with the *abhaya mudrā*, where an open palm is held aloft with the fingers upward in a gesture of reassurance meant to alleviate fear. When reclining, the Buddha image depicts the peaceful trance in which the Buddha is said to have entered before passing away into *parinirvāṇa* at the end of his life.

Artistic representations of the Buddha clearly functioned in part to aid devotees in recalling the Buddha and to edify them about his appearance and attainments. However, such images could sometimes be more than just representations of a Buddha who had passed away long ago. Images could symbolically recall certain moments in the life-story of the Buddha. These images could thus be conceived as commemorative relics (*uddesika-dhātu*) that memorialize the founder of the religion who discovered and taught the Dharma, and that somehow make him present for worship. It has even been argued that early images of the Buddha were often enshrined in special chambers in monastic complexes, where the Buddha was considered to be a living presence that could receive and own property donated to the Saṅgha on his behalf (Schopen 1997: 262–7). There is inscriptional and archaeological evidence pointing to the fact that beginning around the fourth century CE in India, special accommodations in monasteries were routinely set aside for the Buddha who appeared in the form of an icon that was seen as being equivalent to a living presence (Schopen 1997: 276–7). It is unlikely that Buddha images were always understood as the living presence of the Buddha. However, different communities in different times and places likely saw such images as more or less "alive" in the sense of manifesting some form of the Buddha's presence long after he was thought to have attained his *parinirvāṇa*.

2

Foundations:

Mainstream Buddhist texts and communities

The development of the Saṅgha
Elaborations on the Vinaya
Founding the *Bhikṣuṇī* order
Buddhist councils
First Council of Rājagṛha
Second Council of Vaiśālī
Later Buddhist councils
Buddhist canons and texts
Writing canonical texts
Mainstream Buddhist schools
Mahāsāṃghika and related schools
Sthavira Schools I: Pudgalavāda
Sthavira Schools II: Sarvāstivāda
Sthavira Schools III: Vibhajyavāda and Theravāda
Sthavira Schools IV: Sautrāntika
Abhidharma speculation

The development of the Saṅgha

Buddhist texts describe how before the Buddha passed away, he established the Saṅgha comprising an order of monks (P: *bhikkhu*/Skt: *bhikṣu*) and an order of nuns (P: *bhikkhunī*/Skt: *bhikṣuṇī*). While the idea of the Saṅgha may sometimes encompass a "Fourfold Community" of monks, nuns, male lay devotees (*upāsaka*), and female lay devotees (*upāsikā*), the establishment of more formal methods of ordination led to a conception of the Saṅgha as essentially a monastic body of world-renouncers. It is the development and the division of the Saṅgha into various "mainstream" sects (*nikāya*) that marks the next significant chapter in the history of South Asian Buddhism. While the Buddha was alive, the Dharma was transmitted orally and the Saṅgha existed as a more or less unified body. But in the centuries following his *parinirvāṇa*, the Buddha's message or "Dispensation" (P: *sāsana*/Skt:

śāsana) became historically instantiated in Buddhist texts and monastic lineages. And the community of monks and nuns changed from a band of wandering, homeless renunciants into a primarily settled order of monastics dwelling in permanent shelters throughout the year.

This process whereby Buddhists monastics came to live collectively in large monasteries called *vihāra*s that were provided by lay donors is sometimes referred to as the "domestication" of the Saṅgha. The move to adopt permanent residences need not, however, be seen as a compromise or a betrayal of an original ideal. Not only did smaller numbers of individuals continue to live by the ideal of the "forest-monk," the renunciant who lives in relative seclusion and isolation from the civilized world, but monasteries facilitated greater interaction between monastics and the laity as far as religious instruction and ritual donations are concerned. Permanent dwellings allowed for greater numbers of individuals to become monks and nuns, increased lay support of the Saṅgha, and offered the time and resources necessary to produce and study texts on the Dharma. In other words, Buddhism developed in South Asia around the presence and activities of large numbers of monks and nuns who mostly resided permanently in dwellings that the laity gave to them. Their behavior was in turn regulated by one or another monastic code of conduct included in the genre of texts called the Vinaya, which means "to lead away" or "to remove," as in the sense of refraining from morally inappropriate behavior and, it has been suggested, ridding oneself of the false sense of the "I" as a permanent and unique actor in the world (Holt 1983: 4).

Different theories exist to explain why the Saṅgha transformed from a wandering order of homeless mendicants into a settled order of monastic residents. One view holds that once the Buddha instructed his disciples to take up temporary residences during the rainy season, in part since the public expressed opposition to monks wandering around at this time and damaging crops and smaller life-forms in the lush vegetation, the monks found these dwellings conducive to their activities of study and meditation (Prebish 1975: 4–5). Thus, their three-month rainy season retreats gradually grew into longer periods of residence, eventually leading to year-round dwelling places for the Saṅgha near where the laity dwelled. Another view holds that once the Buddha permitted the Saṅgha to accept residences donated by laypersons, this decision resulted in a more sedentary lifestyle in fixed dwellings (Wijayaratna 1990: 21–4). It is possible that both of these theories affected the development of the Saṅgha away from a wandering band of homeless ascetics and into settled communities of renunciants.

The combination of the requirement to spend at least part of the year in fixed shelters and the donation of land and dwellings to the Saṅgha by wealthy lay devotees resulted in a monastic order that became increasingly sedentary as time passed. A tension remained, however, between so-called "town monks" (*grāmavāsins*) who resided in monasteries near the laity and "forest monks" (*araṇyavāsins*) who resided in caves and elsewhere in the wilderness. The former had more frequent contacts with the laity and tended to thrive under the comparative ease in which they gained patronage and new recruits. Forest monks, however, tended to earn greater respect and admiration for their austere way of life, and the laity would periodically seek them out for alms-giving for the sake of earning greater merit by giving to those who are assumed to be highly virtuous. The polarity between "town" and "forest" offered competing visions of the monastic ideal and continued to structure South Asian Buddhist monasticism for centuries.

Elaborations on the Vinaya

The domestication of the Saṅgha in South Asia was made orderly by the adoption and expansion of various disciplinary rules to regulate all aspects of monastic conduct for monks and nuns, wherever they resided. The regulation of monastic conduct was accomplished first by the adoption of the *Prātimokṣa* (P: *Pāṭimokkha*) code of conduct, comprising a lengthy list of offences together with the punishments prescribed for those who commit them. Such a list of rules became necessary as the numbers of monks grew and expanded to new regions. The *Prātimokṣa* code is thus designed to make the lives of Buddhist renunciants conform to a strict and recognizable set of rules that would promote communal harmony, earn the respect and support of the laity, and facilitate progress toward attaining *nirvāṇa*. The institution of such a code and the insistence that it be observed helped to make the Saṅgha a "field of merit," or religiously disciplined practitioners who are worthy of material support and public esteem. By following the path laid out by the Buddha and by adhering to a monastic disciplinary code, Buddhist monks and nuns made themselves into virtuous actors in early South Asian societies. A layperson who offered this ideal Saṅgha some food, robes, or a monastic residence could thus expect to earn great merit, or a kind of spiritual reward that would later materialize as a fortunate karmic result.

Scholars have identified six versions of the Vinaya that are at least partially extent or preserved in Pāli, Sanskrit, Chinese, or Tibetan. These works are attributed to the Buddha and therefore, in theory, quiet ancient. In all likelihood, these works were compiled and developed over several centuries. The six extant *Vinaya*s are linked to the following "Mainstream" Buddhist orders or schools: Dharmaguptaka, Theravāda, Mahāsāṃghika, Mahīśāsaka, Mūlasarvāstivāda, and Sarvāstivāda. The fact that each one of these monastic communities possessed their own *Vinaya* suggests that they each developed a distinctive ordination tradition and corporate identity. In other words, a monk would be considered a "Dharmaguptaka monk," if he was ordained in the monastic lineage that subscribed to the Dharmaguptaka *Vinaya*. The fact remains, however, that the six extant *Vinaya*s share a great deal in common with each other. This is particularly true with reference to their oldest section, the *Prātimokṣa*. Each order's *Prātimokṣa* begins by listing four *pārājika* offences, which are violations or "defeats" deemed serious enough to warrant expulsion from the order. The four "defeats" for monks include (1) engaging in sexual intercourse, (2) theft, (3) intentionally taking or instigating the taking of a human life, and (4) falsely boasting of possessing exceptional religious attainments or superhuman powers. (Buddhist nuns, in contrast, were given eight expellable offences.) Engaging in any one of these activities runs counter to an individual's spiritual progress and risks undermining the trust and support of the laity for the Saṅgha as a whole.

Despite their agreement over the *pārājika* offences, the six *Prātimokṣa* codes contain different numbers of rules. Most of these differences are found in the minor categories of monastic regulations that mainly cover rules of monastic etiquette and composure. The Mahāsāṃghika order appears to have possessed the smallest number of *Prātimokṣa* rules with a total of 218 specific regulations to follow. The Pāli *Vinaya* preserved by the Theravāda order contains 227 regulations. Meanwhile, the Sarvāstivāda *Prātimokṣa* contains the most regulations, which number 263. Nevertheless, the different codes all appear to have contained lists of rules that sanctioned expulsion (*pārājika*), probation, confession and forfeiture, or simple confession depending on the severity of the offence. Examples of offenses that called for probation and the suspension of one's identity as a monk include masturbation, making sexual overtures, and building a hut for oneself that has not been donated and that has involved destroying life. Offences that call for confession and forfeiture typically involve the inappropriate use of articles such as robes, bowls, and money. Types of offences that only require a simple confession include intentionally driving out another *bhikkhu* from his dwelling place, sitting with a woman in private, and sporting in the water. The recital of the entire list of *Prātimokṣa* rules and the requisite acknowledgment of any of their violations took place on the ritual recital of the *Prātimokṣa* by all members of a particular monastic community. These recitals were mandated in the *poṣadha* (P: *uposatha*) ceremonies held every fortnight in conjunction with the new and full moon days, and wherein all Saṅgha members were required to attend.

Each of the Mainstream Buddhist *Vinaya*s also contains a section called the *Vibhaṅga* that represents a commentary to explain the rules of the *Prātimokṣa*. While explaining the *Prātimokṣa*, the *Vibhaṅga* also typically provides additional information regarding the event that led to the rule being made by the Buddha and also the conditions that affect how the rule should be interpreted and applied. It is here that one finds exceptions to the rules. Schopen comments that the *Vibhaṅga*'s "impressive number of loopholes" reflect the ingenuity expressed in Buddhist legal interpretation (Schopen 2004b: 888). Thus, whereas the rules laid down in the *Prātimokṣa* may appear strict and inflexible, the legal commentary in the *Vibhaṅga* suggests that in practice the *Vinaya* could often be interpreted and expressed in a looser manner. In the case of the *Vibhaṅga* from the Pāli *Vinaya* of the Theravāda order, additional specifications attributed to the Buddha appear either to strengthen or to loosen a particular monastic rule or the punishment prescribed for its offense (von Hinüber 1995: 16–17). The *Vibhaṅga*s found in the *Vinaya*s of other orders similarly contain material reflecting legal interpretations that belied the apparently straightforward manner of the *Prātimokṣa* rules. For example, in the Mūlasarvāstivāda *Vinaya*, the rule prohibiting monks from handling money is elaborated upon to allow them to accept permanent money endowments and to lend that money out to gain interest on it (Schopen 2004b: 888). Buddhist *Vinaya*s typically contain separate *Vibhaṅga*s for monks and nuns, with the latter receiving more rules and stricter applications of them.

If the *Vibhaṅga* sections deal with adjudicating the conduct of individual monks and nuns, than the *Skhandaka* (P: *Khandaka*) comprises material that concerns the discipline of entire monastic communities. The Pāli version is divided into the Mahāvagga and the Cullavagga, which relates the institution of rules for the order in the context of biographical material on the Buddha's life as a teacher and organizer of the Saṅgha. Related to this material are statements on the *karmavācanā*s (P: *kammavācanā*s), or judgments on the organization of the life of the Saṅgha as a whole. Among the topics considered in the *Skandhaka* are rules for admission into the order; monthly confession ceremonies; the monastic retreat during the rainy season; the use of medicines, sandals, and clothing; and the procedures for settling disputes and avoiding schisms (Lamotte 1988: 165–7).

The final section of the *Vinaya*s contains various *Parivāra*, or "appendices," many of which vary considerably or are absent in the different monastic orders for which a basket of *Vinaya* texts still exists. These materials often appear as summaries of various sections of the disciplinary texts. Some of these summaries may, however, predate the other sections of the *Vinaya*, and could represent an independent ordering and treatment of monastic rules (Schopen 2004b: 888).

This discussion of the various versions and sections of the *Vinaya* that survived from the ancient period serves to illustrate the fact that the monastic disciplinary code developed over time. Although there is a tradition that states that Upāli, a disciple of the Buddha, recited the entire *Vinaya* at the first monastic council following the Buddha's death, it is more likely that only the *Prātimokṣa*s for the monks and the nuns were rehearsed at this time. Moreover, several different monastic orders lay claim to possessing the original and most authentic *Vinaya*. Such claims, however, cannot be verified with any certainty.

Founding the *Bhikṣuṇī* order

The story of how an order of Buddhist nuns or *bhikṣuṇī*s (P: *bhikkhunī*s) was established illustrates the patriarchal subordination of female renunciants to the male order of monks. In early Pāli texts this event occurred when the Buddha's maternal aunt and stepmother Mahāpajāpati Gotamī approached him to request ordination as a female renunciant. The Buddha is said to have thrice refused her request. Subsequently, Mahāpajāpati and five hundred noblewomen shaved their heads and dressed themselves in robes before approaching the Buddha and again requesting his consent to ordain them. At this point, the monk Ānanda intervened on behalf of the women and asked the still reluctant Buddha whether women were capable of attaining the higher fruits of practicing the Buddhist path. The Buddha acknowledged that women can attain *nirvāṇa* and allowed for their ordination as *bhikṣuṇī*s, in part since the previous Buddhas had allegedly done the same.

Women were permitted to join the Saṅgha as "nuns" provided that they accept eight special conditions or "heavy rules" (*aṭṭhagarudharmā*). These additional rules that appear specifically for *bhikṣuṇī*s alone requires that any given *bhikṣuṇī*: (1) must rise and pay respect to any and all monks, including those who are junior to her in terms of length of ordination; (2) must not spend the rains retreat in an area where there is no monk; (3) must request instruction from the monks twice each month; (4) must declare any fault seen or suspected in her order to the monks; (5) must be disciplined for any suspension before both orders of monks and nuns; (6) must be ordained by both orders; (7) must not abuse or revile any monk; and (8) must not admonish a monk, although the latter may admonish her. These eight rules effectively place the order of nuns under the supervision and control of the monks. But even after allowing for female ordination, the Buddha is depicted in accounts as ruefully commenting that the presence of women in the Saṅgha will eventually hasten the disappearance of the Dharma.

Attempts by scholars and practitioners to explain the Buddha's apparent reluctance to found an order of Buddhist nuns often cite the patriarchal social system of ancient India and either the Buddha's inability or hesitation to deviate from conventional views about women's participation in the ascetic life. In general, women in ancient South Asian culture were required to be under the control of men throughout their lives, with their fathers, husbands, and sons assuming the obligation to control their sexuality and to prevent them from offending social norms (Kloppenborg 1995: 151). In this perspective the Buddha's apparent reluctance to ordain women could reflect an anxiety about transgressing cultural norms about a woman's place in society. Another hypothesis holds that the Buddha was merely concerned to assist the monks in upholding the demands of celibacy, and thus he wished to avoid bringing monks into more contact with women—including nuns (Dhirasekera 1982: 141). A wholly different approach favored by some suggests it is unlikely that these rules were imposed by the Buddha himself, but rather they were the results of efforts undertaken by later writers to subordinate nuns to monks.

Whatever the circumstances behind the founding of the *bhikṣuṇī* order, once female renunciants were accepted into the Saṅgha, they flourished in large numbers in ancient South Asia. Many of these women became renowned for their spiritual attainments and for their donations of Buddha images and monastic dwellings. The idea that *bhikṣuṇī*s could achieve the same degree of spiritual accomplishment as the *bhikṣus*—developing abilities to meditate, adhering to the disciplinary code, performing supernormal powers, and obtaining *nirvāṇa*—is supported by the literature. The text called the *Therīgāthā* is particularly noteworthy in this regard, since it apparently preserves the ancient utterances of several dozen or more elder nuns (*therī*s) in verse. Although it is impossible to know whether these poems were actually composed by the *therī*s themselves, the text does purport to convey the religious goals and experiences of women, and it is likely that portions of it are quite old and were orally transmitted with the help of conventional expressions and stock formula beginning around the third century BCE (Blackstone 1998: 3). Therein, Buddhist nuns express the joys of living a life of renunciation and experiencing the blissful state of liberation. Many of them also draw contrasts between these positive experiences and the negative ones they suffered as female laypersons living in a patriarchal society.

It was precisely this social environment that imposed restrictions and stereotypes on women in ancient South Asian Buddhism. Numerous scholars have noted that early Buddhist views of women were often ambiguous and contradictory. In the ancient literature, certain women are occasionally celebrated for their moral discipline and their attainment of *nirvāṇa* on par with any other revered monk. But in other places, women are reviled as sensual beings whose desire outweighs their intellect. In an oft-cited essay, Alan Sponberg has identified four distinct attitudes toward women in early Buddhist texts. The first attitude is called "soteriological inclusiveness," and it refers to the Buddha's expressed acknowledgement that women are fully capable of following the path and attaining the highest fruits of Buddhist practice (Sponberg 1992: 8). In other words, women may grasp the

Dharma and attain liberation from *saṃsāra* just like men. It is this attitude that supporters of the religion cite as evidence of the Buddhist religion's comparatively progressive attitude towards women in ancient South Asia. Because, according to the Buddha, gender differences are insignificant for realizing Awakening, women and men are instructed to follow the same path toward liberation.

At the same time, however, Sponberg notes another attitude in early Buddhism called "institutional androcentrism" that places restrictions on women to bring them under the control of men. The eight special conditions (*aṭṭhagarudharmā*) that women must accept to become ordained as *bhikṣuṇī*s illustrates this view. Since the various *Bhikṣuṇī Prātimokṣa*s contain many more rules of conduct than the codes for monks contain, it stands to reason that over time the tradition devised additional disciplinary rules to control the women in the Saṅgha and to establish them in a clearly inferior position under male authority. Sponberg believes that institutional androcentrism developed later as female membership in the Saṅgha grew and as Buddhist monastics increasingly came to reside in permanent dwellings (Sponberg 1992: 13). In such a view, the reliance of the Buddhist Saṅgha on public acceptance and lay support compelled its members to establish various methods to control women and to prevent them from challenging broader social norms.

The third attitude towards women found in early Buddhism is "ascetic misogyny." This position was not unique to Buddhism, as there is evidence in other South Asian ascetic traditions of deep suspicion and fear of women. Indeed, any religious system that extolled celibate renunciation could be expected to develop teachings to discourage male practitioners from sexual activity. For example, disturbing images of disfigured, dead, or sleeping women frequently appear in ancient South Asian Buddhist literature to inspire disgust among male monks and to aid them in abandoning their desire for physical pleasures (Wilson 1996). But in case the images of decaying or snoring women are not sufficient to dispel a monk's lust, numerous Buddhist texts contain admonitions in which women are portrayed as wicked temptresses with uncontrolled sexual appetites, ready to impede a man's spiritual progress (Harris 1999: 50). The common portrayal of women as primarily sensual beings who are ill-suited for spiritual pursuits can be found across a wide range of Buddhist texts with different sectarian allegiances. Diana Paul's translation of the following excerpts from the *Mahāratnakūṭa Sūtra*, an early collection of Mahāyāna *sūtra*s, illustrates this view quite well:

> Women can ruin
> The precepts of purity.
> They can also ignore
> Honor and virtue.

Causing one to go to hell
They prevent rebirth in heaven.
Why should the wise delight in them?

...Ornaments on women
Show off their beauty.
But within them there is great evil
As in the body there is air.

...As the filth and decay
Of a dead dog or dead snake
Are burned away,
So all men should burn filth
And detest evil.

The dead snake and dog
Are detestable,
But women are even more
Detestable than they are.

(Paul 1985: 31, 41–2)

Such misogynistic depictions of women may represent either an innate gender bias or a tool for male monastics to control their passions. In either case, numerous texts in South Asian Buddhist traditions contain negative portrayals of women as serious obstacles to progress on the Buddhist path.

Sponberg's fourth category of "soteriological androgyny" developed later around the sixth and seventh centuries CE. This attitude ascribed a much more positive value to the ideal of the feminine, arguing in favor of the active integration of masculine and feminine attributes in the attainment of the liberated state (Sponberg 1992: 25–6). Such a view would become prominent in Buddhist Tantric systems, but was difficult to find in the early centuries of Buddhism in South Asia. It is worth noting, moreover, that this positive reevaluation involves the feminine as an ideal—the complimentary aspect to what is masculine—rather than any actual, embodied woman per se.

One of the major benefits of Sponberg's typology is that it reveals how the views on women in ancient South Asian Buddhism were deeply ambivalent. One can find support for women's aspirations to participate fully in the Buddhist path leading to Awakening. But it is equally possible to find material that could be used to control women and to deny their ability, and perhaps the opportunity, to follow the Buddha's path. The contested nature of early Buddhist attitudes toward women is likely the result of the success that many ancient Buddhist nuns and *upāsikā*s had in practicing the

Dharma and in emerging as important symbols and donors for the religion. The verses in the *Therīgāthā*, for example, supplied material to challenge prevailing stereotypes about women—including those that held women to be stupid, family-oriented, vain, and seductive (Kloppenborg 1995: 153–4). The recognition that some women accomplished the tradition's highest goals meant that any attempts to prevent them from doing so could only be seen as arbitrary and unjust. The *bhikṣuṇī* order eventually died out throughout South Asia sometime between the tenth and twelfth centuries CE. However, for several centuries before their disappearance, *bhikṣuṇī*s (and *upāsikā*s) appeared as prominent figures in the Saṅgha.

In an exhaustive survey of ancient Buddhist inscriptions from South Asia, Schopen has drawn scholarly attention to evidence suggesting that nuns and laywomen were just as active as monks and laymen in participating in early image and *stūpa* cults, at least up to the Gupta period (4th–5th c. CE). With few exceptions, such as the Karoṣṭhī area of the Northwest, there is a preponderance of historical inscriptions that show nuns were present nearly everywhere as active donors supporting the worship of Buddha images and *stūpa*s in numbers similar to those of monks (Schopen 1997: 248–50). From this, we may conclude that women were generally very active and influential members of the Buddhist Saṅgha in the early centuries of the Common Era. Inscriptions reveal that some *bhikṣuṇī*s claimed titles such as "master of the Three *Piṭaka*s" and "versed in the *Sūtra*s," while others had large groups of disciples like leading monks (Schopen 1997: 250).

However, the vitality of female participation in the Saṅgha further to the south in Sri Lanka appears somewhat different. A study of Brāhmī inscriptions in Sri Lanka from around the third century BCE to the first century CE shows that while the number of *bhikṣuṇī*s compared to *bhikṣu*s who donated caves to the Saṅgha for meditation and retreat is small (ten versus around three hundred), the number of *upāsikā*s who donated caves (105) actually exceeds that of male lay devotees (91) (Paranavitana 1970: cxvii–cxviii). In Sri Lanka, therefore, the contributions of female monastics to the Dispensation appear to have been proportionately less than that of female lay devotees. But the role of women in the life of the Buddhist Saṅgha in ancient Sri Lanka still remained influential.

Buddhist councils

According to the idealized self-image of South Asian Buddhist traditions, the formation of the early Saṅgha in South Asia revolved around councils (*saṃgīti*) of monks and the development of canons of authoritative scriptures. These two phenomena were interrelated, at least in theory, since a number of Mainstream Buddhist schools trace the formation of their version of the

Tripiṭaka—the "Three Baskets" of Buddhist scriptures—to a major assembly of monks who met and recited the texts attributed to the Buddha before arriving at a more or less fixed version of their respective canons. However, the notion of an assembly of monks establishing a Buddhist canon, comprised of texts originally recited by the Buddha, may be more ideal than real. The various Buddhist canons that were nominally established were often less fixed and more variable than the term "canon" implies. For one thing, although different *Vinaya*s belonging to Mainstream schools cite one or more Buddhist councils as historical events, their respective descriptions and dates of these events can vary dramatically. And because of these variances, modern scholars have voiced doubts over the historicity of at least some of these councils. Even when they provisionally accept that such a council was held, they often question the accuracy of their literary accounts. These various councils, moreover, were apparently held not only to recite and to standardize canons, but also to settle monastic disputes, to unify the Saṅgha, to preserve the Buddha's Dispensation, and to showcase the authority of the councils' royal sponsors, among other reasons (Hallisey 1991: 147).

First Council of Rājagṛha

The diversity of accounts and opinions on ancient Buddhist councils notwithstanding, it is clear from the literature that such events—real or fictional—were recognized as key moments in the formation of monastic orders and textual canons. The so-called First Council of Rājagṛha is traditionally thought to have been held within a few weeks or months of the Buddha's passing away into *parinirvāṇa*. Scholars of Buddhism have generally dismissed this council as an actual historical event (Prebish 1974: 241). Yet a number of different *Vinaya*s contain accounts of this council, which was held after a monk named Subhadra happily stated that since the Buddha had died, it was then possible for the monks to abandon the regulations he enforced. The *arhat* Kāśyapa responded by calling five hundred monks to assemble and rehearse the Dharma and the Vinaya taught by the Buddha so that moral laxity would not creep into the Saṅgha. The disciple Upāli is said to have recited the Vinaya, while the Buddha's personal attendant Ānanda recited the *sūtra*s, or discourses of the Buddha. These recitations were then accepted as authoritative and memorized by the five hundred *arhat*s to be transmitted to their students for the sake of preserving the Buddha's teachings.

Different opinions also appear over what was recited at Rājagṛha. Although some orders such as the Theravādins and Mahāsāṃghikas maintain that only the Vinaya and Sūtra Piṭakas were rehearsed at the First Council, several other orders such as the Dharmaguptakas and Sarvāstivādins add the Abhidharma Piṭaka to the sections of the canon recited just after the

Buddha's death (Prebish 1974: 245). Summarizing some of the scholarly objections to the alleged historicity of the First Council, Andre Bareau notes that the various narrative accounts of this event offer no description of the canon's contents, that it is unlikely that the objections of a single monk to the Vinaya shortly after the Buddha's death would have necessitated a large council to fix his teachings, and that it seems plausible that the accounts retroactively sought to justify the authenticity of a particular vision of the canon by attributing it as the product of an early assembly of *arhats* (Prebish 1974: 245–6). Nevertheless, this account of the Council of Rājagṛha has served a useful role by explaining how the Buddha's teachings were preserved and transmitted following his death.

Second Council of Vaiśālī

The Second Council of Vaiśālī, traditionally said to have been held about 100 to 110 years after the Buddha's *parinirvāṇa*, is thought by some scholars to have actually occurred. This council was held after a dispute arose between two parties of monks over disciplinary issues. Several different *Vinaya*s specify that a monk named Yaśas objected to ten practices promulgated by a body of monks residing in Vaiśālī. After being chastened for his objections to practices such as receiving more than one meal from different villages, confirming acts of the Saṅgha before an incomplete assembly, drinking unfermented wine, and accepting gold and silver, Yaśas presented his objections to other *bhikṣus*. A council was held under the auspices of some senior monks, who ruled in favor of the delegation that maintained that the ten points violated the Vinaya. Some scholars, citing evidence in the Mahāsāṃghika *Vinaya*, have suggested that the Second Council was prompted only by a rejection of the practice of accepting money (Prebish 1974: 248). In any event, the Council at Vaiśālī highlights the attempt to settle disagreements over monastic discipline.

Later Buddhist councils

The two councils at Rājagṛha and Vaiśālī are universally recognized in the literature of Mainstream Buddhist schools, even if the details of their respective accounts vary substantially. The fact that these events would be described differently should come as no surprise given that each school used the tradition of the councils to demonstrate the authenticity and antiquity of its own version of the canonical writings (Lamotte 1988: 135). A number of other councils beyond these first two meetings are recorded in different texts from different schools. For example, the Mahāsāṃghika School maintains that a council was held at Pāṭaliputra, probably around 137 years after the *parinirvāṇa*, wherein a king recognized that the Sthaviras (or community of "Elder-monks") had imposed more Vinaya rules than was necessary (Prebish 1974: 252–3). For their part, the Sthaviravādins held that the dispute was over the so-called five theses of the monk Mahādeva, who held that *arhat*s had imperfect natures and were still prone to have nocturnal emissions and subject to ignorance and doubt. The outcome of this dispute, whether there was actually a formal council or not, was the first clear schism in the Saṅgha, resulting in the Mahāsāṃghika and the Sthaviravāda Schools.

Some early Theravāda sources record what is by their reckoning the Third Council at Pāṭaliputra sponsored by the renowned King Aśoka approximately 236 years after the *parinirvāṇa*. It is listed third since the Theravādins did not accept the legitimacy of an earlier council at Pāṭaliputra, used to mark the beginnings of the Mahāsāṃghikas. At the council called by King Aśoka, a *thera* named Moggaliputtatissa presided over a body of one thousand monks versed in the *Tripiṭaka* and refuted doctrinal points deemed heretical and inconsistent with the position described as Vibhajyavāda, or "those who profess distinctions." Those monks who held doctrines in violation of the Vibhajyavāda position were, according to some accounts, disrobed and expelled from the Saṅgha in an act of purification. In reality, the major result of this council seems to have been the division of the community into two factions—the Vibhajyavādins and the Sarvāstivādins, who maintained a doctrine that held that past and future things exist just like things in the present, a thesis labeled "eternalism" by its critics.

If, as the story goes, the Sarvāstivādins were formed out of rejecting the Vibhajyavāda doctrines from the so-called Third Council at Pāṭaliputra, they too would be able to point to a council wherein their positions were reaffirmed. Sometime around the turn of the first century CE in Kāśmīra, under the auspices of King Kaniṣka of the Kuṣāṇa Empire in the northwest region of the subcontinent, a large number of monks are said to have held a council that settled monastic differences in favor of the Sarvāstivāda view concerning the continuity of phenomena. Tradition holds that one result of this council was the composition of a work called the *Mahāvibhāṣā* (Great Options), which served as a commentary on the first book of the Sarvāstivāda Abhidharma and served to explain the school's distinctive views on time and matter. The faction that lost this debate, a group that would later be called the Sautrāntikas, split off from the dominant order in this region. More recently, however, some scholars have suggested that rather than a formal debate, the Council in Kāśmīra was really a reunion of the Sarvāstivāda School at which a work called the *Jñānaprasthāna* (Source of Knowledge) was composed to systematize the Sarvāstivāda Abhidharma texts, and it was later linked to King Kaniṣka simply to glorify the ruler in the image of Aśoka (Willeman *et al.* 1998: 118–20). If this view is correct, it shows how different Mainstream

Buddhist schools used the *ideas* of councils to lend their orders and canons greater validity and importance. And the various accounts of such councils offered persuasive models for subsequent monks and kings to replicate in order to direct their own reforms and purifications of the Saṅgha.

Buddhist canons and texts

Even if the narrative accounts of Buddhist councils are often historically suspect, they help us to understand a crucial aspect of canon-formation in the ancient Mainstream Buddhist schools. In the early centuries of South Asian Buddhism, canonical texts derived their authority and significance from the idea that they represented the actual oral teachings of the Buddha. Since there was no record or even claim for the Dharma being put into writing while the Buddha was alive, early Buddhists were confronted with the task of preserving and transmitting his teachings as accurately as possible. Indeed, the Buddha is commonly portrayed as having directed his disciples to take the Dharma as their guide after his departure from *saṃsāra*, and there is every indication that the early Saṅgha quickly developed the will and the means to write down the Buddha's teachings.

Much like the councils, the *idea* of the Buddhist Canon often evokes more coherence and consensus than what was actually the case in history. Although all South Asian Buddhist schools spoke of the *Tripiṭaka* or "Three Baskets" as the source of the Buddha's teachings on monastic discipline (*Vinaya Piṭaka*), discursive sermons (*Sūtra Piṭaka*), and technical reflections on the Teaching (*Abhidharma Piṭaka*), the texts they included in this threefold division of scriptures could vary substantially. Indeed, what we today call a "Buddhist Canon" was likely only constituted gradually over time as certain local traditions and languages became recognized as authoritative and were elevated to a canonical status. There are traces of many distinct corpuses of Buddhist scriptures, most of which were eventually linked to a particular monastic order that studied and preserved them. And yet while it is possible to speak of a Theravāda Canon and a Sarvāstivāda Canon, among others, it is necessary to recall that such textual corpuses were the products of centuries of the transmission, revision, and at times even the loss of texts.

The section of Buddhist scriptures that exhibits the most coherence is the *Sūtra Piṭaka*. The texts contained within represent the doctrinal basis of the Buddhist religion. In theory this material, like the rest of the canonical texts, originates with discourses preached by the Buddha. However, it is likely that only a measure of the texts as we now have them can be directly linked with the Buddha himself. The Pāli Canon of the Theravāda school specifies five *nikāya*s or "collections": (1) *Dīgha Nikāya* (Collection of Long Discourses), (2) *Majjhima Nikāya* (Collection of Medium Discourses),

(3) *Saṃyutta Nikāya* (Collection of Connected Discourses), (4) *Aṅguttara Nikāya* (Collection of Numerical Discourses), and (5) *Khuddaka Nikāya* (Collection of Minor Discourses). Each of these collections includes numerous discourses or texts of varying lengths. A number of schools that preserved Sanskrit canons adopted the same titles of these collections but called them *āgama*s instead of *nikāya*s. Some of these schools recognized only four *āgama*s and either excluded the minor texts of the *Kṣudrakāgama* (cf. *Khuddaka Nikāya*) or included them as independent works or in the other *āgama*s. In general, the various *Sūtra Piṭaka*s display a fair degree of uniformity in terms of doctrinal content and titles of individual *sūtra*s, but they often differ in terms of how they are arranged and in other details such as the setting given for a particular discourse (Lamotte 1988: 155–6).

A discussion of the different *Vinaya*s that appear in the canons of various Mainstream schools appears above in this chapter. Suffice it to say that the different *Vinaya*s share the same basic structure but can deviate from one another in terms of the numbers of rules and the scholastic arguments and narratives found therein. Thus, each *Vinaya* includes a list of offences (*Prātimokṣa*) and a description of the acts and ceremonies (*karmavācanā*s) that the Saṅgha is to perform on certain occasions. Most of the major rules and ceremonies are similar if not identical, but the finer points of the monastic discipline and the explanations given for them could vary from school to school.

The *Abhidharma* (P: *Abhidhamma*) *Piṭaka* contains texts that were likely compiled at a later date compared with the *Sūtra* and *Vinaya* collections. Some scholars maintain, however, that they were based on older summaries (*mātṛkā*s) used to classify and memorize lists of key teachings on the Dharma. As systematic presentations of the "Higher" or "Special" Dharma, *Abhidharma* texts present doctrinal material without the narrative descriptions of *sūtra*s. Whereas most Mainstream schools used more or less identical *Sūtra Piṭaka*s and employed similar *Vinaya Piṭaka*s, it was their *Abhidharma Piṭaka*s that showed the greatest degree of variance between them (Lamotte 1988: 180). This is partly due to the fact that the *Abhidharma* texts were generally composed later, after the different schools split off from each other and began to develop their own traditions and interpretations. Among the schools that possess an *Abhidharma Piṭaka*, their number of works vary from four to seven. The Theravāda and Sarvāstivāda schools both used an *Abhidharma* comprising seven books, but they are entirely different from each other. The Theravādins traditionally ascribe their *Abhidharma* texts to discourses given by the Buddha first in the Tāvatiṃsa Heaven to his mother Māyā shortly after his Awakening. The Sarvāstivādins, in contrast, held that the Buddha only initiated their *Abhidharma* teachings, which were then completed and composed by disciples much later (Lamotte 1988: 186–7).

Writing canonical texts

It is reasonable to conclude that the various Buddhist canons were composed variously by different monastic orders, at first orally and then in writing, over several centuries. All of the early Mainstream schools recognized the *Sūtra* and *Vinaya Piṭaka*s, and many also added an *Abhidharma Piṭaka*. There is some evidence that suggests the writing down of Buddhist scriptures began sometime in the final decades of the first century BCE. And there have been recent discoveries of Buddhist manuscripts and manuscript fragments in birch bark that date back to the first century CE, if not earlier. What is interesting about this evidence is that it locates the earliest writing activity of Buddhist monks in Sri Lanka and in Gandhāra, or the region roughly comprising Eastern Afghanistan and the Peshawar Valley in modern Pakistan. Since these areas are about 2000 miles apart and were the seats of different Buddhist traditions, these events likely occurred independently of one another.

The Sri Lankan case rests on the claims of texts written several centuries later, and thus it represents a somewhat idealistic version of the writing of Buddhist texts. Nevertheless, the many references to the voluminous collection of Buddhist texts in Sri Lanka from the early centuries of the Common Era suggest that it is plausible to conclude that Sri Lankan monks began to write down the Dharma at this early stage in history. Literary and archaeological evidence points to a flourishing presence of Buddhist practitioners from at least around the third century BCE, when King Aśoka was said to have sent his son Mahinda to Sri Lanka in order to disseminate the Dharma in this neighboring kingdom. However, the Pāli Commentaries (*aṭṭhakathā*) report that in the middle of the first century BCE there was widespread political upheaval and famine that caused many monks to flee to India or to perish from lack of support.

Figure 2.1 Abhidharma early commentary, India, 2nd c. CE. (MS 2373/1 (Schøyen Collection). Reproduced from *Buddhist Manuscripts in the Schøyen Collection*, vol. I, eds. Jens Braarvig, Jens-Uwe Hartmann, Kazunobu Matsuda, and Lore Sander, Oslo: Hermes Academic Publishing, 2000).

Subsequently, after order was restored to the island, King Vaṭṭagāmaṇī (r. 29–17 BCE) resumed the royal support of Buddhism, especially to a newer sect called the Abhayagiri-vihāra. Sometime around the year 20 BCE, a group of monks belonging to the Mahāvihāra ("Great Monastery") order met at the Aluvihare monastery, far from the royal capital, to recite and write down the Buddha's teachings. The texts transcribed at Aluvihāra likely included some version of a portion of the Pāli *Tipiṭaka* that was eventually redacted in the form we possess today sometime by the fifth century CE. The tradition in Sri Lanka is to inscribe letters onto dried, rectangular palm leaves, blacken the letters with a mixture of resin oil and charcoal, and bind them together with a cord that is run through two wooden boards. These materials were effective in creating written texts, but they remained susceptible to damage by pests and decay from the island's humid environment. As such, none of these original texts survive today, and the oldest palm-leaf manuscripts from Sri Lanka date only to around the twelfth century CE.

The reasons for transcribing what would become known as the Pāli Canon have been summarized by E.W. Adikaram. He suggests that the monks undertook the task of writing down Buddhist scriptures since (1) they feared that more political unrest and battles threatened to displace monks and endanger the texts that had been memorized and orally preserved, (2) the recent famine in the island drove home how easily the texts could be lost, (3) the entrance of morally lax persons into the Saṅgha threatened to weaken the discipline and learning of monks, and (4) the founding of the rival Abhayagiri monastic order and the patronage it received from the king undermined the position of the Mahāvihāra order (Adikaram 1994: 79). The brief description of this event in the sixth-century *Mahāvaṃsa* portrays the writing of the Pāli *Tipiṭaka* as a result of monks fearing the depopulation of the monasteries and wishing for the Dharma to remain in the world for a long time. Yet it seems just as likely that the sectarian rivalry between the Mahāvihāra and Abhayagiri monasteries motivated the former group to establish a closed canon of scriptures to bolster its claims to be the sole legitimate custodians of Buddhism in the island (Collins 1992: 98). And despite evidence that the Theravāda canon underwent changes and development since the Aluvihāra council, this orientation toward a more restrictive set of scriptural texts attributed to the Buddha has been a hallmark of the conservative Mahāvihāra branch of the Theravāda ever since.

In contrast, the details emerging around recent discoveries of Buddhist birch-bark manuscripts that date roughly between the first and third centuries CE present us with a different picture of how Buddhist canons were formed. Buddhism may have been introduced to the Gandhāran region around the third century BCE by monks dispatched by King Aśoka. The region would eventually become an important center for Buddhist art, *stūpa*s, and intellectual activity well into the Common Era. Known for its Buddha images, including the colossal standing images in Bāmiyan that were destroyed in 2001, Gandhāra was evidently also a vibrant site for the production of Buddhist texts. Located at the primary western gateway to the Indian subcontinent, Gandhāra lay at the meeting point between various eastern and western cultures, and Gāndhārī language texts written in the distinctive Kharoṣṭhī script were spread widely throughout western and central Asia and into western China (Salomon 1999: 4–5). Based upon ongoing research into the newly discovered birch-bark manuscripts and manuscript fragments, some provisional conclusions may be drawn about the ancient production of these Buddhist texts.

Richard Salomon suggests that the various collections of Gāndhārī manuscripts indicate that the formation of a corpus of Buddhist texts occurred in the region beginning around the first century CE and continued at least into the third century CE. Some texts appear to have been directly composed in the Gāndhārī language, whereas others appear to have been translated from other Middle Indo-Aryan languages (Salomon 1999: 165). This fact, along with discoveries of Sanskrit texts in the Brahmī script in the region, suggests that other regions of northern India also engaged in writing Buddhist scriptures from an early date. Many of the texts discovered recently are of the *sūtra* genre, a smaller number are related to *Abhidharma* and other scholastic works, but there appear to be few *Vinaya* texts. This may indicate that the scribes of Gāndhārī manuscripts initially only wrote down select texts, while other better-known works continued to be memorized and orally transmitted (Salomon 1999: 165–6). Texts appear to have been written down for practical reasons, such as to serve as materials for learning and reference, as well as for ritual functions including the interment of manuscripts along with the bodily remains of monks (Salomon 2006: 369).

Clearly, the research being done on these manuscripts, which represent the oldest surviving Buddhist texts in the world, will lead to further revision of our knowledge about Buddhist canons. For instance, based on these finds, it appears that the Gāndhārī materials were not written down as part of a complete canon, but rather they represent unsystematic and unstandardized efforts to write down certain texts or even parts of texts without any obvious concern to produce a formal, complete version of a canon of scriptures (Salomon 2006: 369–70). The texts contain *sūtra*s with titles and material broadly similar to works found in the Pāli Canon and in Chinese translations of works contained in Sanskrit-language canons. However, at this point, it appears that the Gāndhārī materials illustrate a method of textual production that likely was typical throughout the ancient Buddhist world. In them we see evidence of a common fund of basic texts known to all, but which differed significantly in wording, arrangement, and contents between different regions and sectarian communities (Salomon 2006: 375). The first written texts in Buddhism probably emerged displaying strong local variations, and only later were standardized and formed into canons of scriptures recognized by a particular school. This case was probably similar to what occurred in Sri Lanka, although the later textual references to the event represent it as a much more formal and organized production of the entire Pāli *Tipiṭaka*. There may have been other places in South Asia besides Sri Lanka and Gandhāra where Buddhist texts were written around the beginning of the Common Era, but we lack altogether any evidence to suggest which ones.

Mainstream Buddhist schools

The expansion of the Saṅgha led to the development of new formulations of monastic discipline and new interpretations of doctrine. As noted above, different monastic communities eventually created new ordination traditions that were codified in their own *Vinaya Piṭaka*. After the Buddha's *parinirvāṇa*, the Saṅgha lacked a centralized ecclesiastical authority that could enforce uniformity in doctrine and discipline. Each community developed its own system of hierarchy, and monks and nuns were responsible only to the senior monastics within their own ordination lineages. Despite the Buddha's warnings regarding divisions in the Saṅgha, there is evidence that the Saṅgha began to divide into different schools within a century or

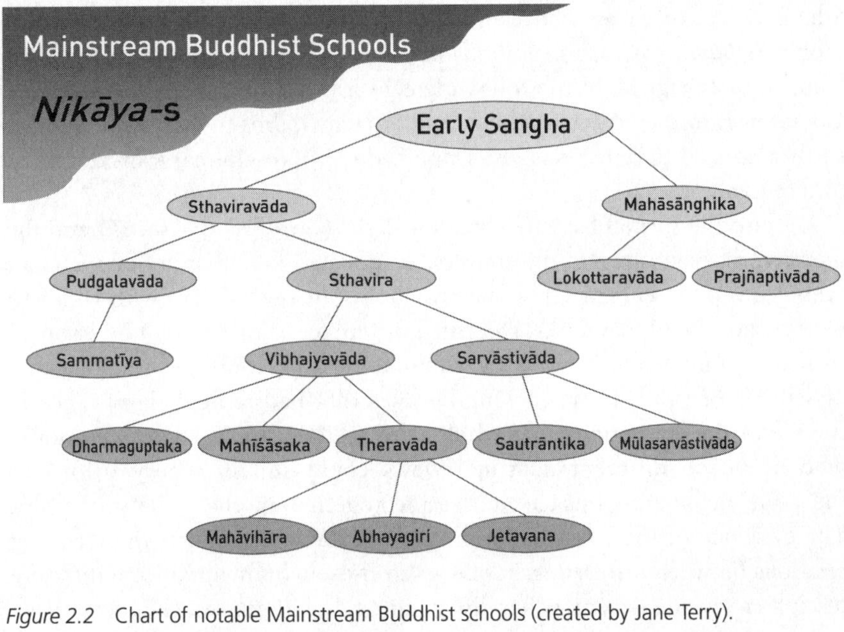

Figure 2.2 Chart of notable Mainstream Buddhist schools (created by Jane Terry).

so after his passing. It is not always clear what constituted a school or a sect in early Mainstream Buddhism. Tradition holds that eighteen distinct Mainstream schools were formed following the first major schism of the Saṅgha. They are called "Mainstream" because they represent the schools that appeared earliest and that possessed a relatively coherent system of thought and practice. They also lacked any clear or direct relationship to what would later become Mahāyāna Buddhism, which in spite of its self-designation as the "Great Vehicle" and its large body of texts was never deemed large or significant enough to be formally addressed and refuted in a text from a Mainstream school (Williams 2000: 97–8). The Mainstream schools, by contrast, constantly debated and refuted each other's positions. The term "Mainstream" is also preferable to that of "Hīnayāna" (Lesser Vehicle), which was a term used pejoratively by some Mahāyāna polemicists to describe these schools.

Mahāsāṃghika and related schools

The development of the Mainstream schools appears to have occurred following the Council at Vaiśālī. Sometime after that dispute over monastic rules, a group of monks split off and formed the Mahāsāṃghika School. The split may also have occurred due to the Mahāsāṃghika position that *arhat*s, although awakened, were still not free of imperfections—e.g., they could still have erotic dreams and nocturnal emissions, and still were ignorant of certain things. This view was rejected by those who called themselves the Sthaviravāda, or those who claimed to profess the teachings of the elder-monks (*sthavira*) who transmitted the Word of the Buddha from the First Council of Rājagṛha. In the following centuries leading up to and after the Common Era, the Mahāsāṃghikas and Sthaviravādins in turn were divided further into different sects or schools due to disciplinary or doctrinal differences.

Despite the formal list of eighteen *nikāya*s ("groups" or "sects") and the mention of even more in the sources, it appears likely that an independent school was only recognized by the presence of its own *Vinaya* with which to ordain and discipline monks. Doctrinal differences alone cannot be assumed to denote independent monastic communities, but only generated names of schools of thought or teaching lineages that had limited significance in the life of the community as a whole (Cox 2004b: 503). Therefore, monks who professed different doctrinal views could still in theory belong to the same ordination lineage and reside together in the same monastery. The evidence of life in early South Asian Buddhism supports the idea that relations between different schools—even those who maintained a different disciplinary code—were generally good and without much antagonism.

Monks from different schools all considered each other to be disciples of the Buddha and professed the reality of *saṃsāra*, *nirvāṇa*, and the law of dependent origination, with their differences arising over merely secondary points of doctrine or discipline (Lamotte 1988: 518–19).

The Mahāsāṃghika (Members of the Great Community) School appears to have been fairly widespread throughout the subcontinent, including the Kathmandu Valley of Nepal. The Mahāsāṃghikas were divided early on into three different schools for reasons that remain unclear. Perhaps the most notable school was the Lokottaravāda, a community of monks that argued the Buddha transcended the ordinary human condition in all his actions and utterances. The idea the Buddha was *lokottara* or supramundane suggested that he was not subject to ordinary human needs such as eating, sleeping, bathing, and undergoing the effects of *karma* (Williams 2000: 128–9). An early text from the first or second century CE called the *Lokānuvartana Sūtra* (Scripture on the Conformity with the World) contains this view of a supramundane Buddha who made a show of being like ordinary humans, disguising his transcendent nature, in order to assist beings along in the path to liberation (Harrison 1982: 212–13). This vision of the Buddha as transcending the normal human condition is also developed in the *Mahāvastu*, which is a text ascribed to the Lokottaravāda School. Both of these works present the general Mahāsāṃghika view wherein the Buddha allegedly hid his supramundane characteristics and acted in conformity with the world in order to show ordinary humans how to attain Awakening. The Lokottaravādins appear to have made the area around Bāmiyan in what is now Afghanistan their center.

Another school that developed later out of the Mahāsāṃghikas was called Prajñaptivāda (Those who profess provisional designations), a group who allegedly claimed that the Buddha spoke of reality in terms of provisional or relative terms. In teaching that all things are mere products of linguistic conventions or provisional designations (i.e., words that only possess a nominal or arbitrary relationship to the realities they designate), the Prajñaptivāda appears to have foreshadowed the teachings on "emptiness" (*śūnyatā*) that would appear in the *Prajñāpāramitā Sūtra*s (Bareau 1989: 202–3). The affinities between the Mahāsāṃghikas and the later Mahāyāna School are striking but insufficient to posit a direct link between the two. Much of what we know about the Mahāsāṃghikas and the groups that developed out of them is limited by insufficient sources.

Sthavira Schools I: Pudgalavāda

The Sthaviravāda community of monks, in contrast, emphasized a more extensive monastic disciplinary code and claimed to belong to the lineage of the "elder-monks" (*sthaviras*) whom they identified with the five hundred *arhats* who met at the First Council of Rājagṛha. Their adherence to a presumed canon of scriptures believed to have come down from that event appears to have given the Sthaviras a fairly strong sense of unity for several generations. The precise nature of their identity, however, is somewhat unclear since we have little in the way of texts in their name and since the label seems to have functioned largely as an umbrella term for all those opposed to the Mahāsāṃghika School. Yet sometime around the third century BCE, a group led by a monk called Vātsīputra split off from the larger body of "Sthaviras" over their affirmation of the existence of an indescribable "person" (*pudgala*)—neither equivalent to the Five Aggregates nor wholly separate from them—that transmigrates and carries the Five Aggregates from one lifetime to the next. The Pudgalavādins or "Personalists" thus emerged as a controversial group that was denounced by most other orders for sneaking in a notion of a permanent Self. The more orthodox Buddhist view held that living beings exist only as a collection of conditioned and impermanent factors, none of which can be said to last indefinitely like the "person."

The Pudgalavāda School, however, maintained that without such an entity, the Buddhist teachings on *karma* and moral responsibility lose their meaning, and that there is no ethical impetus to cultivate benevolence, compassion, and sympathetic joy towards a dehumanized person stripped down to a mere collection of physical and mental aggregates (Priestley 1999: 122). Pudgalavādins argued that when the Buddha spoke about a person that bears the Five Aggregates, he was speaking literally, whereas other Buddhist groups held such scriptural references to be metaphorical. The concept of the *pudgala* offered an explanation for how an individual's acts in the present life (*karma*) can yield corresponding effects in a future life. For the Pudgalavādins, the idea of the *pudgala* was critical to account for the continuity of being that makes sensible the idea of an individual pursuing religious attainments over many lives. But such a "person" was also necessarily conceived as an indefinable entity. If it were the same as the aggregates, it would be conditioned and subject to dissolution and destruction at death; but if it were different from the aggregates, the *pudgala* would be unconditioned and equivalent to an eternal Self—a notion with which the Pudgalavādins did not wish to be associated (Williams 2000: 126). Instead, the *pudgala* was taken to be the ultimate subject of experience—the aspect of individuality that transmigrates and experiences the effects of former acts—and that aspect of an individual that attains *nirvāṇa*.

This doctrine of a discrete, enduring aspect of personhood that characterizes individual existence made the Pudgalavādins particularly controversial in the early Buddhist community. Despite their exclusive commitment to Buddhist sources of knowledge (as opposed to non-Buddhist ones) and a system of argumentation based on a more literal interpretation of the Buddha's words, many of their opponents accused them of smuggling a poorly disguised version of the *ātman* into Buddhist thought. But according to the Pudgalavādins, the claim for the ultimate indescribability of the *pudgala* was supported by other recorded instances when the Buddha refused to answer certain philosophical questions such as is the world eternal or not eternal, and does the Tathāgata exist after death or not. One interpretation of the Buddha's silence on such matters is that he concluded that such inquiries were wholly unrelated to the path leading to liberation and thus merely futile distractions from the primary goal. Yet it was also possible to view his silence as indicating that certain things are unfathomable and beyond discursive thought. For the Pudgalavādins, the "person" was just such a phenomenon, an indeterminate and inexpressible reality that endures through successive lives, allowing us to conceive of moral responsibility and spiritual attainments as extending beyond the span of the present life (Priestley 1999: 54–5).

Although other Buddhist schools developed their own theories to account for causation, rebirth, and other questions related to the continuity of being, the Pudgalavāda School enjoyed great growth over several centuries in certain parts of South Asia. This group in turn divided into four identifiable sects around the beginning of the Common Era, with the Sāṃmitīyas (or Sammatīyas) becoming the most significant one. Some of the works of the Sāṃmitīya group survive in Chinese translations. And this school, named after its founder Saṃmata, eventually grew to have the largest number of monks in western India by the seventh century, while also maintaining significant numbers throughout the Ganges Basin and eastern India (Bareau 1955: 36, 38; 1989: 200). By positing the unknowable *pudgala* as the link between the created *dharma*s or factors constituting the Five Aggregates on the one hand and the uncreated *dharma* of *nirvāṇa* on the other, the Pudgalavādins were able to explain how an individual could actually be said to attain *nirvāṇa* after the destruction of the Five Aggregates at death (Priestley 1999: 218). Judging by the evidence that suggests Pudgalavāda survived and flourished in the subcontinent up to around the eleventh century CE, this school seemingly appealed to numerous monastics that lacked confidence in a strict interpretation of the doctrine of No-Self.

Sthavira Schools II: Sarvāstivāda

Sometime subsequent to the formation of the Pudgalavāda School, another split occurred among those in the community that continued to identify itself with the *sthavira*s at Rājagṛha. As mentioned above, one Buddhist tradition connects this event with the outcome of the Council at Pāṭaliputra, where the monks whose views were rejected broke away and formed a new order called Sarvāstivāda, a group sometimes labeled "Pan-realists" for espousing the conviction that *dharma*s—the momentary, mutually conditioned, fundamental factors that make up existence—exist at all three times: past, present, and future. The Sarvāstivādins adopted the position that a factor (*dharma*) or a discrete existent phenomenon traverses the three periods of time, and this is what enables past causes to give rise to present results, and present causes to give rise to future results. Here is yet another philosophical position that attempts to account for the effects of *karma* and to explain causality within the framework of impermanence.

The Sarvāstivādins affirmed that existence is compounded by factors such as the Five Aggregates, which in turn can be divided into smaller units of phenomenal existence. Such speculation was devoted to reducing a person's psycho-physical existence down to its most basic constituent factors. This effort, which was consistent with older Buddhist meditative traditions, contributed to the rise of *Abhidharma* scholasticism in South Asian Buddhism. The Sarvāstivādins arrived at a list of seventy-five discrete *dharma*s arranged under a taxonomy of five categories: (1) physical form (*rūpa*) including the organs of seeing, hearing, and other senses; (2) mind (*citta*); (3) mental factors (*caitasikā dharmāḥ*) including sensation, memory, faith, and delusion among forty-two others; (4) conditionings disjoined from thought (*cittaviprayukta-saṃskārā dharmāḥ*) such as acquisition, the vital faculty, words, phrases, and syllables; and (5) the unconditioned factors (*asaṃskṛta dharmāḥ*) of space and *nirvāṇa* (Dhammajoti 2002: 24–5). The detailed analysis of such factors was thought to contribute directly to the attainment of wisdom, which would lead to *nirvāṇa*. While maintaining that each one of the conditioned factors is impermanent, the Sarvāstivādins argued that aside from their modes (*bhava*), which are changeable, their underlying nature or substance (*dravya*) remains constant. Thus, according to this view, any given factor will abandon its future mode (as a potential existent) and acquire the present mode (as a current existent), before quickly progressing to the past mode (as a previous existent) where it remains able to exert a karmic effect (Willeman *et al.* 1998: 20–1). The appearance of the factor may change, but its underlying nature and potential force remains constant.

Other Buddhist groups tended to reject the Sarvāstivāda view of the continuity of the factors of existence. While it offered a rational explanation to account for cause and effect within the Buddhist theory of *karma*, it also raised suspicions for seemingly violating the doctrine of impermanence. The Sarvāstivādins did appear to locate something more or less permanent within the impermanence of existence. In time, early Mahāyāna philosophers would present vigorous critiques of the Sarvāstivāda position by arguing in response for the "emptiness" or lack of permanent substance in the *dharma*s.

The Sarvāstivāda School maintained a strong presence in the northwest and in the region around Mathurā. Bareau asserts that they "were clearly in the majority over all of northwest India, from the upper Ganges Basin to Kashmir, from the mid-third century BCE to at least the seventh century CE" (Bareau 1989: 200). The reports of the seventh-century Chinese pilgrim Xuanzang record that the Sarvāstivadins were the third largest school after the Sāṃmitīyas and Sthaviras (or, more specifically, the Theravādins in Sri Lanka and the southern Deccan region), numbering more than 16,000 monks in more than 500 monasteries concentrated in northern and northwest regions (Bareau 1955: 36, 38). They authored a complete collection of *Abhidharma* texts and commentaries in Sanskrit, many of which survive in Chinese and Tibetan translations. Members of this school also composed the voluminous *Mahāvibhāṣā* (Great Commentary), which collected the doctrinal positions of the Vaibhāṣika sect of the Sarvāstivāda.

The Sarvāstivādins appear to have been a fairly heterogeneous order with groups possessing different doctrinal views and textual interpretations. An internal dispute over *Abhidharma* teachings gave rise to a breakaway school that came to be known as Sautrāntika (Those who rely on the *sūtras*). Another school known as Mūlasarvāstivāda (The Basic Sarvāstivāda) also developed, although their relation to the Sarvāstivāda School remains a subject of debate. One view holds that the Mūlasarvāstivāda constituted a distinct order that arose due to sectarian or geographical differences. Another theory points to textual evidence that Mūlasarvāstivāda was merely another name for the same Sarvāstivāda School, thereby claiming the status of being the true basis of all other sects (Enomoto 2000: 247–8). Support for the former view of a distinct Mūlasarvāstivāda order is found in the fact that it had its own *Vinaya* and ordination lineage apart from the Sarvāstivāda School (Willeman *et al.* 1998: 87–8).

It remains clear that the Mūlasarvāstivāda *Vinaya*, which was preserved and adopted by Tibetan Buddhist traditions, comprises a voluminous collection of texts that requires additional study. Research into these texts has begun to yield important insights into the economic activities of ancient Indian monks, including Mūlasarvāstivādins but likely involving other monastic orders as well. The Mūlasarvāstivāda *Vinaya* offers a portrait of a monk who did not renounce personal wealth or property, but instead was given specific rules to govern his business activities. These rules suggest monks were expected to pay debts and tolls, own their own furniture, pay for their own medicine, leave estates, borrow money from laypeople and lend money while charging interest, accept and service permanent endowments, accept money, sell the property of deceased monks, and hire and oversee laborers (Schopen 2004a: 14–15). The Mūlasarvāstivāda *Vinaya* thus reveals that monks in this school were not only involved in abstract philosophizing, but they were also heavily involved in economic affairs, probably like other monks from all the different orders.

Sthavira Schools III: Vibhajyavāda and Theravāda

The *sthaviras* who rejected the Sarvāstivāda teaching on the survival of the factors of existence are depicted as having triumphed at the Council of Pāṭaliputra. They adopted the name Vibhajyavāda (Those Who Make Distinctions) and endorsed the viewpoints articulated at the council by the Elder Moggaliputtatissa as outlined in the *Kathāvatthu* of the Pali Canon. The name Vibhajyavāda was attributed to a variety of communities spread across the subcontinent. Some of these groups were located in the northwest and comprised schools known as Dharmaguptakas, Kāśyapīyas, and Mahīśāsakas. Not much is known about these groups, although the recent manuscript discoveries around Bāmiyan, which can tentatively be connected with the Dharmaguptaka School, may change this. We know that the Dharmaguptakas had an important role in spreading the *Vinaya* to China and enjoyed a measure of dominance there early on (Salomon 1999: 167–8). They also argued that the Buddha is superior to and not included in the Saṅgha, and therefore a gift given to him yields greater fruit than one given to the monkhood (Bareau 1955: 192). Overall, however, the differences between the various so-called Vibhajyavādin groups were fairly minor. The three groups mentioned above, along with the so-called Theravādins, basically accepted the following points: thought is inherently pure, there is no intermediate state (*antarābhava*) between rebirths, comprehension of the Four Noble Truths occurs instantaneously, and *arhats* cannot fall back from their level of religious attainment (Cox 2004b: 506).

The Vibhajyavāda *sthaviras* in the south came to represent monastic communities that favored the use of the Pāli language for the preservation of the Dharma. They became the dominant order of monks in Sri Lanka and in the Tamil country in the Deccan, with both groups enjoying close relations. In time, this order of monks would be called Theravāda, the Pāli term for "Tradition of the Elders," and signified the scriptural legacy of the Dharma and Vinaya purportedly handed down from the Council at Rājagṛha (Jayawickrama 1986: 46, 173). The term Theravāda, however, rarely appears outside of certain historiographical texts before the modern era when it became adopted as the label for Buddhists in Sri Lanka and mainland Southeast Asia. Sri Lanka, as the home of monasteries with important libraries, served as the center for the southern *sthavira* (P: *thera*) community. Buddhist traditions assert that the Dispensation was brought by the monk Mahinda to Sri Lanka in the third century BCE. Mahinda is said to have converted the king to Buddhism, followed by vast numbers of nobles and other inhabitants, in and around the ancient capital of Anurādhapura. Written accounts from the *Mahāvaṃsa* and other historical narratives in Pāli and Sinhala present a fairly consistent picture of the rapid spread of Buddhism, accompanied by the enshrining of various relics of the Buddha in *stūpa*s around the island (Berkwitz 2007).

The monks in Sri Lanka organized themselves into three distinct orders in the first few centuries of the Common Era. The monks associated with the Great Monastery (Mahāvihāra) in Anurādhapura adopted a conservative stance with respect to a closed Pāli Canon, rejecting the Sanskrit scriptures of other schools (Collins 1992: 98). Specifically, it was a group of Mahāvihāravāsins (Residents of the Great Monastery) who met at Aluvihāra to write down the Word of the Buddha. Members of this same order worked assiduously to redact the texts and write commentaries (*aṭṭhakathā*) on them, first in an ancient form of Sinhala and then later in Pāli. The renowned scholar monk Buddhaghosa, author of numerous Pāli *aṭṭhakathā* and the digest of canonical teachings called the *Visuddhimagga* (Path of Purification), is said to have resided in the island and is credited with articulating normative Mahāvihāra views. The textual activity of the Mahāvihāravāsins—including the Pāli Canon, its *aṭṭhakathā*, and numerous historical texts or "chronicles" (*vaṃsa*s)—went a long way in standardizing the order's doctrine and practice, enabling it to assume the role of guardians of Buddhist knowledge and practice in Sri Lanka. The Mahāvihāra interpretation of Buddhist texts and rituals was also exported to lands associated with modern Burma and Thailand by around the eleventh century, although there is evidence of an earlier *sthavira* tradition from around the fifth century CE in the Mon and Pyu kingdoms in those same lands (Gethin 1998: 256).

Near the beginning of the Common Era, a split arose in the Mahāvihāra, leading to the formation of a new sect located in the Abhayagiri Monastery. With support from the king at that time, the Abhayagirivāsins developed a separate monastic order. It appears that Abhayagirivāsins originally formed after their leader Mahātissa Thera was expelled from the Mahāvihāra, possibly for accepting a monastery from the king as an individual or for frequenting the homes of laypersons (Adikaram 1994: 78). In time the Abhayagiri order came to develop a liberal attitude towards Buddhist texts, exhibiting a willingness to study and affirm certain Mahāyāna teachings. For this, they were criticized by the Mahāvihāravāsins for expanding the canon to include illegitimate texts. Later, around the fourth century CE, another sect formed from a breakaway group of Abhayagiri monks at the Jetavana monastery, which was built and offered as a personal gift to a favorite monk of the king. This monk named Tissa was later charged with an offence, expelled, and disrobed, but others from this group carried on under the name of Jetavanīyas. They appear to have been slightly more reluctant to embrace the Sanskrit teachings condemned by the Mahāvihāra as "expansionist" (*vaitulyavāda*), although they began to adopt some Mahāyāna teachings too by around the sixth century CE (Adikaram 1994: 92–3). These three orders comprised the Saṅgha in Sri Lanka through the first millennium.

Sthavira Schools IV: Sautrāntika

After the Council of Kaśmīra sometime around the second century CE a rift developed in the Sarvāstivāda in the northwest. Some members ordained in this school began to voice opposition to the increasing emphasis on the *Abhidharma* exegetical activity that fueled the composition and study of the *vibhāṣā* commentaries among the Kashmiri Sarvāstivāda-Vaibhāṣika branch. These opponents apparently began to refer to themselves as Sautrāntikas (Adherents of the *Sūtras*) because of their conviction that the Word of the Buddha is to be found in the *Sūtra Piṭaka* but not the *Abhidharma Piṭaka*. The orthodox Sarvāstivāda-Vaibhāṣikas referred to their opponents somewhat derisively as "Dārṣṭāntikas" because of their frequent use of examples in their discussion. However, the Sautrāntikas persisted in advocating for an emphasis on *sūtras* in place of the *Abhidharma* texts, a position that ran directly counter to the intellectual and scholarly orientation of the Sarvāstivāda. Nevertheless, there is no evidence of a Sautrāntika *Vinaya* or separate ordination tradition, so they likely offered a distinct doctrinal perspective within the larger Sarvāstivāda School (Cox 2004b: 505).

In addition to expressing skepticism over the legitimacy of the broader Sarvāstivāda engagement with the *Abhidharma* literature, the Sautrāntikas came to reject the Sarvāstivāda position on the survival of *dharmas* during the three times of past, present, and future. Explained differently, the Sarvāstivādins maintained that any given factor goes through four moments: (1) origination, (2) subsistence, (3) decay, and (4) destruction (Conze 1967: 135). Prior to its origination a mental or material factor exists in a latent state of potential, it becomes activated in the present, and following its destruction its substance continues to exist in order to condition a subsequent factor or event later. This occurs, the Sarvāstivādin says, because the person who initiates a thought or act immediately comes to "possess" it, and this possession (*prāpti*) functions to generate a sequence of *dharmas* that continue to possess the intention that originally motivated the thought or act, and that also guarantees that the subsequent fruit or result comes to the individual who first performed it (Williams 2000: 116–17). The Sautrāntikas, however, rejected this line of reasoning outright. They maintained that the *dharmas* do not survive over three periods and four stages, as this would violate the Buddha's teaching of impermanence. Instead, they held that *dharmas* are mental or material factors that exist merely for an instant, so briefly in fact that they can never be directly apprehended. For the Sautrāntika, a *dharma* exists only in the moment of its activity, and thereafter it ceases to be as quickly as it arose. People thus perceive the world indirectly as a series of impressions or traces of factors that linger on in the mind after the instantaneous dissolution of the factors themselves.

The Sautrāntika view supplants the ontological theory of the Sarvāstivāda with an epistemological theory to account for the apprehension of the world that is real but composed of momentary factors. In rejecting the Sarvāstivāda notion of *prāpti*, the Sautrāntikas advanced the idea of mental seeds (*bīja*s) that are deposited in the mental continuum at the time of a thought or an act. These seeds then evolve through a series of momentary factors, each one existing but for an instant before "suffusing" or "perfuming" another factor that performs the same activity (Williams 2000: 121). Eventually, what is nominally called a "seed"—but what really constitutes a series of factors each one conditioned by what preceded it—takes fruit as the karmic result of the initial thought or act. The Sautrāntikas also proposed a theory of a substratum (*āśraya*) akin to a subtle level of consciousness that serves as a depository of positive and negative seeds capable of yielding new seeds related to the former ones, while maintaining that such *bīja*s are neither identical with nor different from the mind (Jaini 1959: 244; Conze 1967: 142–3). This complex line of reasoning resulted from the attempt to explain the philosophical problem of the continuity of experience and of *karma* from within a doctrine founded partly on the notions of impermanence and the lack of a permanent Self. And while there is little evidence that the Sautrāntikas gained a wide following, some of their theories would become influential for the later Yogācāra school of Mahāyāna Buddhism.

Abhidharma speculation

Many Mainstream Buddhist schools structured their thought and scholarship around their respective *Abhidharma* literature. We have already seen that different schools accepted different *Abhidharma* texts and doctrines, often employing these differences to distinguish themselves. These *Abhidharma* works of different schools are united by their methods of seeking to break down and analyze the various factors (*dharma*s) or components of existence. This idea of *dharma*s (P: *dhamma*s) is usefully defined as the basic qualities, both mental and physical, that constitute experience or reality in its entirety (Gethin 2004: 521). In general, the discernment or discrimination of the *dharma*s—factors or events comparable to the basic building blocks of all mental and physical phenomena—is to be performed as the practical counterpart to the theoretical orientation of *Abhidharma* writings. The analytical method to identify the factors conducive to the development of virtue is combined with the process of descriptive analysis that works to reveal the underlying structure of existence in order to weaken attachment to objects of desire (Cox 2004a: 551). Phrased differently, in Abhidharma one strives to analyze the very bases of mental and physical phenomena to cultivate an accurate vision of reality that is conducive toward liberation.

The fact that most of the Mainstream schools developed *Abhidharma* works suggests that, despite the differences in content, early South Asian Buddhists saw considerable value in presenting a technical summary of what the Buddha taught in the *sūtra*s. It is noteworthy that Buddhist traditions recognize that the Buddha's disciples had a direct hand in composing these works. Most scholars would argue for dating them at least a century or two after the *Sūtra* and *Vinaya Piṭaka*s. The *Abhidharma* works likely developed in stages based originally on matrices (Skt: *mātṛkā*/P: *mātikā*) or categorized lists of technical terms compiled by the Buddha or some of his early disciples. Perhaps one of the first such matrices was the so-called thirty-seven Wings to Awakening (P: *bodhipakhiyā dhammā*), which include the Four Foundations of Mindfulness, the Four Right Exertions, the Four Supernatural Powers, the Five Sense-Faculties, the Five Powers, the Seven Limbs of Awakening, and the Noble Eightfold Path (Potter 1996: 121–2). Traditionally held to convey the heart of the Buddha's Teaching, the Wings to Awakening represent a collection of summary lists that appear throughout the *sūtra*s and that are used to distill the core principles of the Dharma. The lists themselves were likely developed to aid in memorizing the structure of the Buddha's discourses.

In time, these *mātṛkā*s were expanded and subject to written exposition, thus leading to a new stage in Abhidharma speculation. As new layers of interpretation overspread older taxonomic matrices, more elaborate *Abhidharma* texts were composed to analyze the *mātṛkā*s found in the *sūtra* texts. In time, the *Abhidharma* works evolved into complex works of doctrinal exegesis and philosophical analysis. Special attention was given to the *dharma*s or the constituent mental and physical factors used to classify and interpret one's existence in the world. These scholastic treatises were in turn subject to extensive commentary and became the focus of much intellectual activity among many Mainstream schools during the early centuries of the Common Era. Given the fact that only the *Abhidharma Piṭaka*s of the Sarvāstivādins and Theravādins survive in their complete forms, much of what we associate with Abhidharma thought in general is based on these schools.

The taxonomies of mental and physical factors developed by the Sarvāstivāda and Theravāda schools contain considerable overlap despite the fact that such topics often spurred lively debate between schools. One tends to find the categories of the Five Aggregates, the Six Sense-Fields (seeing, hearing, smelling, tasting, touching, thinking), the Twelve Sense-Bases (the six senses plus their objects—sights, sounds, smells, tastes, tangibles, discursive thoughts), and the Eighteen Elements (the six types of senses, the six types of objects, and the six types of consciousness—e.g., eye-awareness, ear-awareness, etc.) in most *Abhidharma* classifications (Potter 1996: 130). The matrices tend to group the different *dharma*s according to other characteristics, such as whether they are wholesome (*kuśala*), unwholesome (*akuśala*), or morally neutral (*avyākṛta*); whether they are with-outflow (*sāsrava*) or are outflow-free (*anāśrava*); and whether they are conditioned or unconditioned (Dhammajoti 2002: 26–31). Factors that are wholesome may generate a positive fruit (that is, carrying an outflow) or may not produce any effect if one's mind is detached (outflow-free). Unwholesome factors are thought almost invariably to produce an effect. Conditioned factors arise due to other factors that serve as their causes and conditions. An example of these would be the activity of seeing, which depends on the eye, an object that is seen, and eye-awareness. Unconditioned factors are much less numerous. Sarvāstivāda Buddhism recognizes space (*ākāśa*), cessation through consideration (*pratisaṃkhyānirodha*), and cessation without consideration (*apratisaṃkhyānirodha*) as unconditioned *dharma*s that are essentially permanent, free from arising and passing away as well as modification (Cox 2004a: 556). Theravāda Buddhism recognizes only *nirvāṇa* as an unconditioned *dharma* that does not arise or fall away due to the presence of other causes or conditions.

As mentioned above, the Sarvāstivāda *Abhidharma* views *dharma*s as existing in all three times of past, present, and future, possessed of changeable modes (*bhava*s) and an unchangeable substance (*dravya*). In other words, this view holds that *dharma*s have an intrinsic nature that is stable and immutable, allowing them to function causally in all three periods (Cox 2004a: 572–3). The Theravādins, in contrast, viewed *dhamma*s as possessing only a momentary existence with nothing durable or permanent about them. Moreover, in the Pāli *Abhidhamma* work called the *Dhammasaṅgaṇī* (Compilation of Factors), mental *dhamma*s are implied to be evanescent and insubstantial non-entities that have no real essence of life of their own (Gethin 2004: 523). This comparison suggests that the Abhidharma notions against which some later Mahāyāna schools developed their philosophy of emptiness came primarily from the Sarvāstivāda School. However, both Sarvāstivāda and Theravāda *Abhidharma* were alike in developing similar lists to categorize the factors of phenomenal existence, even if they conceived of the nature of *dharma*s quite differently.

Aside from providing an ontological framework for discerning the nature of existence, Abhidharma speculation provided answers to questions about how consciousness and *karma* function. With the notable exception of the

Pudgalavādins and their doctrine of the ineffable "person" that transmigrates from one life to another, the other Mainstream schools were challenged to come up with an account to describe the continuity of experience and the effects of *karma* without recourse to a permanent Self. The Theravāda tradition, for example, responded by turning to the concept of the Fourfold Higher Reality (*catudhā paramattha*) to reinterpret the Five Aggregates mentioned in the Pāli *sutta*s in terms of *rūpa* (matter), *cetasika* (mental factors), *citta* (consciousness), and the unconditioned state of *nirvāṇa*. These were enumerated into 89 distinctive *dhamma*s and classified into various matrices in the *Abhidhammattha-saṅgaha* (Compilation on the Meaning of the Higher Dhamma), a treatise written around the beginning of the twelfth century to summarize Pāli *Abhidhamma* texts.

Matter is said to be of twenty-eight kinds—including the elements of earth, water, fire, and air; five kinds of phenomena related to the senses; four kinds of objective phenomena grasped by the senses (not including the tangibles of earth, fire, and air); femininity and masculinity; the heart-phenomenon; the life-faculty; and nutriment (Bodhi 1993: 236). *Cetasika*s are mental states, or phenomena, that support the cognitive activity of consciousness. They number fifty-two and may reflect "universal" or rudimentary functions such as contact, feeling, and perception; or they may be "occasional" or found only in particular types of consciousness such as energy or desire (Bodhi 1993: 79). These *cetasika*s are ethically variable and may be either wholesome or unwholesome depending on the type of consciousness in which it arises. It is worth noting further that this form of desire (*chanda*) signifies the ethically variable desire to act and should be distinguished from the always-unwholesome greed or desire for accumulation (*lobha*) and lust or desire for sense pleasures (*rāga*) (Bodhi 1993: 82–3). The possibility for an ethically positive desire to achieve *nirvāṇa* is an example of *chanda*, which can be beneficial and productive of good fruits. The *Abhidhammattha-saṅgaha* also lists a number of unwholesome (*akusala*) and beautiful (*sobhana*) mental factors. The former includes delusion, envy, shamelessness, and hatred among ten others; whereas the latter includes faith, mindfulness, fear of wrongdoing, and non-greed among twenty-one others. The unwholesome and beautiful *cetasika*s possess an ethically fixed orientation as either negative or positive accordingly.

Consciousness or *citta* is arguably the most fundamental element in this system. It is seen as the root of all experience and is crucial for determining how one perceives the world and responds to it. Consciousness, in the *Abhidhammattha-saṅgaha*, is reinterpreted as an activity comprising the process of knowing or cognizing an object (Bodhi 1993: 27). Scholars of the Pāli *Abhidhamma* described consciousness as a stream of thought-moments that appears like an unbroken flow of awareness, but really consists of a series of momentary acts of apprehension. Each *citta* or consciousness-moment may be capable of producing an effect or may be the result of a previous cause. The *citta*s are *dhamma*s or ultimate factors that can be classified by their particular plane of existence—(1) the realm of the senses, (2) the realm of form, (3) the realm of the formless, and (4) the world-transcending realm—and by their nature—(1) wholesome, (2) unwholesome, or (3) indeterminate. Wholesome *citta*s are states of consciousness primarily influenced by generosity, loving-kindness, and wisdom. Unwholesome *citta*s are primarily influenced by greed, hatred, and delusion. Indeterminate *citta*s may be the results of other wholesome or unwholesome *citta*s that precede them, or they may be neither determined by nor productive of *karma* (Bodhi 1993: 32–3). In general, *citta*s are morally identifiable states of consciousness that arise in conjunction with one or more mental factors (*cetasika*s).

The analysis of cognition in the Pāli *Abhidhamma* revolves around the arising of *citta*s and their falling away before in turn generating another *citta* to replace it. Unlike the durable *dharma*s of the Sarvāstivāda, the *dhamma*s of the Theravāda are fleeting, lasting a maximum of seventeen consciousness-moments before falling away. When we see, hear, smell, taste, or touch something, we receive thousands of discrete, infinitesimal cognitions of it. Once a mental (e.g. a thought) or external (e.g. a thunderclap) stimulus disturbs the smooth flow of the subconscious mind (*bhavaṅga*), the flow becomes interrupted and the activity of consciousness is triggered. One first receives an initial, unreflective moment of consciousness of the stimulus. If the stimulus is strong enough to register an impression, the mind then investigates and determines what the object it. Next, the mind assigns the object to a place in one's field of knowledge, thereby dwelling on and forming an attitude toward it. One may like the object, dislike the object, or remain indifferent. These responses give rise to feelings that become registered in the subconscious mind and that may in turn spur craving and attachment with respect to the object. This cognitive process is said to last sixteen thought-moments beyond the initial moment of the arising of the object in our awareness, leading *Abhidhamma* scholars to posit that each *dhamma* lasts a total of seventeen thought-moments before it expires (Kashyap 1954: 125–6). The mind typically repeats this process repeatedly to form a clearer impression of and attitude toward what presents itself to the mind. What seems like a steady flow of thought is actually a rapid-fire sequence of consciousness-moments, each one affecting the next until it dies out for lack of strength or until it registers an impression on the subconscious mind. In time, the subconscious mind may return to its undisturbed state, but those stronger mental impressions may trigger certain acts that are productive of certain karmic fruits later.

The stream of momentary *citta*s works to produce sustained periods of awareness and gives the illusion that the external world is more substantial and permanent than it really is. It also is used by *Abhidhamma* scholars to explain the continuity of *karma* and the phenomenon of rebirth without recourse to a permanent Self or "soul." It is said that at the point of death, a *cuti-citta* or dying consciousness-moment arises and sinks down at the last instance of life. This dying consciousness-moment in turn conditions a subsequent "rebirth-link" consciousness-moment (*paṭisandhi*) that arises in the mind of the life form in which one is immediately reborn. Unlike some Buddhist schools that professed an intermediate period between death and rebirth, the Theravāda School maintained that the process is instantaneous. Once the link is made, the mind returns to its subconscious state, passively waiting for a new stimulus or object to interrupt its smooth flow of unawareness (Kashyap 1954: 165–6). Thus, the link between one life form and the next is not a permanent entity that transmigrates. Rather, it is a stream of *citta*s made up of momentary flashes of consciousness that continue to flow, alternating between subconscious and conscious states, that enables one to speak of rebirth and the continuity of existence in this system.

Connected with this analysis is an explanation linking the kind of *citta*s most often produced in one life and the particular circumstances of one's birth in the next (cf. Bodhi 1993: 30–1). *Citta*s conditioned by the realm of the senses (*kāmāvacara-citta*) as manifest in the craving for sense pleasures are said to lead to rebirth in one of the six sensuous planes of existence—hells, hungry ghost (*peta*), animal, jealous god (*asura*), human, or divine. *Citta*s related to the subtle realm of form (*rūpāvacara-citta*), such as those generated in meditative states based on material objects like parts of one's body, lead to rebirth in one of the divine realms of subtle existence. *Citta*s related to the realm of the formless (*arūpāvacara-citta*), such as those produced in formless meditative states, lead to rebirth in the formless heavens.

Lastly, those who develop world-transcending (*lokuttara*) states of consciousness when the mind attains cessation in the highest stages of meditative concentration obtain one of the four higher attainments that culminate with *nirvāṇa*. At the highest levels of Buddhist practice, one generates *citta*s representing the "paths" and the "fruits" of the Stream-winner (*sotāpanna*), the Once-returner (*sakadāgāmi*), the Non-returner (*anāgami*), or fully awakened as an *arhat* (P: *arahant*). The Stream-winner, who is guaranteed of attaining *nirvāṇa* within seven lifetimes or less and who is assured of only human or divine rebirths, obtains this state by eliminating the fetters of false view, doubt, and confidence in external rites from one's mind. The Once-returner, who is reborn in the world only once more before becoming an *arhat*, further weakens the fetters of lust, hatred, and delusion. The Non-returner, who upon death is not reborn again in the realm of the senses but obtains a higher divine form, attains Awakening in the heavenly realm by first eliminating all traces of lust, hatred, and delusion from the mind. And the *arhat* destroys the remaining fetters that pollute the mind and produce karmic effects causing rebirth. The attainment of *nirvāṇa* is said to be sure to follow.

3

Furcations:

Origins and development of the Mahāyāna

Lay Buddhism in Ancient India

The question of lay practice is important for any survey of Buddhism. But when it comes to discussing the origins and development of the school of Buddhism called the Mahāyāna (Great Vehicle), lay practice acquires even more relevance. Some scholars have attributed the rise of the Mahāyāna in the first few centuries of the Common Era to the efforts of Buddhist laypersons to assert their own devotional interests and non-monastic practices. This view, as we will see, is flawed. But it makes sense to discuss the parameters of lay Buddhist practice in ancient India in order to locate the founding of Mahāyāna Buddhism elsewhere in ancient South Asian culture.

The Buddhist laity was given the responsibility of supporting the Saṅgha, a duty that depended more on generosity and pious confidence in the Dharma than it did on philosophical speculation. It became common early on for Buddhist texts to specify five kinds of virtues of a Buddhist lay devotee (*upāsaka*). Although subject to different degrees of emphasis, these five virtues comprised faith (*śraddhā*), morality (*śīla*), generosity (*tyāga*), learning (*śruta*), and wisdom (*prajñā*), all of which were thought to contribute to the formation of the ideal lay devotee (Lamotte 1988: 67). Faith in Buddhism does not imply an unquestioning acceptance and reliance on what the Buddha said. Instead, the idea of *śraddhā* involves initially placing one's confidence in the truth and efficacy of the Dharma, but then confirming this assessment through personal practice and reflection. More generally it reflects the attitude of esteem and reliance on the Three Jewels of the Buddhist religion, an attitude that is expressed by the formula of "going for refuge" in the Buddha, the Dharma, and the Saṅgha (Lamotte 1988: 69). The second virtue of morality also became a critical quality for a Buddhist layperson to assume. Early Buddhist texts reference lists of five, eight, and ten rules that lay devotees could adopt to guard and promote their moral development. These moral training-precepts (*śikṣāpada*) were patterned after the monastic orders and revolved around the Five Precepts that call for the Buddhist to abstain from taking life, stealing, sexual misconduct, lying, and fermented beverages (Lamotte 1988: 70).

Generosity, in its many forms, comprised the lay virtue that was held in the highest regard. Given the monastic community's dependence on lay support for its basic needs, the virtue of giving (*dāna*) and the good fruits that follow from it were stressed in sermons and narratives. Lay generosity in the form of offering food, robes, shelter, and medicines to the Saṅgha was consistently depicted as praiseworthy and conducive to the attainment of good fruits such as a heavenly rebirth. A lay devotee's generosity, however, could also be shown to others who are not members of the Saṅgha. The Buddhist laity was called to act in meritorious ways to assist needy strangers and travelers and to tend to those who are sick or dying (Lamotte 1988: 72–3). A layperson would generally not be seen as a "field of merit" like a monk or a nun, but giving to someone in need would theoretically still generate some merit, or the unripened, good fruits of a morally good act. Practicing generosity would also serve to lessen selfish attachment and cultivate an active regard for the wellbeing of others.

Despite the emphasis given to generosity as a lay virtue, it was encouraged and practiced by the monastic community as well. As the recipients of material gifts, the Saṅgha was obliged to give the gift of the Dharma by teaching and preaching the Word of the Buddha. Furthermore, the acts of generosity displayed in accounts of the Buddha's previous lives served as a model for later monks and nuns seeking to accomplish higher spiritual attainments. There is considerable archaeological and textual evidence showing that members of the monastic community made donations of images, texts, cave-dwellings, and other items useful to the Saṅgha. Wealth acquired by the Saṅgha in the form of land, properties, and other material goods belonged in theory to the community as a whole. But there are instances where individual monks received or inherited wealth and property that they could in turn bestow as an act of generosity on their own part. In doing so, monastics could join laypersons in making donations to earn merit that could be transferred to others and could benefit oneself.

For the laity, acts consistent with the virtue of generosity tended to overshadow the development of learning and wisdom. Discourses like the Siṅgālovāda Sutta stressed the development of faith, morality, and generosity among *upāsaka*s and *upāsikā*s. Self- discipline and respect for others would serve as the foundation for moral development, which in turn enabled the lay devotee to generate the resources needed to support one's family, friends, and the monastic community (Lamotte 1988: 74–5). Moral restraint allowed one to refrain from wasting one's money on frivolous goods and sensual desires. Adhering to the Five Precepts, one could instead use one's wealth to do good deeds that earn merit and benefit a much wider sphere of people than an act borne out of selfishness. In this sense, the ideal of generosity also encompassed acts of worship (*pūjā*) involving making offerings to the Buddha in the form of his relics or his image. Offerings of flowers, incense, and other aesthetically pleasing items to *stūpa*s, *bodhi* trees, and images represented a common expression of devotion to the Buddha. This early relic cult, centered around *stūpa*s built even before the reign of Mauryan kings like Aśoka, contributed directly to the growth and spread of Buddhism in early South Asia (Trainor 1997: 39–44). Although opinions varied as to whether the Buddha could actually enjoy such offerings or not, as some texts speak of his absence from the world whereas other evidence suggests he had an enduring presence in his relics and images, offering *pūjā* in honor of the Buddha was another method of earning merit and of developing the virtues of generosity, non-attachment, and faith.

Lastly, a different kind of offering appears to have been made regularly by Buddhist laypersons in ancient South Asia. These offerings were directed to spiritual-deities such as *yakṣa*s (P: *yakkha*s) and *preta*s (P: *peta*s) who were believed to exist and to threaten ordinary people with disease, death, and other forms of harm. Offerings made to these deities would in theory help to negate the danger they posed to ordinary villagers and citizens. Seen as malevolent forces, such spirit-deities were held to require regular offerings to prevent them from harming people. From an early point in the history of South Asian Buddhism, the Saṅgha worked to tame and to convert these beings, turning them into devotees of the Buddha whose tendencies to cause harm could be blunted by the merit transferred to them in rites performed by the Saṅgha (DeCaroli 2004: 173, 187). Thus, whether lay devotees sought to give alms to the Saṅgha, make offerings to the Buddha, or remove the harmful influences of spirit-deities, their religious practice often brought them into contact with Buddhist monks and nuns who could share their resources and offer their skills to assist the laity in meeting their goals.

The origins of the Mahāyāna

The preceding discussion on early lay Buddhist practice is relevant to theories on the origins of Mahāyāna Buddhism because a number of twentieth-century scholars extrapolated on the basis of certain *sūtra*s that this school began as a lay-inspired reaction against the elitism and scholasticism of the Mainstream Buddhist schools. Lamotte was one of the advocates of this view that linked the rise of the Mahāyāna with the assertion of lay Buddhist interests. According to him, the aspirations of the laity encouraged early Mahāyānists to emphasize the transcendent Buddha as a supramundane figure, the altruistic ideal of the *bodhisattva* who works for the welfare of all beings, the place given to minor gods in Buddhist worship, and the legitimacy of external rites of worship (Lamotte 1988: 620–2). In this view, laypersons who had become dissatisfied with the Abhidharma speculation in Mainstream orders turned to means of popular devotion. Thus, the Buddhas began to appear more divine than human, and images were developed to facilitate lay worship (Lamotte 1988: 636). Many of these positions appear to have been based more on assumptions about the different spheres of monastic and lay practice than on solid evidence.

Similarly, Akira Hirakawa cited the popularity of *stūpa* worship by the laity as one of the chief sources for the origin of the Mahāyāna. Hirakawa based his claims in part on textual evidence such as the Pāli Mahāparinibbāna Sutta, wherein the Buddha tells his attendant Ānanda that monks should not concern themselves with his funerary remains but instead let laypersons honor his relics (Hirakawa 1990: 271). Hirakawa maintains that *stūpa* worship began immediately following the Buddha's death, and that such structures were originally built and maintained by lay devotees outside of monastic compounds (Hirakawa 1990: 271–3). The association between the laity and *stūpa*s was made, it would seem, out of necessity since these devotees lacked the means to engage in textual study and meditative practice. They were instead awed by the exalted qualities of the Buddha and saw themselves dependent on his compassion for their own salvation (Hirakawa 1990: 270). Seeking to respond to the evident needs of the laity, early Mahāyāna Buddhists supposedly composed texts extolling the worship of *stūpa*s. Hirakawa also maintained that Mahāyāna Buddhism was originally concerned with lay devotees and consequently reserved an important role for lay *bodhisattva*s (Hirakawa 1990: 270). Thus, according to this scholar, some of the fundamental features of Mahāyāna Buddhism developed out of sensitivity to the needs of the laity, a group for whom the Mainstream monks apparently had little regard.

In more recent years, scholars have called into question such theories attributing the rise of the Mahāyāna to a grassroots movement that responded to the devotional interests of laypersons. Conventional scholarly accounts portray the Mahāyāna as a distinct and innovative school that was formed out of a rejection of the *arhat* ideal of the Mainstream Buddhist orders and the censure of "haughty" and "conceited" monks who cared more about Abhidharma than about performing useful service to the laity (Conze 1968: 50–1). But much of this portrayal rests on inferences and lacks good evidence to support it. Significantly, the theory that the Mahāyāna (or the "Great Vehicle") emerged out of a lay-dominated *stūpa* cult has been effectively rejected. In fact, monastic participation in the veneration of relics and the building of *stūpa*s was a regular occurrence. Inscriptional evidence supports the fact that ancient monks and nuns in South Asia actively encouraged and funded the construction of *stūpa*s, not considering activity in the relic cult to violate monastic discipline (Schopen 1997: 92–3, 108). Moreover, several early *sūtra*s associated with the Mahāyāna are virtually silent about *stūpa*s. Instead, one finds attempts to justify the decision of monks and nuns *not* to participate in the relic cult, which suggests that non-Mahāyāna monastics were generally expected to venerate relics and *stūpa*s (Schopen 2005: 90). Furthermore, archaeological evidence shows that most *stūpa*s were located in or near monasteries, indicating that the relic cult was generally controlled by the Saṅgha.

Early Mahāyāna writings were at best ambivalent about the relic cult. Where the veneration of *stūpa*s is mentioned in the literature, it is compared unfavorably with the development of wisdom, the memorization of *sūtra*s, and the practice of meditation (Harrison 1995: 62). In other words, the texts associated with the Mahāyāna actually tend to downplay the veneration of relics and *stūpa*s in favor of other activities that center around texts. The composition of new texts, many of which claimed to have been revealed to the author in the context of meditation, allowed for the early Mahāyāna movement to adopt new stances and ideas that often ran counter to established Buddhist thought. In certain Mahāyāna texts one finds some hints of a "cult of the book," which may have been favored in these communities over the historically primary cult of relics. The ritualized worship of special texts or verses appears to have been modeled largely after the veneration of relics, so that the place where a text was kept then became a sanctified location for offering ritualized veneration in the form of offering flowers, incense, and lamps to the book (Schopen 2005: 44, 52). The extent to which a cult of the book existed in the Mahāyāna is debatable, as there is scant evidence of actual shrines built to worship texts and the worship of texts often appears secondary to the memorization and recital of them (Drewes 2007: 136–7). Nevertheless, whether or not most Mahāyāna practitioners venerated their texts as cultic objects, it appears that they still regarded texts as the focal points for their practice and their attainment of liberating wisdom.

The conventional notion that Mahāyāna began as a grassroots, lay-oriented movement also appears unlikely. Instead, scholars now attribute its origins to religious specialists who retreated to the wilderness in order to engage in intensive meditation and textual study in a more austere environment. Reginald Ray developed this thesis in a work that singles out the ideal of the *bodhisattva* as a forest-dwelling renunciant as depicted in numerous early Mahāyāna texts. Such texts exalt the virtuous forest practitioner in comparison to his less virtuous counterpart, the settled monastic who resides in monasteries located in populated areas (Ray 1994: 259–62). The ideal of life in the forest or wilderness was not exclusive to the early Mahāyāna, however, as other Mainstream schools also praised this form of renunciation. But in the minds of those practitioners who advocated the Mahāyāna, the life of a sedentary monk in civilization interfered with the practice of meditation, a practice that could be better pursued in the wilderness. Early Mahāyāna texts such as the *Rāṣṭrapālaparipṛcchā* (Inquiry of Rāṣṭrapāla) often decry sedentary monasticism and instead emphasize the centrality of dwelling in the wilderness in an effort to recreate the rigorous *bodhisattva* path followed by the Buddha (Boucher 2008: xxii). Meanwhile, another early Mahāyāna text called the *Ugraparipṛcchā* (Inquiry of Ugra) extols the practice of monks who spend most of their time as wilderness-dwelling *bodhisattva*s, pursuing their meditation amidst the dangers of the wilderness, and only returning to their respective monastic communities to engage in rituals when required (Nattier 2003: 94–6). The celebration of a rigorous life in the wilderness—as exemplified by undertaking the thirteen ascetic practices or *dhutaṅga*s (Skt: *dhutaguṇa*s)—allowed early practitioners of the Mahāyāna to distinguish themselves from the more numerous sedentary monastics of the Mainstream schools. It also explains why many Mahāyāna texts emphasize meditation and magical powers, both of which are more easily developed in the context of extraordinary ascetic practices undertaken in the wilderness (Harrison 2003: 129–30). The prominence given to wilderness dwelling and the practice of meditation in Mahāyāna texts makes it extremely unlikely that such practice and writings were the work of laypeople.

Although this movement eventually came to refer to itself as the "Great Vehicle," there are reasons for being suspicious about many of the claims of its popularity and its distinctive status as a separate school early on. Early texts that claim an affiliation with the Mahāyāna typically possess a defensive tone and harshly criticize those people who do not accept the Mahāyāna. Many texts assert that those people who do not accept the Mahāyāna are stupid and evil, and the fact that they often bemoan a situation where their movement is the object of scorn suggests a general feeling of isolation and desperation among the proponents of the Mahāyāna (Schopen 2005: 8–9). Many early Mahāyāna texts exhibit a sense of individuals being maligned by other Mainstream monks, and it is common for such texts to present the movement as a restoration of the Buddha's original message in order to claim for itself a legitimacy and integrity that had been lost among the sedentary monks living in monasteries (Boucher 2008: 64–5). Whereas Mahāyāna texts contain critiques of other Mainstream schools and doctrines, the latter almost never acknowledge the existence of the Mahāyāna at all. Thus, although Chinese sources from the third century CE depict Mahāyāna as the normative form of Buddhism, it remained a marginal and practically invisible movement in India until the latter part of the fifth century CE. An analysis of the hundreds of ancient donative inscriptions in India reveal not one single reference to gifts or patronage given to individuals or groups connected with the Mahāyāna prior to the fifth century, an absence that raises serious doubts about the early influence of this movement (Schopen 2005: 11).

The emerging picture of the Mahāyāna is that of a loose confederation of groups of monks who were ordained in and belonged to one or another Mainstream order but opted to embrace a new vision of Buddhist practice patterned after the figure of the *bodhisattva* as presented in later *sūtra*s. The fact that there has never been a Mahāyāna *Vinaya* indicates that the followers of this movement were ordained according to the disciplinary codes of other Mainstream schools. Early Mahāyāna was in all probability not viewed as a distinctive "school," but rather a particular vision or ideal after which to pattern one's practice. It might be best described as a particular spiritual vocation identified with the rigorous path of the *bodhisattva* as practiced within an existing Mainstream Buddhist community (Nattier 2003: 195). The first proponents of the Mahāyāna called upon monks to retreat into the wilderness and practice meditation in order to take up the difficult path of becoming a *bodhisattva* in imitation of the Buddha. It appears that some forest-dwelling monks who undertook a more severely ascetic lifestyle in order to develop the attainment of meditative concentration (*samādhi*) began to report experiences of visions and dreams that became the sources of new *sūtra*s advocating a new kind of Buddhism (Harrison 2003: 141–2). The production of these Mahāyāna *sūtra*s led to their circulation among limited numbers of monks associated with various Mainstream orders. This could explain why Chinese pilgrims who visited India often found Mahāyāna monks residing with so-called "Hīnayāna" (Lesser Vehicle) monks in the same monasteries.

By envisioning the Mahāyāna as an elite spiritual vocation embraced by a minority of monks who emphasized radical asceticism and meditative trance, recent scholarship has redefined this form of Buddhism in early South Asian Buddhism. It appears that the Mahāyāna had little to do with the laity or devotional ritual. It was practically ignored in gifts given to the Saṅgha and in Mainstream Buddhist texts. It introduced some fairly innovative ideas about the benefits of following the *bodhisattva* path and generated large numbers of new texts attributed to the Buddha, at times through the medium of revelations achieved through meditation and dreams. The latter feature is particularly significant because it may have been responsible for the belief that the Buddha was not really dead but still existed and continued to transmit his teachings out of his immense compassion for the world (Williams 2000: 108–9). These teachings would come to form the basis of the expansive collection of Mahāyāna *sūtra*s, texts whose relatively recent appearance led many Mainstream monks to reject their authenticity.

Nevertheless, the combination of meditation, visions, and the writing of new texts enabled the Mahāyāna to emerge as an alternative form of Buddhism. Outside of these texts, however, there is scant material or cultural evidence that the Mahāyāna made much of an impact on South Asian civilization through the first five centuries of the Common Era. Its early proponents appear as an embattled minority, resentful of the many donations given to sedentary monastic orders and marginalized to the extent that it sought to establish the Mahāyāna in other lands outside of ancient India (Schopen 2005: 16–17). Indeed, when identifiably Mahāyāna communities were established, they tended to take root in peripheral regions in the northwest of the subcontinent where there was less competition with the more established Mainstream orders. While this may have been a sign of weakness in South Asia, this location in the northwest positioned the Mahāyāna to be introduced into Chinese lands, where it would come to enjoy much more success and support.

Mahāyāna texts

The production and study of certain Buddhist texts were central to the development of the Mahāyāna in South Asia. Their preferences for meditation and wilderness dwelling notwithstanding, the early proponents of the Great Vehicle appear to have privileged textual study over other forms of Buddhist practice. Modern views of the Mahāyāna as a devotional movement focused on the needs of the laity might correspond with some East Asian traditions, but they hardly resemble what was found in ancient South Asia. Indeed, it could be claimed that the early proponents of the Mahāyāna went to great lengths to direct the attention of monks away from cultic practices and toward the Dharma as it appears in texts. Mahāyāna *sūtra*s exhibit scant interests in the *stūpa* cult or the cult of images of the period, but instead emphasize the study, memorization, and teaching of texts (Schopen 2005: 138).

The texts privileged by Mahāyāna proponents tended to be *sūtra*s composed between about the first to fifth century CE that reflected the

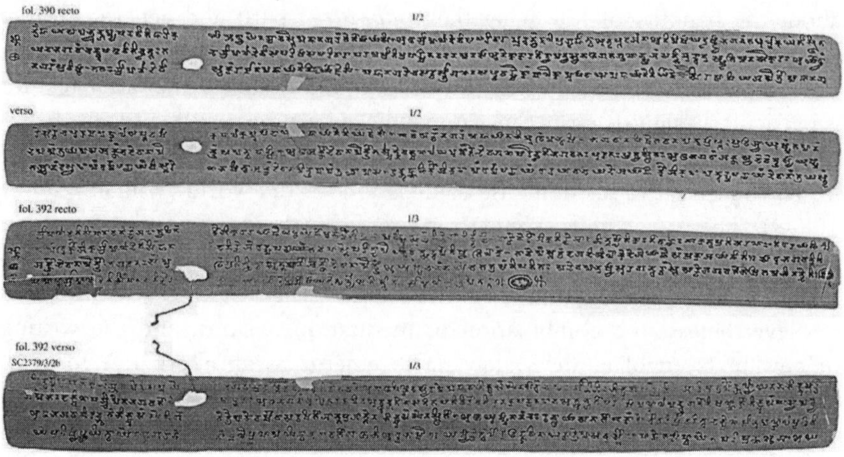

Figure 3.1 Mahāyāna Sutra Manuscript, India, 5th c. CE – MS 2378/1 (Schøyen Collection). Reproduced from Buddhist Manuscripts in the Schøyen Collection, vol. II, eds. Jens Braarvig, Paul Harrison, Jens-Uwe Hartmann, Kazunobu Matsuda, and Lore Sander (Oslo: Hermes Academic Publishing, 2002).

visionary experiences of certain monks and that were products of the emerging technology of writing. Such monks, emboldened by their individual revelations that brought them into direct association with the living Buddha, produced Mahāyāna *sūtra*s that were capable of generating new visions and new movements in the Buddha's name (Boucher 2008: xiv). These visionary experiences enabled the followers of the Mahāyāna to create and legitimate *sūtra*s that otherwise lacked recognition by the Mainstream schools, which privileged the oral transmission of the Buddha's Word. In contrast, some proponents of early Mahāyāna tended to privilege seeing over hearing, implying at times that *bodhisattva*s who saw the Buddha and received his teachings directly were spiritually superior to those who merely memorized and recited texts handed down by others (McMahan 1998: 269).

The problem that the proponents of the Mahāyāna faced was primarily how to demonstrate that their new texts were the authentic Word of the Buddha, who for many other monks had passed away in *parinirvāṇa* several centuries earlier. Although the Mahāyāna *sūtra*s usually opened with the formulaic Sanskrit phrase "*evaṃ me śrutaṃ*," as if to demonstrate that they had originally been heard by Ānanda and recited as such at the First Council (Skilton 2004: 746), they tended to be much more complex and lengthy than the older Mainstream canonical texts. They often contain extravagant descriptions of spectacular visions, and they lack many of the repetitive, mnemonic devices of older texts that were transmitted orally. The followers of the Mahāyāna therefore had to develop justifications for seeing their newer texts as authentic examples of *buddhavacana*. Thus, for example, the

Pratyutpanna-samādhi Sūtra affirms that through their access to visions of the Buddha, practitioners of *samādhi* meditation may receive the Dharma of the Buddha at any time (Harrison 2003: 124). And if this was not enough, the same text also claims that some disciples of the Buddha hid this work underground, in mountains and *stūpa*s, or in the hands of supernatural beings, where it remained concealed until about five hundred years later when it was time for it to be reintroduced into the world (Harrison 2003: 124). Other Mahāyāna texts reiterated these explanations to authenticate later *sūtra*s, while adding a third one in the form of inspiration leading to the spontaneous recital of the Dharma by a practitioner who was moved to do so.

Once these newer *sūtra*s could be accounted for, there was little to prevent the rapid expansion of texts into a voluminous collection of works preserved primarily in a form of Sanskrit, sometimes called "Buddhist Hybrid Sanskrit." The development of writing and better materials for producing texts in South Asia roughly coincided with the period in which the first Mahāyāna texts were produced. The technology of books may have allowed some of the more innovative features and previously unknown texts of the Mahāyāna to survive when other Buddhist works depended on the memorization and recitation practices of large numbers of monks (Gombrich 1990: 29–30). In contrast, a literate monk with access to the materials for producing a book could write down his revelation in a form that could be copied, circulated, and preserved. Such written texts could in theory compete for acceptance and prestige with other orally transmitted works, especially given the tendency of Mahāyāna *sūtra*s to extol written texts and even encourage their veneration.

Some of these early Mahāyāna *sūtra*s have been preserved, although it is likely that many others have not survived the passage of time. Among the earliest examples of such texts is the *Aṣṭasāhasrikā-prajñāpāramitā Sūtra* (Perfection of Wisdom in Eight Thousand Lines). Composed around the end of the first century CE, the "*Aṣṭa*" introduces a number of ideas that would become important for the later development of the Mahāyāna. Its author is unknown, but this work emphasizes that all factors (*dharma*s) are without essential nature, and thus they can be said to be empty (*śūnya*). Those who realize that *dharma*s are empty and do not correlate with any given thing or entity, may give rise to the "perfection of wisdom" as a *bodhisattva* who exists in a spiritually superior state compared with other Buddhists. The principal theme of the *Aṣṭa*—and of the other related *Prajñāpāramitā* texts composed of varying lengths later—is that all things are "empty, like a magical illusion," which is said to mean that they lack any primary, irreducible existence and are merely conceptual constructs generated by thought (Williams 2000: 134–5). This move represents a challenge to the philosophy of *Abhidharma* works, in which existence is analyzed and reduced to a specific number of discrete *dharma*s as mental and physical factors of existence. But the *Aṣṭa* and the works that follow it go further by insisting that even *dharma*s lack discrete existence and must also be said to be empty and without permanent substance.

The repeated insistence on seeing all things as empty becomes equated with the development of perfect wisdom. This vision of the world is held up as the highest accomplishment, as it is compared to the compassionate vision of Buddhas and *bodhisattva*s who vow to help all beings, although without grasping at beings or the notion of "being." The Buddha says as much in a conversation with his disciple Subhuti about the wisdom and compassion of one who helps other beings without seeing the notion of "being" as something substantial.

> *The Buddha:* Here the Bodhisattva, the great being, thinks thus: 'countless beings should I lead to Nirvana and yet there are none who lead to Nirvana, or who should be led to it.' However many beings he may lead to Nirvana, yet there is not any being that has been led to Nirvana, nor that has led others to it. For such is the true nature of dharmas, seeing their nature is illusory. Just as if, Subhuti, a clever magician ... were to conjure up at the crossroads a great crowd of people, and then make them vanish again. What do you think, Subhuti, was anyone killed by anyone, or murdered, or destroyed, or made to vanish?
>
> *Subhuti*: No indeed, Lord.
>
> *The Buddha*: Even so a Bodhisattva, a great being, leads countless beings to Nirvana, and yet there is not any being that has been led to Nirvana, nor that has led others to it.
>
> (Conze 1994: 90)

The seeming paradox of a "great being" helping other beings to *nirvāṇa* without being attached to a false notion of *being* lies at the heart of the *Aṣṭa*. This early text extols the altruistic path of the *bodhisattva*, yet consistently reminds its readers that all things, including *dharma*s, are ultimately empty and exist only as concepts. Conceptual existence may be posited as real and substantial, but perfect wisdom ultimately sees all things as lacking any kind of fundamental or intrinsic existence. This line of thinking becomes further developed and refined in the writings of the second-century monk Nāgārjuna, as we will see below.

Other *sūtra*s that represent the early beginnings in the formation of the Mahāyāna include the *Pratyutpannabuddhasaṃmukhāvasthita Sūtra* (Direct Encounter with the Buddhas of the Present), *Ugraparipṛcchā Sūtra*, and the *Rāṣṭrapālaparipṛcchā Sūtra*, all of unknown authors but likewise attributed to the Buddha. These early texts are similar in that they all discuss the practices to be taken up by *bodhisattva*s. These practices include meditative concentration (*samādhi*) and altruistic giving (*dāna*). The *Aṣṭa* had already introduced a list of six perfections (*pāramitās*): (1) giving, (2) morality, (3) patience, (4) effort, (5) meditative concentration, and (6) wisdom. Early Mahāyāna texts presented these six moral qualities as constituent factors for individuals who have adopted the vocation of a *bodhisattva*. The list of six perfections resembles the longer list of ten recognized in some Mainstream schools. The key difference here is that while non-Mahāyāna schools used the perfections descriptively to account for what the Bodhisattva did in the past on his way to becoming Gautama Buddha, early Mahāyāna texts refer to the perfections prescriptively in order to encourage its readers to make a *bodhisattva* vow and personally adopt the goal of Buddhahood themselves (Williams 2000: 138).

A number of early Mahāyāna *sūtra*s distinguished themselves by emphasizing spectacular visions of other realms inhabited by other Buddhas or this very world as seen through the eyes of one who is awakened like a Buddha. In the context of the wilderness meditation advocated by many such *sūtra*s, a number of Mahāyāna (or proto-Mahāyāna) texts presented readers with vivid and fantastic imagery that was either a guide for, or the result of, meditative techniques. Works such as the *Akṣobhyavyūha Sūtra* (Wondrous Qualities of the Immovable Buddha), *Sukhāvatīvyūha Sūtra* (Wondrous Qualities of the Land of Bliss), and the *Gaṇḍavyūha Sūtra* (Supreme Array Scripture) present their readers with extravagant visions of reality (cf. Osto 2009). The first two texts, composed sometime between the third and fourth centuries CE, describe in vivid detail the heavenly sights to be found in "buddha-fields," that is, heavenly realms created and presided over by Buddhas in other parts of the universe. These *sūtra*s depict marvelous surroundings and describe the heavenly comforts enjoyed by beings that are fortunate enough to be reborn there. For example, the longer Sanskrit version of the *Sukhāvatīvyūha Sūtra* contains numerous vivid descriptions of the celestial Land of Bliss.

> Now, Ānanda, in this Land of Bliss flow rivers of many kinds. There are great rivers one league wide, twenty, thirty, forty, or fifty leagues wide, and rivers as wide as a hundred thousand leagues, and as deep as twelve leagues. And all these rivers flow gently, bringing various sweet-smelling perfumed waters, bearing clusters of various jewel-studded flowers, and resounding with many kinds of sweet sounds ... And, Ānanda, the delightful sound that emerges then from those waters can be heard throughout the Buddha-field ... And each [living being] will hear exactly the delightful sound he wishes to hear, in whatever manner he wishes to

> hear it. For instance, he will be able to hear the word 'Buddha,' 'Dharma,' or 'Saṅgha.' Or he will be able to hear the phrase, 'the perfect virtues of the bodhisattva,' ... And, Ānanda, in this Land of Bliss, the word 'unwholesome' is never heard, the word 'hindrance,' the words 'state of woe,' 'bad destiny,' and 'misfortune' are never heard. The word 'pain' does not occur at all—even the words 'feelings that are neither painful nor pleasant' do not occur there. Ānanda, how, then, could suffering itself or the word 'suffering' ever arise in this land?
>
> (Gómez 1996: 87–8)

This dialogue between the Buddha named Śakyamuni (i.e., Gautama Buddha) and his disciple Ānanda demonstrates that the buddha-field called the Land of Bliss is permeated only by pleasurable things. One's awareness remains focused on the Dharma and the Heavenly Buddha Amitābha who resides there.

By vividly describing such a heavenly realm of inconceivable pleasure, the *Sukhāvatīvyūha Sūtra* helps its readers to imagine and seek out this buddha-field, which is said to exist in a realm of the universe to the west of this earth. It seems likely that many followers of the Mahāyāna would have accepted such visionary texts as portraying accurate images of reality. Still, it may be that such textual images were not only seen as descriptions of things already in existence, but that they also functioned as blueprints for visualization practices that allowed these worlds to be actively constructed in the minds of meditators (Harrison 2003: 122). The world described by this Mahāyāna *sūtra* was meant to be envisioned by practitioners who could then engage with this world and its Heavenly Buddha in the context of heightened religious awareness.

The intensely visual quality of the *Sukhāvatīvyūha Sūtra* is a feature also shared by the *Gaṇḍavyūha Sūtra*. This Mahāyāna *sūtra*, composed prior to the fourth century CE, does not seek to describe a heavenly buddha-field upon which one may meditate. Instead, it describes a journey of a Buddhist pilgrim named Sudhana who gradually learns to view the immediate world in much more fantastic ways. The visions of Sudhana are brought about by the timely interventions of "good friends" (*kalyāṇamitra*) who assist him in his path of spiritual development. Sudhana is shown by advanced *bodhisattva*s such as Maitreya and Mañjuśrī how the world really appears as an interconnected whole, where entities with illusory self-existence appear as reflected in all other things. For instance, inside Maitreya's tower Sudhana sees an infinite number of other towers, all lavishly decorated, wherein he sees reflections of himself and of miraculous scenes where the Bodhisattva Maitreya teaches the Dharma and relieves the suffering of all beings (Cleary 1987: 365–74). The *sūtra* effectively attempts to describe reality as it is seen by one who is awakened and omniscient.

In the pilgrim Sudhana's all-embracing vision, an array of worlds and beings that are defiled and pure appear as an interconnected whole, and he sees numerous Buddhas and their assemblies populating many of these worlds. The *Gaṇḍavyūha Sūtra* depicts a world where a nearly infinite number of Buddhas may co-exist and reside in realms where they continue to preach the one true Dharma to those beings fortunate enough to hear them. And yet this text goes further in implying that Buddhas and advanced *bodhisattva*s are effectively identical with the universe itself, as their immeasurably wise and compassionate presence is said to pervade the universe. At the end of the text, Sudhana is exposed to such a vision when he gazes while meditating upon the body of the Bodhisattva Samantabhadra (Universally Good). Thereupon, he sees infinite rays of light and colorful flames emanating from every pore of the *bodhisattva*'s body; and while meditating on this body, Sudhana perceives infinite numbers of worlds, mountains, cities, and beings within each pore (Cleary 1987: 380–3). This fantastic vision of the Bodhisattva Samantabhadra represents both a commentary on the wondrous, interconnected nature of the world and a template for visualization practice. The text's marvelous description of the *bodhisattva*'s body intermingles with an all-encompassing vision of the universe. The co-existence of the universe with the *bodhisattva*'s body—and with the Heavenly Buddha Vairocana elsewhere in the text—speaks to a vision of the universe wherein "all is empty and therefore seen as a flow lacking hard edges," in much the same way that a meditator might experience it (Williams 1989: 123). Such transcendent visions come to occupy prominent parts in a number of Mahāyāna texts. And they represent a new orientation that privileged seeing Buddhas and *bodhisattva*s who remain available to assist devotees in their spiritual practice and worldly needs.

The Bodhisattva path

It has been suggested that the origins of the Mahāyāna were closely linked with the formation of a new spiritual vocation patterned after the figure of the *bodhisattva*, a being who vows to become a Buddha and devotes countless lifetimes to developing moral perfections in support of this goal. The *bodhisattva* as a spiritual exemplar is likely modeled after the characters aspiring to reach Buddhahood in the *Jātaka* stories, which were popular accounts celebrating the incredible and selfless acts of the Bodhisattva while on the way to becoming Gautama Buddha. The early followers of the Mahāyāna saw in the figure of the *bodhisattva* a much more demanding, yet fulfilling path of Buddhist practice. As a *bodhisattva*, one makes a binding vow and dedicates one's efforts to become a Buddha who can help to release beings from the suffering of *saṃsāra*. As such, this path was extolled as a superior form of practice that the Mahāyāna used to distinguish itself from other Buddhist paths.

It is likely that during the Buddha's time, the idea of other people vowing to become *bodhisattva*s and, eventually, Buddhas was unusual if not wholly unknown. People were encouraged to become *śrāvaka*s or "hearers" who listened to the Dharma and followed the path set out by the Buddha. In time, some individuals began to read *Jātaka* stories as prescriptive models for Buddhist practice, and these same individuals apparently adopted the lengthy and difficult *bodhisattva* path in a heroic effort to follow the "Great Vehicle" that leads to Buddhahood (Nattier 2003: 144–5). The recognition by the followers of the Mahāyāna that one may undertake a *bodhisattva* path opened up a new set of values and practices for South Asian Buddhists. Modeled in part after the idealized Mainstream Buddhist figure of the solitary monk living and meditating in the wilderness, the Mahāyāna *bodhisattva* distinguished himself by consciously striving to become a Buddha rather than merely behaving like one (Ray 1994: 270). It was this motivation that allowed the Mahāyāna to assert the superiority of the *bodhisattva* path in terms of its greater compassion and the magnitude of its eventual accomplishment. To strive to undertake countless lifetimes and unimaginable personal sacrifices to become a Buddha appeared like the ultimate goal—one equivalent to what the Buddha achieved. And although the compassionate concern for all beings is frequently mentioned as the main motivation for the *bodhisattva* path, it appears that early on in the Mahāyāna the goal was pursued less out of compassion for others than out of ambition to transform oneself into a glorious Buddha worthy of veneration (Nattier 2003: 146–7).

It is often thought, based on some *bodhisattva* vows, that the *bodhisattva* path involves the deliberate postponement of one's own Awakening or *nirvāṇa* until all other beings attain this goal first. As a result, electing to postpone one's own *nirvāṇa* to stay in the world and work for the liberation of others is often assumed to be the defining quality of Mahāyāna *bodhisattva*s. Such a view, however, is erroneous as it implies that a Buddha, who by definition has already attained *nirvāṇa*, is somehow spiritually deficient to the *bodhisattva*; and that one should postpone Buddhahood despite the fact that the attainment of Buddhahood is precisely what leads to the greatest benefit for all beings (Williams 2000: 139). One does not postpone *nirvāṇa* to help others achieve it first. It is more accurate to see the *bodhisattva* as transcending the duality of *nirvāṇa* and *saṃsāra* by striving to become a Buddha who remains in the world to assist others in attaining liberation (Williams 2000: 139). The more quickly one attains the goal of Buddhahood, the more quickly one may deliver relief from suffering and the bliss of Awakening to others. In the Mahāyāna, moreover, a Buddha may continue to offer compassionate assistance from his particular buddha-field throughout his unimaginably long lifespan, making the idea of postponing the goal superfluous.

Nevertheless, the *bodhisattva* path of the Mahāyāna called for practitioners to adopt a rigorous path of mental and moral development. As mentioned above, the path eventually came to comprise the cultivation of six moral perfections: giving, morality, patience, effort, meditative concentration, and wisdom. These moral qualities are perfected by undertaking difficult deeds over many lifetimes in *saṃsāra*. Certain *sūtra*s came to emphasize the importance of a single perfection over the others. Thus, the various *Prajñāpāramitā* texts typically cite the perfection of wisdom (*prajñā*) as the highest accomplishment that necessarily completes all of the other perfections. Meanwhile the *Ugraparipṛcchā* highlights the perfection of giving (*dāna*) above the other *pāramitā*s. Regardless of the emphasis given in a particular *sūtra*, the list of six perfections structured the Mahāyāna *bodhisattva* path. And although one might conclude that these perfections brought the *bodhisattva*s into active relationships with other beings that suffered in *saṃsāra*, the actual picture of the *bodhisattva*'s relationship to the wider world appears quite different. In early South Asia, *bodhisattva*s were exhorted to avoid contact with others in order to develop the qualities needed for Buddhahood (Nattier 2003: 132). Having attained Buddhahood, the virtuous actor is now ready to dispense his compassion upon the world of beings. Prior to that, however, the path of the *bodhisattva* in South Asia was a reclusive one rather than an activist one. Even the ideal of generosity could be described primarily as a mental attitude rather than as concrete steps to free the world from suffering (Crosby and Skilton 1998: 34).

In eighth-century India, the scholar-monk Śāntideva composed the *Bodhicaryāvatāra* (Undertaking the Way to Awakening), which became seen as the definitive statement on conduct associated with the Mahāyāna *bodhisattva* path. The text appears like a handbook for aspiring *bodhisattva*s. It begins with praise and a description of the *bodhicitta* ("Awakening Mind" or "Thought of Enlightenment"), which is taken to be the first step on the path leading up to Buddhahood. The *bodhicitta* here appears as the resolution to attain Awakening as a Buddha to release limitless beings from the misery of repeated existence. Śāntideva describes the moral implications of the *bodhisattva*'s "Awakening Mind" in this way:

> That jewel, the Mind, which is the seed of pure happiness in the world and the remedy for the suffering of the world, how at all can its merit be measured?
>
> Worship of the Buddha is surpassed merely by the desire for the welfare of others; how much more so by the persistent effort for the complete happiness of every being? ...

> People honour someone who gives alms to a few people, saying, 'He does good', because he contemptuously supports their life for half a day with a moment's gift of mere food.
>
> What then of the one who offers to a limitless number of beings, throughout limitless time, the fulfillment of all desires, unending until the end of the sky and those beings?
>
> (Crosby and Skilton 1998: 7–8)

With a mind devoted to Awakening, the *bodhisattva*, having articulated the vow to become a Buddha, then begins the long and difficult path of developing the six perfections to attain Buddhahood.

In addition to the six perfections, the Mahāyāna eventually developed a system of ten stages (*bhūmi*s) through which the *bodhisattva* must pass on the way to Buddhahood. Some texts present us with a different number of stages, but the enumeration of *bhūmi*s as found in the *Daśabhūmika Sūtra* (Scripture on Ten Spiritual Stages) has become more or less standard for the *bodhisattva* path in the Mahāyāna. The development of these *bhūmi*s is a testimony to the length of the *bodhisattva* path, as well as the attempt to offer a more systematic means of following it. The stages appear as follows: (1) Joyful Stage—marked by the perfection of giving; (2) Free from Defilements Stage—marked by the perfection of morality; (3) Light-giving Stage—marked by the perfection of meditative trance; (4) Glorious Wisdom Stage—marked by the perfection of patience; (5) Very Hard to Conquer Stage—marked by the perfection of energy; (6) Face-to-face stage—marked by the perfection of wisdom; (7) Proceeding Afar Stage—marked by the perfection of skillful means (*upāya*); (8) Immovable Stage—wherein one perfects vows to save all sentient beings; (9) Good Insight Stage—wherein one perfects the power to lead all beings; and (10) Dharma-cloud Stage—wherein one perfects knowledge (Kawamura 2004: 59). The elaboration of the *bodhisattva* path in terms of six perfections and ten stages provided further guidance to those seeking to become Buddhas, and it also served to increase the magnitude of the *bodhisattva*'s accomplishments.

As the Mahāyāna worked to popularize the *bodhisattva* ideal, it picked up on some earlier critiques of the *arhat* made by the Mahāsāṃghikas. In the context of views that stressed the incomparable altruism of the *bodhisattva*, some Mahāyāna polemicists began to argue that the *arhat* was a spiritually inferior and incomplete attainment. In earlier works such as the *Ugraparipṛcchā*, the *bodhisattva* path was presented as an optional pursuit for the relatively few monastics and householders interested in pursuing a more difficult and rarefied Buddhist goal (Nattier 2003: 86). The ideal of becoming a *bodhisattva* was neither expected of nor recommended for everyone. Yet, in time, as the followers of the Mahāyāna grew more self-assured (or perhaps more frustrated with its minor influence in South Asia), efforts were made to make what was once a difficult path for the few into a universal path for all Buddhist devotees. The *Saddharmapuṇḍarīka Sūtra* (Scripture on the Lotus of the Good Dharma)—a Mahāyāna text that enjoyed much more popularity in East Asia than in South Asia—described the *bodhisattva* path as the "one vehicle" (*ekayāna*), implying that the paths of the hearer (*śrāvaka*) and the solitary Buddha (*pratyekabuddha*) could not lead to any meaningful Buddhist goals. This view, which reinterprets the *bodhisattva* path as the only authentic one, was likely less common in South Asia than the view that held the *bodhisattva* as the most exalted of a number of good options for Buddhist practice.

The *bodhisattva* ideal of the Mahāyāna represented a newer religious path inspired by the Buddha himself. Certain texts speak of the possibility of both monks and laypersons making a *bodhisattva* vow and undertaking the path of accumulating merit that eventually leads to the attainment of Buddhahood. Of the two, however, certain texts assert that the monastic lifestyle is more conducive to fulfilling one's lofty aims as a *bodhisattva*. The *Ugraparipṛcchā*, for example, advocates ordination, renunciation and minimizing one's contact with others in order to accumulate merit and amass the "roots of goodness" for attaining the state of a Buddha (Nattier 2003: 121–2, 133). Such a program of practice appears to depart from the common view of a *bodhisattva* as being intimately involved with reducing the suffering of others. Indian Mahāyāna texts generally portray the *bodhisattva* path as a reclusive one, wherein one cultivates an attitude of compassion but delays offering active assistance to others until after reaching Buddhahood (Nattier 2003: 134–5).

The major exception to this image of the monastic *bodhisattva* appears in the figure of Vimalakīrti in the *Vimalakīrtinirdeśa Sūtra* (Scripture of the Teaching of Vimalakīrti). In this early *sūtra*, Vimalakīrti appears as a wise and worldly lay *bodhisattva* who humiliates the Buddha's leading monastic followers with his flawless argumentation on the non-dual nature of reality. Using skillful means (*upāya*) by feigning an illness to draw the Buddha's disciples to him, Vimalakīrti explains to the advanced *bodhisattva* Mañjuśrī how a *bodhisattva* may live in the world without becoming attached to it (Potter 1999: 193). The *Vimalakīrtinirdeśa Sūtra* thus presents a rather different image of a *bodhisattva* for the Mahāyāna in South Asia. Renunciation here appears unnecessary, as demonstrated by the layman Vimalakīrti's superior display of wisdom and skillful means. Aware that the non-duality of existence nullifies the difference between monastic and lay lives, the ideal *bodhisattva* in this text remains in the world without being defiled by its sensory delights. The cultural impact of this text in South Asia appears to have been minimal if not negligible, but the assertion that laypeople may attain the highest wisdom and religious goals helped to make the *Vimalakīrtinirdeśa Sūtra* a particularly influential Mahāyāna *sūtra* in East Asia, where the ideals of renunciation and monasticism conflicted with social norms.

If the Mahāyāna *bodhisattva* ideal was generally not envisioned to be traversed by laypersons, neither did it appear exceptionally available to women. Although female *bodhisattva*s are referenced in Mahāyāna texts, female Buddhas are virtually nowhere to be found. The early images of *bodhisattva*s and the virtues associated with their lengthy and arduous path were apparently cast in masculine terms in the South Asian environment, and unlike the *arhat*, which was a goal open to women, Buddhahood was a goal attainable only by men (Nattier 2003: 99–100). Consequently, the Mahāyāna prescription of the *bodhisattva* path and the goal of Buddhahood may have effectively contributed to a decline in the status of women in the religion. Owing to such masculine ethical ideals, the ability of women to pursue the same path and achieve the same goal was subject to question and debate. Mahāyāna Buddhists were neither uniformly misogynist nor uniformly egalitarian when it came to assessing women's abilities to achieve the highest religious goals (Mrozik 2007: 126). Yet modern interpretations of the *bodhisattva* ideal often wrongly conclude that its universalistic concerns to alleviate suffering led to a correspondingly inclusive, egalitarian view of gender, which it actually lacked.

Philosophical systems of the Mahāyāna

The Mahāyāna movement in South Asia owed its development to more than the articulation of the *bodhisattva* path, the growth of technologies of writing, and the veneration of texts. Some of the followers of the Mahāyāna were also concerned with the analysis of Buddhist thought. These thinkers composed sophisticated philosophical treatises that came to define important Mahāyāna doctrines and supplied the theoretical basis for what would later become a Mahāyāna "school." These systems, in part, grew out of the speculation on emptiness found in the *Prajñāpāramitā* literature. The concepts that stand out as particularly influential in Mahāyāna philosophy include that of emptiness (*śūnyatā*), consciousness (*vijñāna*), and the "womb of Buddhahood" (*tathāgata-garbha*). The important early schools of Mahāyāna philosophy in South Asia include the Madhyamaka or "Middle Way" School and the Yogācāra (Practice of Yoga) School. Nevertheless, it is important to note that such "schools" were actually just schools of thought that lacked any formal ordination tradition.

Madhyamaka

The Madhyamaka or "Middle Way" school of Mahāyāna Buddhist thought originated in the influential and intellectually sophisticated writings of Nāgārjuna, a Buddhist monk who is generally thought to have lived around the late second and early third centuries of the Common Era in the Andhra region of southern India. Nāgārjuna's philosophy has received a great deal of commentary and analysis both by the Buddhist scholars that followed him and by modern western scholars. As the subject of numerous legends and hagiographies, Nāgārjuna remains a largely enigmatic figure. We know that he authored the *Mūlamadhyamaka-kārikā* (Fundamental Verses on the Middle Way), a work that in twenty-seven chapters demonstrates that all factors (*dharma*s) and entities (*bhava*s) arise conditioned upon other factors and things, and thus must be said to be "empty" of inherent, independent existence. Many other works have been attributed to him, but only about four or five other works including the *Ratnāvalī* (Garland of Jewels) and the *Śūnyatāsaptati* (Seventy Verses on Emptiness) display sufficient coherence in doctrine to be attributed to him with confidence (Ruegg 1981: 8–9, 19–23).

Nāgārjuna, it has been argued, was the pioneer of a distinctively Mahāyāna approach to Buddhist thought. By extending the implications of the traditional Buddhist notions of impermanence and dependent arising, Nāgārjuna went further to argue not only that the constituent factors of existence (e.g. Five Aggregates) lack permanence, but they also lack substance or essence and cannot even be said to *exist* momentarily. His work draws on the notion of emptiness (*śūnyatā*) from the *Prajñāpāramitā* texts. According to him, any factor or entity posited to exist, can only be said to exist *conventionally*, which is to say that its existence is dependent on other factors. It cannot be said to exist independently or inherently at all. Ultimately speaking, it is "empty"—empty of own-being or self-existence (*svabhāva*). Whereas while most other Mainstream Buddhist schools recognized the non-substantiality of the Self or individual, Nāgārjuna expanded the idea of non-substantiality—or the lack of any permanent essence or property—to include the factors of existence (*dharma*s) enumerated and analyzed by scholars of Abhidharma (Ruegg 1981: 5–6). Thus, even *dharma*s lack substance and are not irreducible elements that exist independently.

Nāgārjuna demonstrated the fallacy of maintaining inherently existing entities through recourse to his system of "fourfold argumentation" (*catuṣkoṭi*). Logically, as David Seyfort Ruegg describes, one can posit four different positions with regard to the relations between allegedly self-existent entities: (1) a positive relation, (2) a negative relation, (3) a conjunction of both positive and negative relations, and (4) an indeterminate relation consisting of neither positive nor negative relations (Ruegg 1981: 39). For

Nāgārjuna, one may use this analysis to show how it is absurd to posit that two self-existent entities are (1) the same, (2) different, (3) both the same and different, or (4) neither the same nor different. For example, to posit that milk and curds are the same is to suggest that they lack any distinctive qualities essential to them, and thus one can question whether curds come from milk or milk comes from curds. To posit that they are different is to hold that there is no relation between them whatsoever, and that one cannot give rise to the other. To posit that they are both the same and different is merely to replicate the problems found in both theses. And to claim they are neither the same nor different is to be left without ascribing any meaningful relation between milk and curds. The problem with all of the above propositions is that each one relies on an errant view of the inherently existing nature of milk and curds. Whenever one posits that a given entity exists independently in terms of an unchanging essence, it is impossible to show how it comes into relation with any other thing. One needs to learn how to see "milk" and "curds" differently, as things that are empty of self-existence.

Nāgārjuna's critique of views that posit or imply the real existence of entities is founded upon his conviction that all things are not independent but *interdependent* and exist only in relation to other things. He led the Madhyamaka School to reinterpret the doctrine of Dependent Co-Arising (*pratītyasamutpāda*) to mean that since all phenomena are produced from various conditions, all phenomena must be said to be empty of any inherent existence (Lang 2004: 479). Nothing can be said to exist in and of itself. To be "non-empty" is to exist without change and conditions. Any notion of "essence" implies an unchanging, characteristic property—a feature that defines the very existence of an entity. But in the *Mūlamadhyamaka-kārikā*, Nāgārjuna argues that the notion of essence would require recognizing that it is eternal, independent, and does not arise dependently on anything else (Garfield 1995: 220). Such a mistaken view of essence lies behind the tendency of deluded beings to posit real, substantial existence to things, which causes grasping and desiring what one cannot possess or maintain indefinitely. The conditioned nature of all "things," for Nāgārjuna, means that everything is empty and without essence.

Much of Nāgārjuna's analysis revolves around the distinction between conventional truth (*saṃvṛti-satya*) and ultimate truth (*paramārtha-satya*). Conventional truth refers to tacit, agreed-upon methods of describing the world of experience as it appears to us. Thus, conventionally speaking, we can refer to a flat surface supported by four legs as a "table," and say that a table exists because we write or eat upon it. We will eventually stop writing or eating and leave the table for a period of time during which it is outside our sensory experience. However, at some point, when we return to the "table" again, we notice that it remains in the same place and how little it has changed; and thus we begin to conclude that there is something substantial and permanent about it. And yet the designation of an object as "table" merely reflects the conventional usage of language and certain assumptions about the nature of its continued presence in the field of our sensory experience. At the level of ultimate truth, we must conclude that the "table" does not exist as such; that its existence is dependent on many factors related to its materials, the process of its production and assembly, and an entire system of sensory factors including light and our abilities to see and touch. The table is actually empty, which is another way of saying that it does not and cannot exist independently of other factors. To speak of the table as substantial, independent, and self-existent is to be deluded about the true, interdependent nature of all phenomena.

Nāgārjuna's efforts to deconstruct the tendency of un-awakened beings to reify things and attribute innate, independent existence to them are based on a method that charts a "middle way" between the false doctrines of eternalism (i.e. eternal, self-existence) and nihilism (i.e. non-existence). Both views, according to him, must be rejected since they involve the reification of an entity or the denial of any existence whatsoever. The middle way out of this dilemma is to acknowledge that all entities exist in dependence on other entities, none of which may be said to be independent, unchanging, or self-existent. What is conceived as existing independently is merely the linguistic construction (*vikalpa*) of an entity whose presumed self-existence (*svabhāva*) is merely conceptual or imaginary, based on the discursive nature of the thought of it and the speech used to describe it (Ruegg 1981: 42). This can be simplified to mean that the practice of assigning a given entity a name carries with it the tendency of attributing independent existence to it. But ultimately speaking, a table is just the dependently arisen notion of "table" as conventionally labeled and described. The notion of "I" as an independent being with an unchanging essence (e.g. an *ātman* or a *pudgala*) is likewise a conventional designation that is useful for everyday discourse, but should not be confused as something real and substantial in itself.

We learn from the *Mūlamadhyamaka-kārikā* that the basic Buddhist notions of conditions, aggregates, elements, desire, suffering, bondage, *karma*, time, the Tathāgata (or the Buddha), *nirvāṇa*, and the Twelvefold Chain of Dependent Co-Arising, among other things, are all "empty" in that they arise due to conditions. Importantly, "empty" does not mean unreal or non-existent. It means that to speak of the existence of any thing, one must qualify it as being dependent on other things. Nāgājruna concludes that "emptiness" is itself empty, a conventional designation used to describe the dependently arisen nature of all things and concepts. In this sense, the ultimate truth of emptiness is merely another way of stating the conventional truth that all factors and entities arise due to conditions.

Whatever is dependently co-arisen
That is explained to be emptiness.
That, being a dependent designation,
Is itself the middle way.

Something that is not dependently arisen,
Such a thing does not exist.
Therefore a nonempty thing
Does not exist.

If all this were nonempty, as in your view,
There would be no arising nor ceasing.
Then the Four Noble Truths
Would become nonexistent.

If it is not dependently arisen,
How could suffering come to be?
Suffering has been taught to be impermanent,
And so cannot come from its own essence.

(Garfield 1995: 69–70)

In this way Nāgārjuna equates emptiness with dependent co-arising; both are means to describe the ultimate lack of self-existence in all phenomena. Emptiness, moreover, is what allows for change and transformation. By definition, that which is allegedly unconditioned and possesses inherent existence cannot be subject to arising and ceasing. And without the possibility of change and transformation, there would be no suffering or liberation from suffering.

Perhaps Nāgārjuna's most radical claim is to posit that since *saṃsāra* and *nirvāṇa* are both empty of self-existence, there is no meaningful difference between them. Neither *saṃsāra* nor *nirvāṇa* can be said to be substantial, for if they were then there could be no change in one's condition. Events and experiences would then in theory be un-caused, and thus it would make no sense to speak of the conditions leading to rebirth or the liberation from suffering. The difference between *saṃsāra* and *nirvāṇa* is relational, not absolute. To posit that they are essentially different is to attribute them with unchanging, innate properties that disallow the possibility of conditioned experience and spiritual transformation. To be "in *saṃsāra*" is to see things as they appear to a deluded mind—as existing inherently and independently, whereas to be "in *nirvāṇa*" means to see things as they really are—as empty, dependent, impermanent, and nonsubstantial, but not to be or to go anywhere else (Garfield 1995: 332). In this sense, *nirvāṇa* is finally only *saṃsāra* as a

Buddha experiences it. One realizes the emptiness and interdependence of all things, and thus refrains from reifying and grasping after them.

The effects of Nāgārjuna's work on Mahāyāna thought were lasting and considerable. His writings spurred numerous other Buddhist scholars, such as his disciple Āryadeva, the author of *Catuḥśataka* (Four Hundred Verses), to address and expand upon his ideas about emptiness, the non-duality between *saṃsāra* and *nirvāṇa*, and the relationship between conventional and ultimate truth. To be sure, however, Nāgārjuna and Madhyamaka philosophy had their critics. It is likely that most South Asian Buddhists familiar with the various Abhidharma theories received Nāgārjuna's contention that all "things" are ultimately conceptual constructs with doubt and suspicions of nihilism, since to say that all things only possess a secondary, conceptual existence is to insinuate that there is nothing primary and non-conceptual out of which to construct them (Williams 2000: 150). Such a view would be equivalent to positing a world made up of signs but no referents.

The later proponents of Madhyamaka philosophy rejected such critiques and set out to demonstrate the truth and utility of the system of thought outlined by Nāgārjuna. Buddhapālita, who lived around the beginning of the sixth century, wrote a commentary on the *Mūlamadhyamaka-kārikā*, in which he employed the so-called *prasaṅga* method of pointing out the necessary but undesired consequences resulting from a thesis used to prove something about an entity (Ruegg 1981: 60). Bhāvaviveka (ca. 6th c. CE) wrote commentaries and original works that developed Nāgārjuna's ideas in a different direction. Bhāvaviveka maintained the Madhayamaka needed to do more than just annul the theses of its opponents, but that it must also introduce an independent (*svatantra*) inference or a positive thesis consistent with the logical structures recognized by other philosophical systems (Williams 1989: 58–9). Worldly phenomena remain empty, but one can do more than just assert the absurdity of views that presuppose the nonempty nature of things. Later, in the seventh century, Candrakīrti responded by reaffirming the *prasaṅga* method of reasoning and criticizing Bhāvaviveka's syllogisms as introducing the notion of an independent entity that could be positively verified by two parties in a debate. For Candrakīrti then, Bhāvaviveka's reliance on independent proofs in argumentation could not escape the charge of positing the existence of independent things and concepts that could be analyzed and affirmed positively. Subsequently, the work of Nāgārjuna and his followers made a large impression upon Tibetan Buddhists, many of whom studied their works on the philosophical implications of emptiness and its importance for developing wisdom.

Yogācāra

Within the elite circles of Buddhist philosophy, there were apparently many individuals who concluded that Madhyamaka thought, if not nihilistic, was overly intellectual and rested too firmly on abstract reasoning. Some were drawn instead to another major Mahāyāna "school" of philosophy called Yogācāra (Practice of Yoga) or Cittamātra (Mind Only). In the fourth century CE, two monks and (half-)brothers named Asaṅga and Vasubandhu authored works that gave rise to a new philosophical system emphasizing the primacy of the mind (*citta*) or consciousness (*vijñāna*) in accounting for one's ordinary experience of the world. Herein, it is the workings of a deluded mind afflicted by the misperception of the real nature of the world that gives rise to ignorance and suffering. For Yogācāra, the mind is both the cause of misperception and the means for liberation. Instead of following Nāgārjuna and explaining how all factors and entities are ontologically empty, the Yogācārins focused on the epistemological perception of factors and entities. In other words, they set out to show how the mind works in both its deluded and purified conditions, as this analysis could then bring delusion to an end and generate a clear awareness of experience.

Asaṅga and Vasubandhu developed some of their ideas in conjunction with some early Mahāyāna *sūtra*s that address the role of consciousness in determining one's experience. These formative texts from around the third century CE include *Saṃdhinirmocana Sūtra* (Scripture Unfolding the Real Truth), the *Avataṃsaka Sūtra* (Flower Ornament Scripture), and the *Laṅkāvatāra Sūtra* (Scripture on the Descent into Laṅka). These works, attributed to the Buddha, introduced a greater emphasis on the phenomenology of the mind. Inspired by the terminology and orientation of these texts, Asaṅga and Vasubandhu composed their own treatises to outline the workings of the mind in an effort to analyze meditative states and facilitate progress toward Awakening. Asaṅga authored a number of important works including *Yogācārabhūmi* (Stages in the Practice of Yoga), a lengthy compendium of Buddhist doctrine and terminology intended to serve as a guide for practice; *Mahāyānasaṃgraha* (Compendium on the Great Vehicle), a more concise summary of key Buddhist ideas; and the *Abhidharmasamuccaya* (Compilation of Works on the Higher Dharma), which deals with the insubstantiality of *dharma*s and yet illustrates that Abhidharma thought was not completely rejected by some Mahāyāna thinkers. Meanwhile, Vasubandhu composed the *Viṃśatikā* (Twenty Verses) and the *Triṃśikā* (Thirty Verses), which concisely summarize Yogācāra thought.

One of the important innovations by Asaṅga and Vasubandhu in developing Yogācāra was to incorporate a threefold system to explain the basic spheres of experience with reference to the mind. This doctrine is called *trisvabhāva* ("three natures"), and it is used to reinterpret the notion of emptiness in terms of how the mind mistakenly apprehends experience and, in turn, how it *should* apprehend experience. First, there is the "constructed nature" (*parikalpita-svabhāva*), which refers to impressions based on the polarization of subject (or "the grasper") and object ("the grasped") into a duality as perceived by the un-awakened mind (Williams 2000: 156). Next, there is the "dependent nature" (*paratantra-svabhāva*), which refers to the flow of consciousness as a series of dependently arisen cognitive experiences that appear to the mind (Williams 2000: 157). Finally, there is the "perfected nature" (*parinişpanna-svabhāva*), which is the complete abandonment of the false subject–object duality in the context of the dependently arisen flow of consciousness. The perfected nature thus reflects a purified mental state devoid of imaginary mental constructions of experience that reinforce the false notions of "I" as subject and "things" as objects. This leads Yogācāra to redefine emptiness in terms of seeing the causal flow of consciousness in the dependent nature as being empty of the seeming subject–object duality that the un-awakened mind mistakenly constructs based on its apprehension of experiences (Dunne 2005: 1211).

The metaphor of a mirage in the road may be helpful to illustrate the three natures in Yogācāra. When driving down a long stretch of road on a warm, sunny day, one might see what appears to be a puddle of water. This puddle of water that appears to the eye represents the constructed nature of the mind, which is to say, it is a sense-object that is falsely cognized as a puddle of water. However, based on experience and the recognition that the car never catches up to this puddle of water, one realizes that the water is simply a mirage. The mirage that is a dependently arisen factor of rays of light, the dry surface of the road, and the eye's visual capacities represents the dependent nature, or the flow of consciousness that results from various conditions. The recognition that there is no difference between the puddle of water and the dry road, that both are simply things that appear to one's mind based on various factors, is the perfected nature. Thus, what sets Yogācāra apart from the Madhyamaka School is that its analysis of experience is not content to deconstruct all things into emptiness, but rather it presupposes that underneath all appearances lies a substratum of consciousness that can perceive things correctly or incorrectly. Emptiness here refers to the absence of subject–object duality in the mind—since it must be admitted that the ordinary sense of subjectivity is dependent on and inseparable from the objects perceived by the subject, but at the same time this interpretation rests on the undeniable reality of consciousness itself (Dunne 2005: 1210–11). Underneath all the conceptual constructions of experience lies the mind that apprehends and analyzes the infinite variety of factors that present themselves to it. This move that differentiates Yogācāra from Madhyamaka—and which may have been responsible for the greater influence of Yogācāra in South Asian Mahāyāna thought—accepts that the mind or consciousness has the status of a primary existent or a substratum in which all experiences are processed (Williams 2000: 156–8).

This understanding of ignorance as stemming from the false conceptualization of experience in terms of subject and object led Yogācāra to offer a more extensive analysis of the mind. If the mind in its "constructed nature" consistently misperceives reality in terms of discrete objects that can be grasped and a discrete subject that grasps them, then one must develop a more sophisticated account of consciousness to remedy this problem. Most Buddhist thinkers described consciousness events in relation to the six senses: eye-consciousness, ear-consciousness, nose-consciousness, tongue-consciousness, skin-consciousness, and the consciousness of the mind-organ. Yogācara made two additions to this list. First, the concept of *manas* refers here to the faculty of the mind that processes all sensory data and produces a coherent picture of reality based on the accumulation of experiences (King 1999: 97). For all who are un-awakened, the *manas* is deemed to be afflicted and prone to produce a false sense of an egoistic subject that experiences or "grasps" the infinite variety of stimuli and objects that enter into one's awareness. Thus, the Cartesian formula of "I think therefore I am" is illustrative of the afflicted *manas*—a false sense of subjectivity based on the activities of objective awareness. The operations of the six senses lead most people to associate a distinct, subjective reality—*manas*—that apprehends the objects of physical and mental experience.

The final level of consciousness posited by the Yogācārins is the *ālaya-vijñāṇa* or "storehouse consciousness." The *ālaya-vijñāṇa* is understood as a kind of mental substratum identifiable with the stream of consciousness-events that appear to the mind and are stored as "seeds" (*bījas*) that may later sprout and "perfume" or affect one's resulting states of consciousness. According to Yogācāra, the previous moments of consciousness linked to karmic actions produce seeds that become stored in the *ālaya-vijñāṇa* until which time they sprout and shape subsequent moments of consciousness. Generally speaking, for one whose *manas* is afflicted, the seeds of consciousness reinforce the false subject–object duality that lies behind ignorance and conditions grasping for "things." Aligned with the dependent nature, the *ālaya-vijñāṇa* is nonetheless perfumed by the constructed nature, which leads to the imagination of experience in terms of the deceptive and ultimately unreal notions of subjectivity and objectivity (Kochumuttom 1989: 13). When in the perfected nature, however, the *ālaya-vijñāṇa* ceases to be defiled by dualistic thought. For one who is awakened and who has purified his or her mind of the defiling subject–object dualism, the flow of consciousness is non-dual and pure. The false conceptualization of experience into subjects and objects ceases, grasping ceases, and Awakening is attained.

The Yogācāra school redirected early Mahāyāna thought away from the negation of all views in Madhyamaka toward the recognition of the mind as the substratum of all experience. Followers of the Madhyamaka school accordingly criticized Yogācāra for reifying the existent, "dependent nature" of the mind and for espousing a form of idealism wherein nothing is said to exist except for the mind itself (King 1994: 663–4). This charge of idealism has been repeated by some modern scholars who have interpreted Yogācāra as asserting that only the mind exists and that the external world is unreal and imaginary. This view, however, is misleading when one considers the works of Asaṅga and Vasubandhu. Their contention that all things appear as mere representations of consciousness reflects a theory of experience, not an ontological claim about the nature of the world (Kochumuttom 1989: 4–5). It entails the recognition of the ordinary activity of consciousness that is gained through the practice of meditation. The notion of "mind-only" or "consciousness-only" does not imply a sort of monism wherein the only reality is a type of universal mind. Instead it means that the experiences of "objects" in the state of *saṃsāra* merely appear "objective" through the representational activity of consciousness (Kochumuttom 1989: 204). Although the totality of all experience is dependent on the mind, one should not conclude that there is nothing outside of the mind. The mind simply filters all experience and conditions one's views and responses.

Later Yogācāra authors developed further the ideas presented by Asaṅga and Vasubandhu. The sixth-century scholars Sthiramati and Dharmapāla studied and commented upon older Yogācāra works. Associated with different monastic universities, these two Yogācārins differed over the philosophical question of the nature of consciousness. Dharmapāla, for example, maintained that the transformations of consciousness into subjectivity and objectivity are real events, albeit the products of an afflicted mind (Williams 1989: 93–4). Sthiramati, on the other hand, rejected the reality of the transformation of consciousness into subject and object, instead maintaining that there always is only the non-dual flow of consciousness that may or may not misperceive the illusions of subject and object (Williams 1989: 94). The writings of Yogācāra Buddhism became influential within scholastic circles, as they were perhaps more palatable to early medieval Buddhist monks than those of the Madhyamaka school, which could be viewed as nihilistic. Yogācāra ideas and works were transported to China and Tibet, where they were received even more eagerly than they were in South Asia.

Tathāgatagarbha thought

The teaching of the *tathāgatagarbha* ("womb of Buddhahood") arose in South Asia in certain *sūtra*s associated with the early Mahāyāna. The notion itself refers to an image used to illustrate the conviction that all beings possess an innate capacity to achieve the condition of a Buddha. Its genesis is likely related to the Mahāyāna idea that the awakened status of a Buddha is qualitatively different from and superior to the so-called "Awakening" of *arhat*s. Thus, one should strive to become a Fully Awakened Buddha, a being whose infinite wisdom is complemented by measureless compassion for the plight of all sentient beings. This view sustained the ideal of the *bodhisattva* path in the Mahāyāna, beginning with the step to rouse the "Awakening Mind" (*bodhicitta*). The idea of the *tathāgatagarbha* appears to have developed in conjunction with these foundational Mahāyāna positions. It appears first in two third-century texts: the *Tathāgatagarbha Sūtra* (Scripture on the Womb of Buddhahood) and the *Śrīmālādevī-siṃhanāda Sūtra* (Scripture on the Lion's Roar of Queen Śrīmālā). Therein, the "Womb" of Buddhahood appears as a kind of latent force for Awakening found within the impure bodies of ordinary beings. The latter text significantly reinterprets the notion of emptiness again, as in this instance it refers neither to the emptiness of inherent existence (as in Madhyamaka) nor to the emptiness of duality (as in Yogācāra) but rather to the emptiness of defilements in the *tathāgatagarbha* (Skilton 1994: 132). The *sūtra* then equates this undefiled "Womb," or the capacity to become a Buddha, with the *dharmakāya*, or "truth-body," of a Buddha whose goal has been fully realized.

The *tathāgatagarbha* teaching was never used to found a distinctive philosophical "school" in South Asia. Although mentioned in a number of Mahāyāna *sūtra*s, the *tathāgatagarbha* is not subjected to detailed analysis except in the *Ratnagotravibhāga Sūtra* (Scripture on the Analysis of the Source of the Jewel [of Buddhahood]). Therein, the *tathāgatagarbha* is again presented as representing the intrinsic purity of consciousness in a being that has not yet removed the defilements that taint and obscure the awakened mind (Williams 2000: 166). It follows from this that all beings possess an innately pure and luminous mind, one that is comparable to the mind of a Buddha, but they are usually unable to realize this fact. In general, however, the idea of the womb of Buddhahood appears to have been largely understood in South Asia symbolically to encourage one to realize the highest spiritual goal, not as a real entity with an ontological existence (Williams 2000: 161–2). The objectively real *tathāgatagarbha* becomes a commonly accepted notion in East Asia, in part due to the sixth-century Indian monk Paramārtha, who reinterpreted Yogācāra thought in line with the *tathāgatagarbha* teachings. In East Asia, the *tathāgatagarbha* became identified with the *ālaya-vijñāṇa* and taken as the substratum of individual existence that represents an inner "Buddha-nature" that holds the potential for Buddhahood in everyone.

The Mahāyāna pantheon

Heavenly Buddhas

While some followers of the Mahāyāna dedicated themselves to becoming Buddhas by traversing the long and rigorous *bodhisattva* path, others focused their practice on the visualization of Heavenly Buddhas who reside in celestial realms along with advanced *bodhisattva*s. The result of such meditative practices and the concurrent revelations of new *sūtra*s was the expansion of the traditional Buddhist cosmology to incorporate new heavenly spheres populated by accomplished Buddhas and *bodhisattva*s who could actively intervene in the world out of great compassion. As such, this strand of the Mahāyāna employed visualization techniques to become aware of celestial paradises and to seek them out as a means for attaining *nirvāṇa*. The Heavenly Buddhas and Bodhisattvas associated with these realms, moreover, became conceived as powerful intercessors that could assist Buddhist practitioners in their worldly goals and rebirths.

The expansive Buddhist cosmology in Mahāyāna likely arose in conjunction with interpretations of Gautama Buddha's own *bodhisattva* path and early traditions surrounding the views that he was merely the latest Buddha in a long line of Awakened Ones. Although no one could dispute that Gautama Buddha no longer lived in India, the adherents of the Mahāyāna posited that he exists in a different realm from which he continues to reveal the Dharma to those advanced practitioners who are able to "see" him in visions. Such is the explanation behind the source of the *Lotus Sūtra*, which claims to be a text preached by the Buddha on the Vulture Peak Mountain. If the Buddha, whose lifespan is much longer than that of ordinary human beings, continues to reside somewhere else, than it would seem to follow that there should be other Fully Awakened Buddhas residing in other realms as well.

There is reason to believe that the ideas of celestial paradises inhabited by Heavenly Buddhas and Bodhisattvas developed early on in the Mahāyāna. These magnificent and pleasurable places were understood to be the products of Buddhas who created them out of compassion for living beings who suffer in *saṃsāra*. In the case of the *Sukhāvatīvyūha Sūtra*, a *bodhisattva* named Dharmākara vowed to dedicate the merit he earned from traversing the *bodhisattva* path over many lifetimes to create a marvelous buddha-field called Sukhāvatī (Land of Bliss), where all beings may share in the benefits of his merit (Gómez 1996: 27). This text probably dates to around the third or fourth century CE. The older *Akṣobhyavyūha Sūtra* contains many similar features regarding the creation of another world-system called Abhirati

(Great Delight) by a Buddha who seeks to assist other beings in eliminating suffering. Given the numerous references to the Buddhas Amitābha and Akṣobhya in early Chinese translations of Mahāyāna *sūtras*, it is reasonable to assume that these two figures were originally the most popular Heavenly Buddhas in South Asia.

However, there are notable differences between the *Akṣobhyavyūha Sūtra* and the *Sukhāvatīvyūha Sūtra*. The *Akṣobhyavyūha Sūtra* appears to illustrate an earlier stage in the development of views and practices related to buddha-fields and Heavenly Buddhas. Therein Akṣobhya is said to have created an entire world-system that includes heavens but excludes the miserable states of existence such as hells. Abhirati, the paradise in the east, is said to possess many of the same delightful features of the western buddha-field Sukhāvatī. However, rebirth in this world-system is said to require dedicated efforts to earn merit through doing good deeds, the *bodhisattva* path leading to Buddhahood is an optional pursuit, and most beings attain the condition of the *arhat* with Akṣobhya's help (Nattier 2000: 100–1). In these respects, rebirth in the Abhirati realm resembles some Mainstream Buddhist notions about the pursuit of a heavenly rebirth resulting from merit. The *Sukhāvatīvyūha Sūtra*, in contrast, recognizes only the spiritual path of *bodhisattva*s and stresses the role of faith in attaining rebirth in Sukhāvatī. The aspirant to the Land of Bliss should "cultivate the roots of merit," but rebirth in Sukhāvatī is ultimately guaranteed by the virtue and the solemn promise of Amitābha Buddha to create a buddha-field and to bring to this paradise all beings wishing to go there (Gómez 1996: 31).

An attempt to categorize the different views about the existence of the Buddha, or multiple Buddhas, was made early on by some Yogācārins, who developed a theory on the "three bodies" (*trikāya*) of the Buddha. This effort served to systematize earlier Mahāyāna notions about the Buddha by outlining how he could exist in different states and realms simultaneously. While this would become a popular idea in Mahāyāna, there were precedents in some Mainstream schools. The Sarvāstivādins developed a two-body theory consisting of the *rūpakāya* and the *dharmakāya*, wherein the former refers to the Buddha's physical attributes including the thirty-two major marks and the eighty minor marks, while the latter consists of his moral qualities and powers (Xing 2005: 19). Mahāsāṃghika Buddhists, for their part, developed a vision of a transcendent Buddha, for whom the historical person in India was merely a manifestation. The *Mahavastu*, which may be attributed to the Mahāsāṃghikas, refers to innumerable Buddhas and innumerable buddha-fields throughout many universes (Williams 1989: 224). Furthermore, a number of inscriptions from around the fourth or fifth centuries in India suggest that images of the Buddhas installed in monasteries were viewed as living persons with whom the residents could come into daily contact, implying that the spread of Buddha images may have likewise contributed to notions about multiple bodies of the Buddha (Schopen 1997: 262–3, 276–8).

The earliest analytical description of the Yogācāra *trikaya* theory appears in Asaṅga's *Mahāyānasūtrālaṃkāra* (Ornaments of the Treatises of the Great Vehicle), a lengthy compilation of numerous Mahāyāna teachings. First, the *dharmakāya*—the "body of the doctrine" or "truth body"—represents the Buddha's body at the abstract level identified with the entire corpus of his teachings. The notion of the *dharmakāya* was developed in stages, even appearing in early Mainstream texts. Initially, early Mahāyāna writers took *dharmakāya* metaphorically to mean that the Buddha could be identified with his teachings that constitute the realization of Buddhahood and with the qualities he developed as a result of this attainment (Harrison 1992: 74–6). In time, however, it appears to have been reinterpreted as a metaphysical absolute, the hypostasization of a kind of unitary cosmic principle comparable to the *tathāgatagarbha*. It should be noted, however, that this cosmic reinterpretation of the *dharmakaya* appears later and particularly in Chinese translations of Mahāyāna texts (Xing 2005: 81). For the Yogācārins, the *dharmakāya* was understood to be the true way of things, the *tathatā* or "thusness" equivalent to the intrinsically radiant consciousness of a Buddha that serves as a support for the compassionate manifestation of other forms of the Buddha who appear to teach and save others (Williams 2000: 174). As the aspect or "body" of the Buddha that is related to the foundation of Awakening, the *dharmakāya* retains a transcendent and eternal quality.

The second aspect of the *trikāya* theory is the *saṃbhogakāya* or the "enjoyment body" of the Buddha. The *saṃbhogakāya* refers to the glorified Buddhas who reside in buddha-fields that they have created as paradises to assist sentient beings in escaping the miseries of worldly existence. These Buddhas are said to enjoy the comforts of the great merit they earned over countless lifetimes striving to attain Buddhahood. At the same time, those *bodhisattva*s (and, in some cases, *arhat*s) who are lucky enough to be reborn in their magnificent buddha-fields are said to enjoy gazing upon the beautiful bodies of Heavenly Buddhas that are also the results of their vast stores of merit. The *saṃbhogakāya* appears in multiple forms in different buddha-fields scattered throughout unimaginably vast universes, preaching the Dharma to beings who listen in rapt attention despite the beautiful surroundings. The notion of the *saṃbhogakāya* as a glorified body of the Buddha that enjoys the fruits of his merit while being surrounded by a great retinue of *bodhisattva*s may have been developed in part to reaffirm the great fruits of the *bodhisattva* path (Xing 2005: 134–5).

Third, the *nirmāṇakāya* or "apparition body" represents a conscious borrowing of the Mahāsāṃghika idea that the historical Buddha who appeared in India was merely the magical manifestation of the *dharmakāya* to help show sentient beings the path. In this case, Gautama Buddha's appearance and eighty-year lifespan represents a magical projection rather than a real, ordinary human existence. The appearance of the *nirmāṇakāya* on earth reflects an attempt to show sentient beings the way to Awakening. Thus, in a number of Mahāyāna scriptures like the *Saddharmapuṇḍarīka Sūtra*, the life and apparent death of Gautama Buddha are said to have been simply displays in which he pretended to pass away in *parinirvāṇa*. It is out of compassion and skillful means that the Buddha pretends to be an ordinary, un-awakened human in order to convince sentient beings of the greatness of Buddhahood and the efficacy of the path. By arguing that the Buddha in the world was merely an apparition or a phantom, the *trikāya* theory offered an account for the Buddha's seemingly limited lifespan and his withdrawal from the world when many beings still suffered.

The *trikāya* theory provided a basis to comprehend and justify the numerous references to Heavenly Buddhas in Mahāyāna *sūtra*s. As mentioned above, Akṣobhya ("Immovable") Buddha and Amitābha ("Measureless Light") Buddha were likely among the earliest non-historical Buddhas recognized as inhabiting heavenly realms. Neither Akṣobhya nor Amitābha, however, appear to have had much of a cult following in South Asia. The appeal of rebirth in Sukhāvatī among South Asian Buddhists became detached from the figure of Amitābha per se, and it appears to have become more of a generalized goal as early as the fourth century for those seeking a heavenly reward for hearing or preserving the name of a particular Buddha, copying or worshipping a sacred book, and so forth (Schopen 2005: 166–7, 180–3). In other words, the allure of the vivid and delightful descriptions of that buddha-field caused some followers of the Mahāyāna in India to seek it out, sometimes independently of any particular devotion to Amitābha. When the longer and shorter *Sukhāvatīvyūha Sūtra*s were translated into Chinese and disseminated in East Asia, these texts helped to spur a large cult following for Amitābha Buddha that led to a "Pure Land" school of Buddhism in East Asia. Notably, there is no evidence for a similar organization in South Asia.

Other Heavenly Buddhas that appeared later and were more marginal in South Asia include Vairocana (Shining Out) and Bhaiṣajyaguru (Master of Healing). Vairocana may have originated from an epithet of Gautama Buddha that eventually gained a separate identity as a wholly different Buddha. Vairocana grew in importance in Tibetan Buddhist thought and in the esoteric Shingon School of Japanese Buddhism. Bhaiṣajyaguru may have originated in Central Asia, but he is recognized in Mahāyāna as a Buddha who specializes in healing those who are sick.

Heavenly Bodhisattvas

Along with Heavenly Buddhas, the Mahāyāna recognized a class of advanced *bodhisattva*s on the verge of attaining Buddhahood that also exist in celestial realms. When named, these figures usually represented *bodhisattva*s who were in the tenth *bhūmi*, or the "Dharma-cloud stage." A number of Mahāyāna *sūtra*s make reference to specific *bodhisattva*s such as Maitreya, Avalokiteśvara, and Mañjuśrī, who apparently were the most popular in South Asia. These and other Heavenly Bodhisattvas are sometimes depicted in texts as members of the vast assemblies who gather to hear the Buddha preach or as members of the retinues of Heavenly Buddhas such as Amitābha.

What distinguishes the Heavenly Bodhisattvas from Heavenly Buddhas in the Mahāyāna pantheon is that they come to personify great beings (*mahāsattva*) who may come to the assistance of devotees in the present world, whereas Buddhas like Akṣobhya and Amitābha were primarily associated with auspicious rebirths in the next world. The figure of Maitreya was also recognized by many Mainstream Buddhists as the next Buddha to appear in the world after Gautama Buddha. This *bodhisattva* is understood to be currently residing in a heavenly realm, waiting for the proper time to take his final rebirth as a human and to attain Buddhahood. While he resides in heaven, however, he may hear and respond to the requests of those beings that seek his assistance. The name "Maitreya" may be translated as "loving-kindness" or "benevolence," which indicates the quality most associated with him. Maitreya is also credited with revealing some Mahāyāna *sūtra*s including some of the foundational Yogācāra texts to Asaṅga. And Maitreya appears to have been the focus of a popular cult in Kashmir and Central Asia, where he was fashioned in sculpted images and venerated.

Avalokiteśvara, the "Lord Who Looks Down," is an advanced heavenly *bodhisattva* associated with great compassion. He is portrayed as looking down from heaven ready to assist the beings of the world who are suffering or who are in danger. He appears to have emerged as an important savior-figure in the *Saddharmapuṇḍarīka Sūtra* around the third century CE. His compassion to help sentient beings in need is described by the Buddha in this text in vivid detail.

> Good man, if incalculable hundreds and thousands of myriads of millions of living beings, suffering pain and torment, hear of this bodhisattva He Who Observes the Sounds of the World [*avalokitasvara* (sic)] and single-mindedly call upon his name, the bodhisattva He Who Observes the Sounds of the World shall straightaway heed their voices, and all shall gain deliverance.
>
> If there is one who keeps the name of this bodhisattva He Who Observes the Sounds of the World, even if he should fall into a great fire,

the fire would be unable to burn him, thanks to the imposing supernatural power of this bodhisattva.

If he should be carried off by a great river and call upon this bodhisattva's name, then straightaway he would find a shallow place.

(Hurvitz 1976: 311)

Accordingly, Avalokiteśvara became seen as a powerful and compassionate great being who could rescue those who called upon him for help. The *Saddharmapuṇḍarīka Sūtra* also describes Avalokiteśvara as being able to grant fine sons and daughters, and affirms that those who worship him will attain the limitless benefits of great merit (Hurvitz 1976: 313). This Heavenly Bodhisattva is mentioned in other *sūtra*s as well, and he comes to be depicted iconographically as holding a lotus and as possessing anywhere from two to one thousand arms to signify the tremendous help he can offer his devotees. Avalokiteśvara became a popular figure of devotion in Tibet, Nepal, and to a lesser degree in Sri Lanka. In East Asia, Avalokiteśvara became recast and venerated as the female *bodhisattva* of compassion named Guanyin or Kannon.

Mañjuśrī or "Gentle Glory" is the Heavenly Bodhisattva associated with great wisdom. He too plays various roles in a number of Mahāyāna *sūtra*s,

Figure 3.2 Avalokiteśvara, Pala period, from Bihar (Indian School/Museum of Fine Arts, Boston, MA/Marshall H. Gould Fund Frederick L. Jack Fund/The Bridgeman Art Library).

including the interlocutor chosen to question the wise householder in the *Vimalakīrtinirdeśa Sūtra* and the spiritual guide for the pilgrim Sudhana in the *Gaṇḍavyūha Sūtra*. Sometimes portrayed as a young prince, Mañjuśrī nevertheless is often seen as the embodiment of supreme wisdom, a figure capable of guiding other *bodhisattva*s along the path to Buddhahood (Williams 2000: 189–90). It is difficult to establish the exact dates of his appearance in the Mahāyāna pantheon, but he is mentioned in the *Saddharmapuṇḍarīka Sūtra* and thus must have already been recognized by around the third century CE. He is often portrayed iconographically as holding a sword of wisdom in one hand and a book in the other. Mañjuśrī became highly venerated in Tibet and was credited in numerous legends with bringing civilization to Nepal and establishing the first king.

Many other Heavenly Bodhisattvas appear in various Mahāyāna texts. None of these, however, reach the scale of popularity and influence in South Asia as Maitreya, Avalokiteśvara, and Mañjuśrī. The idea of Heavenly Bodhisattvas, beings willing to use their extensive compassion, knowledge, and power to intercede in the lives of ordinary folk, must have appealed to numerous Buddhists in South Asia. These figures represented spiritual heroes and guides able to assist devotees in the circumstances of their present lives. It is also likely that their appearance in numerous Mahāyāna *sūtra*s helped to popularize these texts and traditions, allowing the Mahāyāna to take root in other parts of Asia.

4

Consolidations:

Medieval systems of thought and practice

Buddhist scholasticism
Vasubandhu (4th–5th c. CE)
Buddhaghosa (5th c. CE)
Dharmakīrti (ca. 600–670 CE)
Śāntideva (ca. 685–763 CE)
Buddhist Tantra and the Vajrayāna
Tantric Buddhist texts
Tantric Buddhist rituals
Legacies of Buddhist Tantra

Buddhist scholasticism

The development of Buddhist schools and canons in the centuries following the beginning of the Common Era invited efforts to systematize the diversity of ideas in South Asian Buddhism. The sectarian trends in previous centuries gave rise to an increasing variety of texts and teachings that were all attributed to the Buddha or, in the case of the Mahāyāna, one or more Buddhas. As South Asian Buddhism began to mature around the fourth and fifth centuries of the Common Era, we find new and concerted efforts to consolidate the gains made by previous generations in the study and composition of Buddhist texts. Scholastic activity in monasteries started much earlier with the Abhidharma texts. But in this era, which is sometimes called the "Middle Period" of South Asian Buddhism, exegetical writings and treatises (*śāstra*) begin to overshadow the composition of original *sūtra*s conveying the Word of the Buddha. Compilations and commentaries emerge as popular genres of Buddhist writing. And the focused efforts by monks to analyze and codify Buddhist *sūtra*s also created sharper distinctions between Buddhist schools, contributing to an environment of increased debate with other Buddhists and non-Buddhists in South Asia.

It is probably not coincidental, therefore, that the Middle Period of South Asian Buddhism coincides with the emergence of Mahāyāna as an institutionally distinct Buddhist movement. The name "Mahāyāna" begins to appear in inscriptions only in the latter part of the fifth century, suggesting that this movement lacked a distinctive and visible institutional identity prior to this period (Schopen 2005: 11). Even the apparently vast collection of Mahāyāna *sūtra*s beginning from around the first century CE is deceiving, since few of these titles have appeared in the earliest manuscript finds along the Silk Route before the fifth century (Walser 2005: 27–9). However, by the end of the fifth century, the Mahāyāna name begins to become more recognizable in South Asia, and its texts become more widely dispersed. Its popularity in the region does not measurably increase, but it does start to be acknowledged as a distinct Buddhist movement apart from the Mainstream schools.

Buddhist scholastics from the fourth and fifth centuries onwards were active in analyzing texts and classifying teachings. This scholastic turn towards explicating and arranging the Buddha's Word continued the work of the earlier scholars of the Abhidharma. However, authors in this later era began to emphasize more the activities of exegesis and debate over memorization and revelation. Developments in writing and the production of written texts certainly helped to move Buddhist literature in these directions. The growth of large monastic universities also contributed to these trends. And the steady centralization of power and wealth in the hands of kings as the early medieval period wore on contributed to sharper debates among Buddhist groups and with non-Buddhists, all of whom sought the patronage of South Asian rulers. In short, a number of technological, institutional, and political developments from the fifth century onwards supported the growth of the scholastic enterprise in South Asian Buddhism.

Many South Asian Buddhist scholastics received crucial material support from large universities and libraries. As certain monasteries developed large libraries to support their educational efforts for training monks in the Dharma, they increasingly attracted scholarly monks with interests in the study and explication of texts. While it is certain that many monks and nuns continued to focus their efforts on treading the austere path of renunciation and meditation apart from society, a growing number of monastics affiliated themselves with educational institutions that are comparable to universities in their focus and breadth of training. Some of these institutions like Taxila had ancient roots, while others were founded and endowed in the Middle Period or later. The university at Nālandā became renowned as a major center for Buddhist learning during the first millennium of the Common Era. Endowed by the Gupta emperors in the fifth century and located a few miles north of Rājagṛha, Nālandā became the paradigmatic center for Buddhist scholastic activity where as many as ten thousand students were taught Abhidharma, Madhyamaka, epistemology, logic, linguistics, astronomy, medicine, poetry, and literary

Figure 4.1 Ruins of Nālandā University (photo courtesy of Prince Roy, USA, www.princeroy.org)

criticism among other subjects (Warder 1991: 467–8). It had one thousand teachers, one hundred lectures per day, and two libraries.

Monastic and lay students from all over South Asia and beyond attended this institution. Some were trained according to a monastic education, but others studied secular subjects as preparation for other careers. It seems that students at Nālandā were taught by several teachers in various religious and secular subjects rather than by a single teacher who was traditionally responsible for the complete training of his disciple (Scharfe 2002: 152–3). Buddhist thinkers of great renown such as Vasubandhu, Asaṅga, Dignāga, Dharmakīrti, Sthiramati, and Śāntideva were affiliated with this university, and many different schools of Buddhism were represented there (Scharfe 2002: 148). The vast material and intellectual resources at Nālandā supported the growth and vitality of this institution for several centuries before its eventual demise and destruction at the end of the twelfth century.

There are accounts of several other Indian Buddhist universities in the travel records of Chinese Buddhist pilgrims. One of the more notable institutions was Valabhī in Western India. Attracting several thousand students, many of whom were affiliated with the Pudgalavādins (i.e., Saṃmitiya) and Yogācārins, Valabhī became second only to Nālandā in size until its destruction in the eighth century (Warder 1991: 467, 509). Like Nālandā, Valabhī received the patronage of Buddhist and non-Buddhist rulers, and it taught a wide-ranging curriculum. Many other universities were founded in the northeast and supported by the rulers of the Pāla dynasty in the medieval period. These included Vikramaśilā, Jagaddala, and Uddaṇḍapura, among several others. Vikramaśilā had a Mahāyāna orientation and an emphasis on Tantric beliefs and practices, which eventually led to the formation of close ties with Tibet and Nepal, as illustrated by the work of its one-time chief monk Atīśa in propagating Buddhism in Tibet (Scharfe 2002: 155–6). Vikramaśilā was eventually destroyed and razed around the beginning of the thirteenth century by Muslim armies.

Meanwhile, a few monasteries in Sri Lanka developed large educational centers (*piriveṇa*) in the early centuries of the Common Era. The Mahāvihāra sect in Anurādhapura possessed an impressive collection of Buddhist texts in Pāli, Sanskrit, and Sinhala, which attracted students and pilgrims from other countries. A *piriveṇa* was founded in the fourth century within the precincts of the Mahāvihāra, and it provided facilities to train thousands of monks not only in the canonical texts of the Pāli Tipiṭaka and its commentaries, but also subjects such as grammar, poetics, logic, and arts among others (Adikari 2006: 100–2). A number of other educational centers were established to train monks, including one associated with the Abhayagirivihāra that incorporated the writings of the Mahāyāna along with other Mainstream texts. In the southern part of the island, the monastery at Tissamahārāma was recognized as a center of learning that attracted large numbers of monks (Adikaram 1994: 116).

Many of the Middle Period's most famous and influential Buddhist thinkers were associated with major universities and *piriveṇa*s and drew upon their textual resources and intellectual environments to produce important scholastic works. Access to texts and the presence of debates and lectures on the doctrines of Buddhist schools as well as Hindu and other religious systems enabled the more talented scholar-monks to author influential commentaries and compendia. Among the Buddhist tradition's scholarly luminaries, we may count figures such as Vasubandhu, Buddhaghosa, Dharmakīrti, and Śantideva as among the most influential authors between the fourth and eighth centuries of the Common Era. Of course there were many other important Buddhist authors during this period such as Dhammapāla the commentator on the Pāli Tipiṭaka, Dignāga the Buddhist logician, and Candrakīrti the Madhyamaka philosopher. However, the four Buddhist scholars mentioned previously will serve here as an illustration of the impressive array and achievements of Buddhist scholasticism in the Middle Period of South Asian Buddhism.

Vasubandhu (4th–5th c. CE)

The figure of Vasubandhu, a Buddhist scholar who lived sometime between the fourth and fifth centuries CE, looms large in the history of South Asian Buddhism. Renowned enough to be the subject of a biography by Paramārtha, the sixth-century Indian monk who founded a Yogācāra school in China, Vasubandhu's life story nevertheless remains obscure and subject to debate. The crucial point of contention is whether the Vasubandhu who composed the *Abhidharmakośa* (Treasury of Abhidharma) and its *bhāṣya* or "commentary," is the same Vasubandhu who composed the *Viṃśatikā*, *Triṃśatikā*, and other Yogācāra treatises. Much Mahāyāna tradition says that the authors of these disparate works are one in the same. But another theory proposed in 1951 by Erich Frauwallner holds that there were in fact two different authors named Vasubandhu. Scholarly consensus on this point is elusive, but there recently seems to be a tendency to hold that the tradition may be correct. The view that the scholar of the Sarvāstivāda Abhidharma was later converted to the nascent Mahāyāna movement by his half-brother Asaṅga is supported by scholars such as Padmanabh Jaini and Alex Wayman. Jaini maintains that Frauwallner's thesis is doubtful based on evidence from a different Kashmiri Sarvāstivāda text that indicates how the author of the *Abhidharmakośa* already displayed some Mahāyāna leanings and converted to the "Vaitulika" (or "expansionist") doctrine of the Mahāyāna (Jaini 1958: 50–3). Wayman points out that both the Chinese and Tibetan traditions agreed on the identity of a single Vasubandhu, and he additionally contends that the Sarvāstivāda master Saṅghabhadra would not have challenged an older Vasubandhu to a debate if the latter had not become a renowned exponent of Yogācāra thought (Wayman 1997: 117–18). In short, he raises doubts over whether the *Abhidharmakośa* would have ever become an influential text for later Mahāyāna communities if it were not linked to Vasubandhu the Yogācārin.

According to the Chinese and Tibetan sources, Vasubandhu was born in Gandhāra to a mother who had given birth to his half-brother named Asaṅga from a previous marriage. He was ordained in the Sarvāstivāda lineage, which enjoyed considerable popularity in the region of his birth. But while Asaṅga eventually came to subscribe to the Mahāyāna movement and began to develop Yogācāra, Vasubandhu remained committed to his original school. He later traveled to study with a teacher in the center of Vaibhāṣika learning in Brahmapura, where he was initiated into the Sarvāstivāda Abhidharma and developed some sympathy for the Sautrāntika doctrine (Pereira and Tiso 1987: 452). Subsequently, Vasubandhu moved to Ayodhyā, the capital of the Gupta Dynasty, composed the *Abhidharmakośa* and gained the favor of two Gupta kings. The accuracy with which Vasubandhu presented the Vaibhāṣika Sarvāstivāda views in the *Abhidharmakośa* at first delighted the orthodox Sarvāstivādins in Kaśmīra, and they requested a commentary on the work. However, Vasubandhu's auto-commentary on the six hundred verses that made up his *Abhidharmakośa* represented a critique of Sarvāstivāda positions from the point of view of Sautrāntika, which gave rise to indignation among the orthodox Vaibhāṣikas (Anacker 1984: 17–18). In the latter part of his life, Vasubandhu was attracted to the Mahāyāna by his half-brother, who evidently feared that his younger sibling might one day turn his formidable intellect to undermine the Mahāyāna doctrines (Nagao 2005: 9526). Vasubandhu then studied and wrote numerous commentaries on *sūtra*s and *śāstra*s (treatises), as well as original works detailing the views of the Yogācāra school of Buddhist thought. He is said to have died in his eightieth year.

Vasubandhu's earlier works

As an expositor of Sarvāstivāda Abhidharma, Vasubandhu compiled his voluminous *Abhidharmakośa* with his prose commentary (*bhāṣya*) to outline the basic structure of Abhidharma thought. The broad scope of this work stands as a monument to Buddhist systematic thought at a time when scholars devoted considerable efforts toward outlining, classifying, and summarizing Buddhist *sūtra*s. Vasubandhu's *Abhidharmakośabhāṣya*, with its summary verses and prose commentary, maps out the structure of Vaibhāṣika Sarvāstivāda thought, reveals its flaws, and relates the Sautrāntika critique, at times in his own words (Poussin 1988: 6). The work itself generated much debate and, later, acclaim for the author as it came to be adopted as the standard work on the theoretical positions of the Abhidharma by students of the Mahāyāna, who doubtless appreciated Vasubandhu's critiques of Sarvāstivāda positions more than the Sarvāstivādins did.

Vasubandhu's *Abhidharmakośabhāṣya* covers a broad range of doctrine in an analytical manner. The work covers topics such as the ontology of conditioned factors of existence (*dharma*s), the Buddhist cosmology, moral and mental discipline, the theory of *karma*, the nature of liberation, the nature of knowledge, meditative states, and theories of the "soul" or other such permanent substrata of individual existence. Thus, for instance, he discusses the distinction between conditioned, impure *dharma*s and unconditioned, pure *dharma*s, and then outlines the differences between the five *skandha*s (aggregates), the twelve *āyatana*s (sense faculties), and the eighteen *dhātu*s (sense spheres). When it comes to cosmology, Vasubandhu describes the three different spheres of transmigratory existence—sense-desires, form, and formless, which encompass six different forms of existence from hells to heavens. He discusses the four stages of life, which include birth, existence, death, and the intermediary stage between death and rebirth (*antarābhava*) (Chaudhuri 1983: 49). Vasubandhu discusses another key element of Sarvāstivāda thought when he asserts the reality of past, present, and future elements.

An example of Vasubandhu's detailed exposition of Abhidharma thought may serve to illustrate the general tenor of this work. In discussing the two types of mental absorption in the chapter on sense faculties, Vasubandhu contrasts the Vaibhāṣika Sarvāstivāda view with that of the Sautrāntika School. Verses from the *Abhidharmakośa* first distinguish between (1) non-conscious absorption (*asaṁjñisamāpatti*), or the arresting of the mind and its mental states, and (2) the absorption of extinction (*nirodhasamāpatti*), or the meditative state wherein one realizes the cessation of factors leading to suffering and rebirth. Vasubandhu expands upon their distinctive properties respectively in his *bhāṣya*, eventually describing a doctrinal difference between two Buddhist schools.

> Should one consider the two absorptions as existing in and of themselves? Yes [answer the Sarvāstivādins], for they thwart the arising of the mind. No [answer the Sautrāntikas], it is not what you term 'absorption' that hinders the arising of the mind; rather, it is the 'mind in absorption,' the mind that precedes the state of absorption: this mind, being opposed to the arising of the mind, causes other minds to not arise for a certain time ... What is called 'absorption' is simply the non-existence of the mind for a certain period of time; not a thing in and of itself, but a 'thing of designation' (*prajñaptidharma*).
>
> (Poussin 1988: 232)

This short excerpt shows how Vasubandhu examines Abhidharma thought by presenting the orthodox Sarvāstivāda view and adding a critique from the Sautrāntika position. Thus, contrary to the Sarvāstivādins, the two meditative absorptions leading to non-consciousness and extinction should not be seen as self-existent states.

Vasubandhu's doctrinal analyses of Abhidharma thought eventually gave way to his numerous treatises on Mahāyāna thought. Using the evidence of cross-references in Vasubandhu's works and in the works of his commentators, as well as the evidence of his distinctive style—learned and replete with citations from numerous texts and schools, it appears that the Vasubandhu who wrote the *Abhidharmakośa* is the same author of at least eleven other later works including the *Vyākhyāyukti* (Principles of Exegesis), *Karmasiddhiprakaraṇa* (Discussion of the Demonstration of Action), and *Pañcaskandhakaprakaraṇa* (Discussion of the Five Aggregates), among others

(Skilling 2000: 298–9). The scholarly method of Vasubandhu's writing, which is evident in his efforts to present the views of different schools and to explicate their theories, is a prominent feature of the works attributed to him. There are other key features in Vasubandhu's works that appear to signal a more gradual and consistent development in his views in contrast with his alleged dramatic conversion to the Mahāyāna as portrayed in some later hagiographical accounts. For instance, his works typically expound the theory of the *ālaya-vijñāna* ("storehouse consciousness") and cite the *Saṃdhinirmocana Sūtra* as an authoritative text (Skilling 2000: 307). And despite his growing interest in Yogācāra ideas, he continued to attend to many of the same doctrinal issues and arguments that he first took up in the *Abhidharmakośa* and its *bhāṣya*.

Vasubandhu's later works

Later in his career, Vasubandhu wrote shorter works of verse that attempted to systematize the viewpoints of Yogācāra thought. His *Viṃśatikā* and *Triṃśikā* became renowned summaries of Yogācāra ideas about the origins and workings of individual consciousness. Therein he argues, among other things, that all distinctions between subject and object, or the individual who apprehends something and the apprehended phenomenon, are merely the representations of consciousness (Kochumuttom 1989: 158). In other words, the apparent reality of subject and object as two distinct things is the result of the workings of an ordinary, un-awakened mind (*manas*) that represents experience of objects as discrete phenomena apart from the individual mind that cognizes them. For Vasubandhu, the ineffable nature of things-in-themselves remains unknowable to the un-awakened, since the operations of ordinary consciousness consistently overlay various conceptualizations, which imagine those things in dualistic terms of subject and object. One cannot know anything apart from the way that one's consciousness apprehends it. However, for one who realizes that the notions of subject and object are merely non-substantial constructions of the mind, one's false imagination of experience that obscures liberating wisdom is removed and replaced by the accomplished or consummate knowledge of correct perception (Kochumuttom 1989: 162).

Vasubandhu's *Trisvabhāvanirdeśa* (Exposition on the Three Natures), which may have been his final work, serves to summarize his explanations for the Yogācāra doctrine that distinguishes between the imagined, other-dependent, and accomplished natures of reality as it exists and as it is perceived. In thirty-eight verses, Vasubandhu lays out the fundamental threefold character of reality, showing how they are all distinct but ultimately related.

Arising through dependence on conditions and
Existing through being imagined,
It is therefore called other-dependent
And is said to be imaginary.

The eternal nonexistence
Of what appears in the way it appears
Since it is never otherwise,
Is known as the nature of the consummate.

(Garfield 2002: 136–7)

The impressions one receives due to the representations of consciousness may be said to be both imaginary and other-dependent. That which is imagined as an independently existing thing, actually arises due to other conditions—both external factors and the workings of one's mind. However, once one learns through careful reflection and meditation that reality is actually different from the way it appears, one views reality with a consummate or accomplished mind, which rightly perceives the non-existence of the apparent reality (Garfield 2002: 137). In other words, the only difference between the perceptions of imagined reality and the "consummate" reality is that the former views what is non-dual as dual (i.e., as subject and object), whereas the latter realizes that reality is fundamentally non-dual. The nature of reality is the same, but it is only the perfected mind that sees the true nature of reality as it is.

In order to illustrate how the three natures are all reconciled when duality as either imagined or dependent is seen as non-existent, Vasubandhu employs the image of a magician who creates an illusion of an elephant by means of *mantra*s. The illusory elephant that appears to an audience represents the unreal, imagined nature. The perception of the elephant as experienced by the audience corresponds to the dependent nature, as it arises due to the *mantra*s and the mental representations of the audience. Meanwhile, the realization of the non-existence of the imaginary elephant is said to be the accomplished or consummate nature. In each case, however, the non-dual nature of reality is affirmed. The direct perception of non-duality in what is imagined, dependent, and consummate is then linked with the attainment of liberation, or the result of seeing things as they truly are. And thus, beginning with a comprehensive summary and critique of Sarvāstivāda Abhidharma, proceeding with various compendia and commentaries on Mahāyāna texts, and ending with a number of treatises that defend and explain Yogācāra positions, Vasubandhu's works gained tremendous recognition and respect from Buddhist scholars in South Asia, Tibet, and China in the centuries that followed.

Buddhaghosa (5th c. CE)

Further south in the fifth century CE, an Indian monk named Buddhaghosa achieved great fame as a scholar and commentator of canonical texts in the Theravāda School. Author of the *Visuddhimagga* (Path of Purity), the renowned text that sets out what would become the standard Theravāda interpretation and application of the Pāli Tipiṭaka, Buddhaghosa apparently spent most of his scholarly career in Sri Lanka composing not only the *Visuddhimagga* but also editing and translating commentaries on the Buddha's Word that had been preserved primarily in the local Sinhala language. According to tradition, the *arhat* Mahinda, son of King Asóka, traveled to the island of (Śrī) Laṅkā in the third century BCE to promote the Dispensation of the Buddha in a neighboring land. Accompanied by four other monks, Mahinda is credited with quickly converting the local king and most of his subjects to the Buddha's religion. He is said to have preached discourses of the Buddha, and he selected his colleague Mahā-Ariṭṭha to recite the *Vinaya* to establish the Buddha's Dispensation formally in the island (Rāhula 1993: 55–6). Mahinda and his fellow monks introduced not only texts that would later form part of the Pāli Canon, but also the oral commentarial tradition comprising definitions and exegetical remarks made by senior *thera*s during the Buddhist councils held in India (Malalasekera 1994: 90–1). In time, these commentaries were further developed and written down in Sinhala. They were then stored in the Mahāvihāra, or "Great Monastery," along with the written texts of the Tipiṭaka.

According to the narrative traditions on Buddhaghosa's life, he was a Brahmin youth from northern India who was converted to Buddhism by an Elder-monk named Revata. Wishing to write a commentary on the Tipiṭaka, he was told that he should travel to Sri Lanka in order to consult the commentarial tradition preserved there, but which was apparently lost in India by the fifth century CE. Statements in Buddhaghosa's own commentaries (*aṭṭhakathā*) make reference to the fact that he authored at least two works while residing in Kañcipuram and perhaps other places in South India. Kañcipuram was an important center for Buddhism in the south during Buddhaghosa's time, and the account of the seventh-century Chinese pilgrim Xuanzang records that it had more than one hundred monasteries and ten thousand monks belonging to the Sthaviravāda School (Desikan 1998: 150). It appears that the Sri Lankan Mahāvihāra order had close contacts with some monasteries around India, including those in the south. Recent research holds that Buddhaghosa may have been South Indian by birth, locating his home village of Moraṇḍakheta, which is mentioned in the colophon of the *Visuddhimagga*, in the southern Andhra district (Panabokke 1993: 112). After spending some years as a monk in the Coḷa kingdom in Tamil-speaking South India, Buddhaghosa traveled to Anurādhapura and took up residence with the Theravāda monks of the Mahāvihāra. Legend holds that before being granted access to the books at this monastery, Buddhaghosa was challenged to explain two stanzas from the *Saṃyutta Nikāya* of the Pāli Canon. This incident allegedly was the cause that led him to compose the *Visuddhimagga* as a comprehensive explanation of the entire *buddhavacana*. This story, however, is likely an exaggeration, as the *Visuddhimagga* contains material showing that Buddhaghosa already had access to the ancient Sinhala commentaries at the Mahāvihāra when he wrote the text.

Buddhaghosa's works

The *Visuddhimagga* is widely recognized as the definitive statement of Theravāda Buddhist thought. Buddhaghosa begins this work by quoting two stanzas attributed to the Buddha: "When a wise man, established well in virtue, develops consciousness and understanding; then as a *bhikkhu* ardent and sagacious, he succeeds in disentangling this tangle" (Ñāṇamoli 1991: 6). He then goes on to say that he will explain what the Buddha meant by these lines, expounding on the methods and benefits of developing virtue (*sīla*), concentration (*samādhi*), and wisdom (*paññā*), while relying on the teachings of the monks from the Mahāvihāra in Anurādhapura. This lengthy text serves as something like a one-volume guide to the doctrinal teachings contained in the Pāli Tipiṭaka, arranging them in a systematic fashion to enable the reader to make progress on the path of purity and ultimately liberation. His own method of composition in the *Visuddhismagga*, as well as in the various *aṭṭhakathā* attributed to him, was to adhere closely to the teachings he learned from the Elder-monks of the Mahāvihāra and the texts they preserved.

> Now in teaching this dependent origination, the Blessed One [i.e., the meritorious Buddha] has set forth the text in the way beginning 'With ignorance as condition there are formations' … Its meaning should be commented on by one who keeps within the circle of Vibhajjavādins ["Distinctionists," or the term used for the Sthaviras at the Council of Pāṭaliputra], who does not misrepresent the teachers, who does not advertise his own standpoint, who does not quarrel with the standpoint of others, who does not distort the *suttas*, who is in agreement with the Vinaya, … who illustrates the law (*dhamma*), who takes up the meaning (*attha*), repeatedly reverting to that same meaning, describing it in different ways.
>
> (Ñāṇamoli 1991: 531)

By insisting on fidelity to the Word of the Buddha as understood by the Mahāvihāra, Buddhaghosa presented his works as expositions on the doctrines and the meanings of what the Buddha taught.

In certain instances, however, Buddhaghosa introduced new ideas into the literature of the Mahāvihāra. Not only as a codifier of texts but also as an innovator, Buddhaghosa may have drawn from the ideas of other Mainstream schools, introducing the idea of the heart as the basis of the mind (*hadaya-vatthu*) and the *bhavaṅga* theory of the sub-consciousness into works that would come to define Sri Lankan Theravāda thought (Skilling 1993: 173). Nevertheless, his written works consistently emphasize his adherence to the traditions of the Mahāvihāra. He usually deferred to the explanations of the "Ancients" (Porāṇas) who were credited with composing the Sinhala commentaries, but he still allowed himself to correct and emend the Sinhala texts in order to compose a "re-compiled commentary," that is, a more coherent and correct account in Pāli of the meanings behind the Word of the Buddha as handed down by tradition in Sri Lanka (Jayawickrama 1986: xv–vi). Buddhaghosa's choice of Pāli as the language in which to render the *aṭṭhakathā* material anew was the result of his desire to make these exegetical works accessible to monks outside of the island in the same language in which the canonical texts themselves were preserved.

Given Buddhaghosa's stated interests in explicating the Dharma in a manner consistent with the Elder-monks of the Mahāvihāra School, it is not surprising that the *Visuddhimagga* reads like a manual of Buddhist thought and practice based on the canonical texts themselves. The first part of the text deals with virtue or morality (*sīla*), defining this concept in terms of the volition behind one's actions, the accompanying state of consciousness that one has in mind, the restraint one shows in moral discipline and in one's composure, and the non-transgression of the moral precepts (Ñāṇamoli 1991: 10–11). After outlining the various ways in which one exhibits virtue and composure, Buddhaghosa discusses the benefits of the thirteen ascetic practices (*dhutaṅgas*) of those who choose to adopt a stricter form of monastic discipline. For Buddhaghosa, the purification of virtue forms the basis for the development of meditative concentration (*samādhi*).

Much of Buddhaghosa's discussion of *samādhi* in the *Visuddhimagga* relates to the various subjects that may be taken to focus one's mind in meditation. He begins with an analysis of concentration, dividing it into different types depending on the mental factor or factors under examination. This analysis leads into lengthy discussion of the forty different meditation subjects available to one who wishes to develop concentration. Depending on one's particular qualities and temperament, one can choose from ten *kasinas*, or objects, such as earth, water, fire, color, light, and so forth. Or one can meditate on foul objects such as a corpse in its stages of decomposition.

Or one can recall certain qualities associated with the Buddha, the Dharma, and the Saṅgha, or develop mindfulness in terms of one's body or breathing. Or one can meditate on the Four Divine Abidings (*brahmavihāras*) of loving-kindness, compassion, universal friendliness, and equanimity. All forty subjects of concentration are analyzed and explained by Buddhaghosa, with occasional references made to canonical and commentarial texts, as well as common lore. The one who develops virtue along with mental concentration may then attain wisdom (P: *paññā*/Skt: *prajñā*).

The section on wisdom in Buddhaghosa's *Visuddhimagga* contains some discussion and analysis on the mental and material aspects of existence, including the Five Aggregates, the various organs of sense and sense faculties. A short discussion of the Four Noble Truths leads to a more substantial treatment of Dependent Co-Arising. The work ends with chapters on the purification of knowledge and the benefits for engaging in this pursuit. Buddhaghosa remarks that the development of wisdom leads to four main benefits: (1) the removal of various defilements including the mistaken view of individuality, (2) obtaining the taste of the higher attainments of one who is progressing towards *nirvāṇa*, (3) the ability to attain *nirvāṇa*, and (4) the achievement of worthiness to receive gifts as one who has trodden the path of the Buddha to become an incomparable field of merit in the world (Ñāṇamoli 1991: 726–7, 738). For Buddhaghosa, all Buddhist practice should be in conformity to what the Buddha taught and what the Elder-monks who have transmitted the Dispensation have clarified. This ultimately leads to *nirvāṇa*, which for Buddhaghosa refers to the absence of passion, the destruction of pride, the extinction of craving, the freedom from attachment, and the destruction of all sensual pleasures (Law 1923: 170–1).

After having written the *Visuddhimagga*, Buddhaghosa turned his full attention toward editing and translating the Sinhala *aṭṭhakathā*. Judging from the cross-references made in his Pāli commentaries, Buddhaghosa first completed the *Samantapāsādikā* (All-Pleasing), his commentary on the five books of the Pāli *Vinaya*, which signifies that he took the Vinaya to be the foundation of Buddhism (Law 1923: 77). He prefixed this text with an account of the origins (*nidāna*) of the Vinaya, which relates how the Dharma was transmitted down through the three councils and the lineage of teachers recognized as authoritative by the Theravādins. In the *Samantapāsādikā*, as in other commentaries written by him, Buddhaghosa includes copious references to the teachings of the Porāṇas, or the ancient disciples believed to have received and transmitted the Buddha's Dharma faithfully and accurately. It is the comments of the Porāṇas that made up the kernels around which the *aṭṭhakathā* texts were formed. He also evidently approached his task of writing commentaries in a comprehensive and systematic fashion. He consulted a number of the old Sinhala *aṭṭhakathā* along with the corresponding texts from the Pāli Tipiṭaka, pointing out instances where variant readings or accounts were found (Adikaram 1994: 2). After finishing the lengthy *Samantapāsādikā*, Buddhaghosa wrote a separate commentary on the Pāli *Paṭimokkha*, or monastic code.

It appears that Buddhghosa then turned to composing commentaries in Pāli on the main books of the Sutta Piṭaka. His *Sumaṅgalavilāsinī* (Shining Forth with Great Auspiciousness) comments on the *Dīgha Nikāya* from the Pāli Tipiṭaka. Therein, he claims to have written this work on the basis of the Sinhala *aṭṭhakathā* as well as the accepted interpretations of the Mahāvihāra (Panabokke 1993: 110). The *Sumaṅgalavilāsinī* not only explains the words and meanings found in this canonical text, but it also relates historical accounts, folklore, and a vivid picture of ancient South Asian society (Law 1923: 78–9). Buddhaghosa continued his work by compiling commentaries on the *Majjhima*, *Saṃyutta*, and *Aṅguttara Nikāya*s. Among the so-called "smaller works" of the *Khuddhaka Nikāya*, the Pāli commentaries on the *Dhammapada* and *Jātaka* are traditionally attributed to Buddhaghosa. However, scholarly opinion on whether these works were actually written by him is mixed. Buddhaghosa also wrote commentaries on each of the seven books in the Theravāda Abhidhamma, likewise based on the Sinhala *aṭṭhakathā* and the interpretations of the Mahāvihāra on these works.

After finishing his Abhidhamma commentaries, Buddhaghosa apparently returned to India, where he passed away at an old age. Some Theravādin traditions in Southeast Asia claim that Buddhaghosa visited their countries after his period of residence and writing in Sri Lanka. For example, a Burmese tradition holds that Buddhaghosa propagated Buddhism in Burma, while a Khmer tradition holds that he passed away at a monastery called Buddhaghosa-vihāra in Cambodia (Law 1923: 40–2). Neither tradition, however, has demonstrable historical evidence to support its truth. Instead, Buddhaghosa's fame and influence in the Theravāda tradition appear to have inspired additional legends whereby different communities claimed connections with this great scholar-monk. Buddhaghosa reinforced the conservative traditions of the Mahāvihāra in Sri Lanka, enabling this tradition to make persuasive claims for legitimacy and eventually to emerge as the authoritative form of Buddhism in the island.

Dharmakīrti (ca. 600–670 CE)

The Indian monk Dharmakīrti represents another landmark scholar who composed works that shaped aspects of Buddhist thought in the medieval period. Little is known of his life story, although he is thought to have been a teacher at Nālandā. Often linked with the earlier Buddhist logician Dignāga (ca. 480–540 CE), whose works he commented upon and developed along new lines, Dharmakīrti emerged as an influential scholar of Buddhist epistemology. In this role, he participated in debates that Dignāga and others had with various non-Buddhist thinkers in India over the issues of what constitutes valid knowledge or cognition (*pramāṇa*) in one's attempts to discern reality as it is. Dharmakīrti secured a lasting place in Buddhist philosophy not only for defending the arguments of Dignāga, but also for refining his predecessor's claims and resolving some of the shortcomings therein. The efforts such authors made toward analyzing and explicating the sources of valid knowledge and the means to arrive at it were related to the general Buddhist goal of removing the obstacles to wisdom and liberation. While almost every Buddhist author shared this objective, the logicians were distinguished by their efforts to arrive at more generally applicable propositions for debate with other communities in South Asia such as Hindu Brahmins and Jains.

Dharmakīrti's thought and works

Dharmakīrti, in his eight philosophical works, engages in efforts to determine the means for arriving at reliable knowledge for the sake of attaining liberation. Unlike many other Buddhist thinkers, Dharmakīrti often cites and engages non-Buddhist theories of the instruments of knowledge (*pramāṇa*), and he rarely cites Buddhist *sūtra*s to make his points (Dunne 2004: 16–17). Instead, his works address arguments proffered by theorists on epistemology from various religious communities. Perhaps his first work is the *Pramāṇavārttika* (Commentary on Reliable Knowledge), which includes a commentary on an older work by Dignāga called the *Pramāṇasamuccaya* (Compendium on Reliable Knowledge). The *Pramāṇavārttika* is a work of verse consisting of four chapters on the subjects of inference, valid cognition, perception, and proof; while one of his important later works called the *Pramāṇaviniścaya* (Exegesis of Reliable Knowledge) similarly treats the same subjects albeit in a more mature way (Steinkellner 1994: 214). All of Dharmakīrti's works may be said to deal with subjects centrally related to Pramāṇa Theory and its concerns for establishing the means to arrive at reliable knowledge that remains defensible in the face of debates with opponents holding different views on the nature of reality.

Following Dignāga, Dharmakīrti argued that reliable knowledge is derived from basically two sources—perception (*pratyakṣa*) and inference (*anumāna*). The former employs direct perceptual awareness of a particular, existing object; while the latter consists of knowledge that is obtained indirectly through the presence of an identical or causal relationship between two things. Knowledge gained from direct perception of an object or event is a relatively straightforward matter. Inference, however, is related to indirect knowledge, and thus may be used for obtaining valid knowledge of phenomena that are not directly available to the senses. One definition holds that inference leads to knowledge of an object by means of knowledge of another object that is invariably related to it, such as the appearance of smoke may lead one to infer the presence of fire (Dunne 2004: 25–6). In arguing that perception and inference are the two primary means for arriving at reliable knowledge, Dharmakīrti followed Dignāga in presenting a theory of knowledge that did not specifically rely on authoritative tradition or scripture. This move allowed the Buddhist logicians to engage in debates with their non-Buddhist counterparts based purely on reasoning. However, in matters of radically inaccessible matters that elude perception and ordinary inference, scriptural authority is retained by Dharmakīrti as a means for gaining knowledge that could not be gained by any other way (Tillemans 1999: 29–30).

For all his commitment to rigorous logical argumentation, Dharmakīrti remained a Buddhist monk, and his epistemological work was directed toward the higher goal of eliminating ignorance and attaining liberation from suffering, death, and rebirth. Dharmakīrti even argued that perception and inference can be used to demonstrate that the Buddha is also a source for valid knowledge, thus providing a philosophical foundation for everyday Buddhist practice (Steinkellner 2005: 2336). But for the most part, the Buddha and his Dharma remained in the background of Dharmakīrti's work. Instead he was primarily occupied with establishing the bases for reliable knowledge that might be used in debate and in the process of removing ignorance about reality. The development of sound reasoning, for Dharmakīrti, is critical for both polemics and spiritual progress. And such reasoning rests on the use of perception and inference to gain knowledge about the real nature of entities. In this sense, although sometimes associated with the Yogācāra School, Dharmakīrti appears to have espoused views that are more characteristic of the Sautrāntika School as evinced by Vasubandhu's *Abhidharmakośa-bhāṣya*. According to Dharmakīrti, any particular object may be considered ultimately real if it is perceptible, that is to say, if it presents itself to the causal process of perception in a manner that is momentary and without conceptual thought or language (Dunne 2004: 91). The notion of momentariness is important here not only because of the Buddhist truth of impermanence, but also because whatever may trigger a moment of perceptual awareness is by definition part of a causal process and thus subject to change.

Inferential knowledge, on the other hand, is based on establishing conceptual relations between entities, and thus inferences are related to "universals" in the sense of predictable concomitances or invariable relationships between X (e.g. smoke) and Y (e.g. fire). While not ultimately real, as in the case of perceptible objects that possess a particular, unique existence at a specific moment in time, universal objects or concepts may still be a valid means of knowledge. It is here that Dharmakīrti introduces his approach to concepts called *apoha* (exclusion) theory. This theory posits that one may establish a universal category such as "cow" by excluding objects that lack the same characteristics that are used to generate the category under examination (Dunne 2006: 502–3). Thus, for example, if we judge "cowness" in terms of a certain appearance, diet, and anatomical features such as a stomach with four compartments, we may infer that a particular entity is a cow or is not a cow. This knowledge is not ultimately real, however, since even different cows will be perceived as distinct creatures. But the conceptual awareness of a category such as "cow" may still be judged as reliable knowledge (1) if it is based on a fundamental relation of an essential quality and (2) if it helps one to accomplish one's goal—such as, for instance, developing wisdom that leads one closer to liberation. The knowledge of ultimately real particulars through the means of perception and the knowledge of conventionally real universals through the means of inference combine to enable one to grasp reality and overcome the ignorance that impedes Awakening.

The logical operations performed by Dharmakīrti to establish the bases of reliable knowledge are complex and cannot be fully illustrated or explained here. Suffice it to say that he picked up where Dignāga left off in presenting a systematic method of logic and argumentation that allowed Buddhists to participate in debates with non-Buddhist thinkers in early medieval India. One view holds that this move was shortsighted and ultimately undermined the earlier Buddhist focus on the Dharma on its own terms as an efficacious message to realize liberation. Instead, this epistemological turn led medieval Indian Buddhists to focus on pan-Indian intellectual ideas and syllogistic argumentation that were more familiar to other philosophical schools such as Nyāya and Mīmāṃsā among Hindus, as well as the Jains, than to traditional Buddhist thought (Davidson 2002: 103–4).

Nevertheless, the works of Dignāga and Dharmakīrti would become tremendously influential in Indian philosophy as a whole and in Buddhist thought more specifically. Their works were used as a means to defend the Buddhist tradition from the philosophical charges leveled by Hindus and Jains. And Dignāga and Dharmakīrti can be credited with having advanced Buddhist philosophical discourse beyond the ontological concerns of Abhidharma thought to the fields of epistemology and logic in a method that privileges the perception of particular objects while allowing for the inferential cognition of abstract objects (Arnold 2005: 14–17). The knowledge gained from both would pragmatically assist the thinker in engaging the vigorous debates of medieval Indian philosophy. The goal of such logical operations, moreover, is to advance the Buddhist insight on the false notion of the Self through reflection on the idea that the fleeting sensations we perceive are precisely that—uniquely particular and evanescent events, which fosters a grasp of reality that assists one in moving closer to liberation (Arnold 2005: 206). The value and philosophical precision found in Dharmakīrti's works bestowed the author with lasting renown in Buddhist thought. His works were practically overlooked in China, but they were eagerly received in Tibet, where they formed an essential part of the philosophical training of Buddhist monks.

Śāntideva (ca. 685–763 CE)

The monk Śāntideva is another influential systematizer of Mahāyāna Buddhist thought in the early medieval period of South Asian Buddhism. Leaving aside the legendary accounts of Śāntideva's life, we have reason to believe that he was an accomplished scholar who resided for part of his career at the university at Nālandā. He is also affiliated with the school of Madhyamaka philosophy. Śāntideva composed at least two important works that contributed to the mature development of Mahāyāna thought in South Asia. In his *Sikṣasamuccaya* (Compendium of Training), he assembled and arranged quotations from around one hundred, mostly Mahāyāna *sūtras* and other scriptures to compose a training manual for aspiring *bodhisattvas*. Similarly, his *Bodhicaryāvatāra* (Undertaking the Way to Awakening), a lengthy work of eloquent verse, describes the path of the *bodhisattva* in terms of the six Mahāyāna perfections. His name is also at times associated with a text called *Sūtrasamuccaya* (Compendium of Discourses), but there is a lack of scholarly consensus over this attribution.

Śāntideva's works

Śāntideva's *Śikṣāsamuccaya* represents the product of a learned scholar who likely had access to a vast library of *sūtras* like the one at Nālandā. As a compendium of works written mainly by others, the *Śikṣāsamuccaya* is often seen as a derivative work that nonetheless shows how texts were circulated and read in a culture where handwritten manuscripts were the norm and anthologies were commonly used in place of entire texts (Mrozik 2007: 10–11). Seeking to distill the teachings on the discipline needed for *bodhisattvas* found in various scriptures, Śāntideva compiled this work for practical purposes. Scholars have often said that the *Śikṣāsamuccaya* lacks originality, but it nevertheless offers a systematic summary of Mahāyāna teachings, many of which are taken from texts that no longer exist in their Sanskrit forms (Clayton 2006: 38). However, a recent reconsideration of this text has noted that the author of the *Śikṣāsamuccaya* used his sources creatively to advance particular arguments about *bodhisattva* practice, arguments that were sometimes absent in the original sources themselves (Mrozik 2007: 26). And furthermore, some of the sections of the text that have been long thought of as quotations now appear to be the work of Śāntideva himself. Paul Harrison has noted the presence of at least 160 verses—including the 27 "memorial verses" (*kārikās*)—scattered throughout the *Śikṣāsamuccaya* that appear to be composed by Śāntideva, which suggests that the text is more original than previously thought (Harrison 2007: 219–22).

Śāntideva's *Śikṣāsamuccaya* nevertheless contains excerpts from numerous other works that have been fashioned to form a new work instructing its readers on how to adopt the discipline needed on the path of a *bodhisattva*. As seen earlier, the emphasis given to the *bodhisattva* path was a characteristic feature of the early texts out of which the Mahāyāna eventually arose. By the time of Śāntideva, the idea of the Mahāyāna as a distinctive path was widely recognized. His written works pick up and develop some of the earlier themes associated with *bodhisattva* practice. The first verse of this work sets out a central theme for Śāntideva's work—the identity of oneself and others. He explains that since all beings dislike fear and suffering, there is no basis for privileging one's own protection or suffering over that of others (Clayton 2006: 41). With this idea we get a glimpse of Śāntideva's broader ethical project. Each one who wisely undertakes the *bodhisattva* path should develop the insight that one is ultimately no different from anyone else since the notion of one's own identity is a false, insubstantial construct. Realizing this fact, the aspiring *bodhisattva* may set out with the utmost degree of care and compassion for others, treading the lengthy and arduous path leading up to Buddhahood for the sake of all beings.

The *Śikṣāsamuccaya* prescribes a variety of practices to be taken up by aspiring *bodhisattva*s and maintained by those further along on the path. These include the study of scripture, confessional liturgies, forms of meditation, codes of ethical conduct, and forms of monastic comportment, all of which are intended to give rise to virtuous bodies and minds (Mrozik 2007: 5). Relevant scriptural excerpts are stitched together with some of Śāntideva's own writings to show how one comes to embody the exalted and beneficial status of a *bodhisattva*. Such a person assists all other beings through his (rarely her) body, speech, and thoughts. The Word of the Buddha as found in a variety of texts offers some direction, as does the presence of a "beautiful friend" (*kalyāṇamitra*) whose moral and physical beauty jointly serve to help other, less advanced *bodhisattva*s along the path to Buddhahood. The text defines the *bodhisattva* discipline in terms of giving away, protecting, purifying, and increasing one's body (*ātmabhāva*), one's goods (*bhoga*), and one's merit (*śubha*, *puṇya*) for the sake of the welfare of all other beings (Mrozik 2007: 21). In this way, whatever is of use to oneself should be made useful to others first.

Śāntideva's second work, the *Bodhicaryāvatāra*, shares the *Śikṣāsamuccaya*'s project for the ethical development of aspiring *bodhisattvas*. But rather than relying on material collected from other scriptures, the *Bodhicaryāvatāra* comprises a wholly original poetic work that is organized around a step-by-step path for becoming an advanced *bodhisattva*. In this work we also see the great emphasis that Śāntideva put on prayer and devotion to Heavenly Bodhisattvas such as Mañjuśrī, of whom he was an earnest devotee. This work begins with verses praising the *bodhicitta* or "Awakening Mind," which is of two kinds: the mind resolved on attaining Awakening and the mind that is already proceeding towards that goal (Crosby and Skilton 1998: 6). The text affirms that one who forms the resolution to attain the *bodhicitta* earns great merit, although the merit from that resolution is vastly outweighed by that which is earned by the being who undertakes the practice leading toward Awakening. Then the *Bodhicaryāvatāra* outlines preliminary practices for the aspiring *bodhisattva*. These include liturgical acts such as offering worship to various Heavenly Bodhisattvas and Buddhas, confessing one's faults committed in all previous lives before the same array of Bodhisattvas and Buddhas, rejoicing in the merit done by all beings, dedicating the merit one will earn by traversing the *bodhisattva* path, and finally arousing the *bodhicitta*. Throughout these preliminary practices we see how the text works to cultivate a mental attitude of generosity.

Having taken on the awesome responsibility of providing for the welfare of all beings like a Buddha, the aspiring *bodhisattva* is enjoined to be vigilant in following the path. To abandon this noble effort is equated with doing a most wicked deed, since one would in theory deprive all beings from the benefits of having a *bodhisattva* work to increase their welfare and to alleviate their suffering (Crosby and Skilton 1998: 25). With these preliminaries and admonishments out of the way, the *Bodhicaryāvatāra* proceeds to discuss each of the perfections (*pāramitā*) in varying amounts of detail. For instance, regarding the perfection of forbearance, one learns that hatred and anger towards others are senseless and misplaced and only harm oneself, as the true source of one's suffering are one's own mental afflictions and not someone else. Next, the perfection of vigor is praised for it helps one adhere to the path leading toward Buddhahood, no matter the pain and difficulty that one encounters over many eons. The perfection of meditation (*dhyāna*) is the subject of a lengthy chapter in Śāntideva's work. Its practice involves various techniques, including the meditation on the foulness of the human body to remove feelings of lust and passion for others. For example, verses 58 and 59 in this chapter seek to produce non-attachment to the bodies of women, which, we are told, might look and smell nice but actually comprise that which is disgusting.

> If you do not want to touch something such as soil because it is smeared with excrement, how can you long to touch the body which excreted it?
>
> If you have no passion for what is foul, why do you embrace another, born in a field of filth, seeded by filth, nourished by filth?
>
> (Crosby and Skilton 1998: 93)

Just as in many older South Asian Buddhist texts that highlight the foulness of the human body in order to foster detachment from the objects of lust, the *Bodhicaryāvatāra* seeks to disabuse its readers of the foolish desire for pleasures of the flesh.

The chapter on meditation proceeds to outline another form of meditation that is recognized to be central to the text. Here Śāntideva extols the meditation on the identity of oneself and others, which refers to a sustained reflection on how one's person is really neither more valuable nor that different from anyone else. The text emphasizes that since all experience suffering equally, it is incumbent upon the *bodhisattva* to work to allay the suffering of others. Conversely, since all beings seek happiness, it is profoundly unethical for one to strive after the happiness of oneself alone (Crosby and Skilton 1998: 96). Implicated in this meditative practice is dissolving the false notion of "I" that inhibits the selfless dedication to helping other beings. Verses 110 through 112 exemplify this ethical stance that arises from not seeing oneself as unique or unconditioned.

> Therefore, just as I protect myself to the last against criticism, let me develop in this way an attitude of protectiveness and of generosity towards others as well.
>
> Through habitation there is the understanding of "I" regarding the drops of sperm and blood of two other people, even though there is in fact no such thing.
>
> Why can I not accept another's body as my self in the same way, since the otherness of my own body has been settled and is not hard to accept.
>
> (Crosby and Skilton 1998: 98)

The apparent purpose of this meditation is to come to value others as much as, if not more than, oneself. One should dissolve the idea of oneself as a persisting enduring subject—a uniquely existing "person"—by engaging in repeated and intensive thought experiments in which one exchanges one's (illusory) identity for the (equally illusory) identity of another (Griffiths 1994: 62). With the fiction of the "I" or "self" dissolved, one is freed to work tirelessly for the benefit of all beings.

The chapter on the perfection of wisdom (*prajñā*) near the end of the text involves complex debates between Madhyamaka views and those of other Buddhist and non-Buddhist schools. The chapter opens by reminding the reader of the importance of developing wisdom for the sake of attaining liberation, and by distinguishing between conventional and ultimate truths, the latter of which is beyond all intellection or discursive thought (Crosby and Skilton 1998: 115). Many of the verses therein involve Śāntideva's refutation of false ideas about the ultimate reality and substance of such notions as the "Self", the mind, God, atoms, and other entities considered by some to be substantial, independent phenomena. Various affirmations on the understanding of the emptiness of the inherent existence of all phenomena as the proper point of view for eliminating ignorance and suffering bring Śāntideva's chapter on wisdom to a close. Finally, the *Bodhicaryāvatāra* ends with a series of vows in which Śāntideva models how a *bodhisattva* should dedicate the merit earned from one's efforts to all other beings.

Compiling the writings of others and composing his own, Śāntideva succeeded in producing works that gave greater coherence and persuasiveness to the *bodhisattva* ideal in the Mahāyāna. He broadened the scope for the ethical justification behind the *bodhisattva* path, and his authorial skills helped to establish his lasting renown in Buddhist communities both in and far beyond South Asia.

Buddhist Tantra and the Vajrayāna

The growth in efforts to systematize Buddhist thought in medieval South Asia not only reflected a response to the growth and diversity of Buddhist texts, but it was also implicated in encounters that Buddhists had with non-Buddhist communities. The period between around the sixth to the twelfth century CE in early medieval India was initiated by the fall of large ruling states such as the Guptas and the political and military struggles led by newer clans and houses to assume influence in the face of a vacuum of power. The rise of new, regional powers in what Ronald Davidson has described as a "culture of military adventurism" generated new challenges to Buddhist monasteries that remained heavily dependent on the patronage of wealthy, stable rulers (Davidson 2002: 74). The fragmentation of Indian society altered the social and political landscape, usually to the detriment of Buddhist institutions. And while Buddhist thinkers such as Vasubandhu produced influential doctrinal treatises, and others such as Dharmakīrti devoted themselves to articulating a system of logic that could engage and respond to other traditions, their works also generated severe critiques from various Hindu and Jain thinkers.

Nevertheless, the weakening of Buddhism's position throughout much of early medieval India was due primarily to the political and economic upheavals of the age. In the interests of patronage and survival, Buddhists moved to adapt their thought and practice to these new realities. The militarism that became commonplace in India from the seventh century on had the effect of glorifying kings and princes that exhibited martial power. These new ruling-elites did not typically come from the traditional *kṣatriya* class of warrior-nobles, and this may have led to their willingness to depart from patronizing the same religious institutions that their predecessors supported. In fact, Hindu Śaiva values and rhetoric that privileged violence, power, and self-aggrandizement seemed to complement the conduct of the militaristic leaders, whereas Buddhist values of loving-kindness, forbearance, and non-violence appeared out of step with the political realities of the time (Davidson 2002: 86). Hindu rituals and images of divine kingship were more appealing to these new regional rulers, as they offered actual and symbolic sources of power from which to draw and enhance one's capacity to rule and to conquer. Once these rulers deviated from the Aśokan model of the *dharmarāja* (righteous king) who rules in accordance with the Dharma and supports monastic institutions, the Buddhists were compelled to revise their relationships with local kings.

In this environment, the figures of the *siddha* ("perfected one") and *vidyādhara* ("knowledge-bearing" sorcerer), charismatic wielders of esoteric powers who came from the margins of Brahmanical society, gained more influence. These persons made themselves necessary to militaristic rulers by offering them a means to gain power and by providing ethically dubious services—such as prophecy, spirit possession, demonic control, love potions, wealth generation, and magical killing—to influence worldly affairs (Davidson 2002: 187). These *siddha*s and *vidyādhara*s obtained their powers through a variety of means, including yoga, magic, and the deliberate overturning of conventional social norms. An important type of meditative practice known as *deva-yoga* (deity-yoga) was also utilized to bring about the ritual identification of the practitioner with a deity, whereby having assumed the identity of the deity one could then employ its divine powers to accomplish one's desired worldly and spiritual ends.

The figures of *siddha*s and *vidyādhara*s emerged in the early Tantric movements that emphasized the generation of powerful, even immortal bodies through non-Brahmanical rituals. These figures practiced an archaic form of spirituality that relied on alchemy, yoga, and erotico-mystical rites that endowed the practitioners with supernatural powers and even the immortal bodies of gods, often conceived as a form of Śiva (White 1996: 330–1). The growth of the influence of *siddha*s in medieval India soon led many in the Buddhist community to adopt the techniques and values of these figures in an effort to gain the favor and patronage of the regional rulers. This esoteric, ritualistic tradition called "Vajrayāna," or "Tantric," Buddhism emerged around the seventh century and flourished in north and central India. The term Vajrayāna may be translated as the "Thunderbolt

Vehicle" on account of the rapid path to Awakening it promises to deliver, or the "Adamantine Vehicle" on account of the indestructible ground out of which Buddhahood is attained. Alternately seen as a subset of Mahāyāna Buddhism for its shared goal of attaining Buddhahood, as the highest fruit of Buddhist practice for the great power it bestows, or as a separate path used by sorcerers, Vajrayāna Buddhism claimed to offer its adherents a quicker and easier path to Awakening through a process of visualizing and identifying with Heavenly Buddhas, Bodhisattvas, and other supernatural deities (Davidson 2004: 875–6). The practices and conceptions typically employed in Vajrayāna often closely resemble those of Hindu Tantra, and thus the term Buddhist Tantra is also commonly used to describe this medieval tradition.

The definitive quality of the term Vajrayāna partly masks the fact that Buddhist Tantra developed along divergent paths following the composition and use of a wide variety of texts called *tantra*s. The effort to give a comprehensive, all-inclusive description of Buddhist Tantra thus remains an elusive goal. Some of the aspects widely found in Vajrayāna forms of Buddhism are not unique. The recitation of protective *mantra*s, visualizing other worlds, elaborate ritual liturgies, and the propitiation of Heavenly Buddhas and other beings are likewise found in other types of Buddhism. Leaving aside the transgressive practices of sexual yoga and the ingestion of socially forbidden or impure substances found in some (but not all) examples of Buddhist Tantra, what may best define Buddhist Tantra as a particular current within the broader category of Mahāyāna Buddhism is the universal presence of a ritual initiation (*abhiṣeka*) to consecrate the practitioner and permit him to invoke and identify with specific Heavenly Buddhas, Bodhisattvas, or other deities (Kapstein 2005: 1221). Buddhist Tantra is thus generally characterized by the use of a variety of esoteric rituals that are reserved only for those individuals who have been initiated by the *guru* or Vajra-master into his or her teaching lineage. Certain aspects of Vajrayāna Buddhism are exclusive and esoteric, since its advanced yogic practices are deemed to be so inherently powerful that they could cause great harm to those improperly trained in their use.

The Vajrayāna borrows from the pantheon of Mahāyāna spiritual beings and expands upon it, largely by adapting elements and imagery from the Śaiva traditions that enjoyed tremendous growth in the medieval period. These deities can be seen as spiritual guides and protectors but more generally function as sources of power from which the Tantric practitioner draws to accomplish his or her goals. In earlier forms of Buddhism, deities were acknowledged but distinguished from Buddhas as being lesser in terms of both wisdom and efficacy in accomplishing spiritual aims. However, in esoteric Buddhist traditions, deities are envisioned to share the same ontological status as the Buddha and become integral forces that assist the practitioner in attaining the highest spiritual goals (Wallace 2005: 118–19). In many of the later *tantra*s, which were composed between the ninth and eleventh centuries, these deities come to feature wrathful and terrifying qualities while often exhibiting strong sexual symbolism. Some prominent examples of wrathful Tantric deities include Hevajra, Cakrasaṃvara, Caṇḍamahāroṣaṇa, and Kālacakra, figures who at times embody wild enlightened beings that dwell in cemeteries, drink from and adorn themselves with skulls, and engage in sexual yoga with female consorts (English 2002: 4). Wrathful and peaceful deities alike are typically aligned within one or another "Buddha families," or spiritual lineages linked to a particular Heavenly Buddha. Arrayed in the circular, geometric designs of *maṇḍala*s, a particular Buddha is often depicted in the center being surrounded by various Heavenly Bodhisattvas and deities. The Buddhas who are typically featured in the texts and *maṇḍala*s of Vajrayāna Buddhism include the various emanations of Vairocana, Amitābha, Akṣobhya, Ratnasambhava (Jewel-Born), Amoghasiddhi (Unerring Attainment), and Vajrasattva (Adamantine Being).

Tantric Buddhist texts

With this backdrop of manifold and powerful spiritual forces in the universe, Vajrayāna texts—specifically the *tantra*s—were composed and transmitted selectively to those initiates who sought to wield such powers to attain various goals. Thus these texts, many of which appear only after the seventh century, became seen as the instruments to access both inner and outer divine powers for the sake of protection from harmful forces and illness, the destruction of crops and one's enemies, as well as for visualizing supernatural beings and hidden realms to attain the highest, non-dual state of Awakening where the illusion of "self" and "other" dissolves completely. Moreover, there was a clear lack of unanimity over how to categorize or identify Buddhist *tantra*s. Different Tantric communities employed different texts, as well as different ways to classify them. Some of these classes of *tantra*s included: (1) *kriyā tantra*s ("action *tantra*s"), (2) *cārya tantra*s ("performance *tantra*s"), (3) *yoga tantra*s, (4) *mahāyoga tantra*s ("great yoga *tantra*s"), (5) *yoganiruttara tantra*s ("highest yoga *tantra*s"), (6) *yoginī tantra*s ("divine female *tantra*s"), and (7) *advaya tantra*s ("non-dual *tantra*s"), among others.

The *kriyā tantra*s and *cārya tantra*s generally appeared earlier (although some *kriyā* texts were composed through the twelfth century) and refer to rituals used to obtain both worldly goals and liberation. Many of these texts contain *dhāraṇī*s, which consist of verses that deploy words and symbols as magical utterances held to have a direct impact on reality when recited by one with the requisite training and access to such texts (Gray 2005: 428).

The words and syllables of *dhāraṇī*s represent the distilled forms of larger texts or bodies of knowledge. They may thus be seen as aids to meditation and memory. *Dhāraṇī*s were already present in Mahāyāna sources, and in its earliest phase Tantric Buddhism identified itself as the "*dhāraṇī* method" (*dhāraṇīnaya*). The *kriyā tantra*s and *cārya tantra*s also often contain the preliminary steps for initiating and empowering the practitioner to wield esoteric powers. They typically thus supply instructions not only on recitations of *mantra*s and *dhāraṇī*s, but also on performing *mudrā*s (or ritual hand gestures and bodily poses), constructing *maṇḍala*s that represent esoteric realms in two-dimensional images, and offering fire sacrifices (*homa*). Through such practices one becomes empowered to invoke the assistance of supernatural powers to achieve one's desired ends. *Kriyā* and *cārya tantra*s emphasize external practices and approach deities as external entities rather than as pure manifestations of one's own mind, which is more characteristic of *yoga* and *yoginī tantra*s.

Meanwhile, *yoga tantra*s and *yoginī tantra*s (which can include *mahāyoga* and *yoganiruttara tantra*s as well) express more directly the soteriological goal of Awakening gained through meditation and yogic practices. These later works begin to appear in the late seventh century and clearly diverge from Mahāyāna texts. The *yoga tantra*s, such as the *Sarvatathāgathatattvasaṃgraha Sūtra* (Compendium of the Truths of All the Buddhas), typically emphasize identification between the practitioner and Vairocana Buddha. This identification is established ritually through the use of *mantra*s, *mudrā*s, and *maṇḍala*s that enable the meditator to assume the form of Vairocana and to inhabit his cosmic realm. Through the medium of the *yogatantra*s, one is able to receive the experience of Awakening as bestowed directly by Buddhas.

The *yoginī tantra*s, which begin to appear around the ninth century, include such works as the *Cakrasaṃvara Tantra* (Binding of the Wheels Tantra) and the *Hevajra Tantra* (The Tantra of the Deity Hevajra). And it is the *yoginī tantra*s that present us with the most unconventional and socially transgressive features of Buddhist texts. Features such as a focus on sexual yoga, the consumption of impure substances (such as bodily effluvia), female deities such as *yoginī*s and *ḍākinī*s, and fierce male deities reveal that these texts adopted much material from the antinomian Śaiva groups with their subculture based in funerary charnel grounds and celebration of the *siddha* ideal (Gray 2007: 7–8). These features suggest that these texts often originated outside of Buddhist monastic contexts, although they would later be firmly incorporated into them. Moreover, the strong emphasis on the enlightened female *yoginī* in this texts, either in sexual union with a male deity or appearing alone, set the stage for the rise of Tantric cults of female deities such as Vajrayoginī (English 2002: 4–5). The *yoginī tantra*s encourage the use of meditative practices and transgressive rituals to attain the blissful state of non-dual Awakening. At times, the designation *yoganiruttara tantra* was used in place of *yoginī tantra* to refer to the same class of texts containing advanced meditative and ritual practices.

Tantric Buddhist rituals

The great variety of esoteric Buddhist *tantra*s, numbering several thousand texts by some reckonings, belies a nearly universal focus on ritual performance. Often referred to as *sādhana*, the meditative ritual acts used to visualize a Buddha or a deity directly before oneself or within oneself lie at the heart of Vajrayāna practice. In addition to the aforementioned initiation rites, fire oblations, the recitation of various *mantra*s or *dhāraṇī*s, and the construction of *maṇḍala*s, other forms of ritual practice employed by practitioners include the manipulation of internal bodily forces and sexual yoga.

All Tantric rituals are outlined or at least mentioned in the *tantra*s, but their esoteric nature requires the guidance and exposition of a *guru*. The importance of the *guru*, the enlightened teacher and ritual master, cannot be overestimated in the Vajrayāna. It is the *guru* who initially admits the aspiring practitioner into the Tantric lineage, and it is the *guru* who instructs and prepares the pupil to engage in the secret rituals that are held to yield great power and Buddhahood. The *tantra*s regularly describe the figure of the *guru* as equivalent to the Buddha, a figure to whom worship should be offered and whose instructions should never be violated (English 2002: 28). An example of the great reverence for the *guru* that is typically demanded by Buddhist *tantra*s appears in the twelfth-century *Guhyasamayasādhanamālā* (Garland of Secret Pledge *Sādhana*s):

> The guru is the Buddha, the guru is the Dharma, and the guru is the Saṅgha. The guru is the glorious Vajradhara; in this life only the guru is the means [to awakening]. Therefore, someone wishing to attain the state of buddhahood should please the guru.
>
> (English 2002: 28)

Thus, unlike earlier forms of Buddhism that stress one's individual striving or the intercession of a Heavenly Buddha or Bodhisattva, the Vajrayāna emphasizes the absolute dependence on one's personal *guru* for spiritual advancement.

Doctrinal background of Buddhist Tantras

As important as the *guru* is to this system, there also exists a broader theoretical context that is equally critical for understanding the development and practice of Tantric Buddhist rites. Philosophically, much of Buddhist Tantra accepted certain Mahāyāna notions as foundationally correct. Hence its ritual system recognizes the truths of emptiness and the non-dual perspective of reality that is gained in higher meditative states. Buddhist Tantra seeks to reconcile conventional distinctions such as *nirvāṇa* and *saṃsāra*, male and female, wisdom and skillful means into a single reality that transcends such arbitrary identities to arrive at a single, unifying truth (Snellgrove 1959: 23–4). Tantric rituals can in theory lead one to the supreme state of Awakening wherein all conventional, discursive thought falls away to reveal the true nature of reality. Furthermore, the efficacy of the esoteric rites is based on a theory of analogues whereby the various elements of the rite are believed to hold correspondences with other beings, objects, and principles, enabling the practitioner to manipulate the elements of the rite to control and affect that to which they are related (Robinson *et al.* 2005: 136). In this way, the control of the components of the ritual, which may include items such as jars, various foods and liquids, diagrams and so forth, would theoretically extend to all the entities that are related to them by analogy. The Tantric rite thus enables the practitioner to wield power and control over an increasingly wide sphere of reality, both worldly and divine.

Language and liturgies

In addition the power of Tantric rituals is enhanced by the esoteric and antinomian qualities they possess. As mentioned before, Tantric ritual techniques are guarded by an atmosphere of secrecy. Revealed only to initiates rather than to the public at large, relatively few individuals are shown and trained in the rites. The secrets of Buddhist Tantra were also protected by a system of coded language, sometimes called "twilight language" (*saṃdhyābhāṣā*) that concealed the identity of certain ritual elements by using the names of analogous objects in their place. Thus, for example, in the *Hevajra Tantra* one learns that wine is equivalent to passion, flesh is strength, musk is urine, frankincense is blood, camphor is semen, and so on (Snellgrove 1959: 99–102). The use of such correlates in Tantric texts created coded terms and hidden meanings that prevented the uninitiated from accessing their significance and power. Coded language also served as interpretive tools whereby the later commentators of the *tantra*s unpacked their meanings and created increasingly complex, multilayered texts that could be read in more than one way (Davidson 2002: 262). This quality of the texts would prove useful when Buddhist monastics, who under their vows of celibacy sought to domesticate and adopt the *yoginī tantra*s by interpreting the sexual rites in purely symbolic terms.

The socially transgressive qualities of these texts, however, cannot in every case be explained away in terms of mere symbols. Drawing from the antinomian *siddha* traditions in which ascetic renunciation involved the deliberate transgression of Brahmanical norms, Buddhist Tantra embraced the ideas of ingesting polluting substances and engaging in ritualized sex. Indeed, it is the explicitly taboo nature of these rites that serves to render them effective and powerful for Vajrayāna practice. Whereas other individuals might find drinking urine from a skull, contact with a corpse, or engaging in intercourse with a low-caste maiden repulsive, the *siddha* recognizes that within the taboo lies the means to transcend ordinary thought and conventions that make something taboo to begin with. The un-awakened mind fails to see the illusory and empty nature of distinctions such as "pure" and "impure." The Tantric practitioner, however, uses the repellent and the sensual to transcend the constraints of ordinary thought. One actively uses passions such as lust and wrath to overcome—homeopathically, as it were—the passions of desire and hatred that inhibit Awakening (English 2002: 42). What may appear in certain *tantra*s as shocking and disgusting to ordinary people is actually perceived with equanimity as the means to attaining the state of non-dual bliss characteristic of Buddhahood.

The particular liturgies of Buddhist Tantra vary by text and are subject to refinement by an individual *guru*. Nevertheless, there are some basic features that appear in many later *tantra*s that elaborate upon the recitation of *mantra*s for worldly ends, as emphasized in earlier *kriyā* and *cārya* texts. These works, as exemplified by the *kriyā tantra* called the *Mañjuśrīmūlakalpa Sūtra* (Primary Ritual Manual of Mañjuśrī) depend primarily upon the beings from the Mahāyāna pantheon (such as the Bodhisattva Mañjuśrī) and dedicate *mantra*s and *maṇḍala*s to them in an effort to assist the practitioner in proceeding towards the aim of becoming a *bodhisattva*, often modeled after the *cakravartin* or "Universal Monarch" (Snellgrove 1987: 233–4). The *Mañjuśrīmūlakalpa Sūtra* appears mainly as a collection of *mantra*s to be used in conjunction with guidance from a *guru*. Ascribed to formulae uttered by Buddhas, such *mantra*s are conceived to possess the power to purify, protect, and remove all obstacles for the yogic practitioner who seeks worldly benefits and higher spiritual attainments (Wallis 2001: 100–2). These kinds of practices employing *mantra*s, *maṇḍala*s, and *mudrā*s comprise the ritual structure of texts that were later classified as *kriyā* and *cārya tantra*s. Such texts contributed ritual material to the *yoga* and *yoginī tantra*s, although they tended to be replaced by them in later centuries since the latter, so-called "higher" *tantra*s utilized a wider variety of practices to achieve more supramundane goals (Snellgrove 1987: 234–5).

All Tantric Buddhist texts evince a keen interest in recognizing and manipulating sources of power in the world. Differences appear mainly in the methods they use to appropriate such power and in the ends to which power is used. Earlier esoteric texts focused on the use of *mantra*s and *maṇḍala*s to obtain the power of an overlord modeled after the central Buddha in a *maṇḍala* and the feudal system of power prevalent in early medieval India (Davidson 2002: 114–15, 131). Later esoteric texts, while retaining an interest in wielding worldly power, also added the goal of Awakening as a Buddha. The latter goal of attaining Buddhahood in one's current lifetime appears in the *tantra*s as a radically new notion that distinguished Vajrayāna from earlier Mahāyāna ideas about the lengthy path of the *bodhisattva* (Snellgrove 1959: 40–1). The *yoga* and *yoginī tantra*s came to be seen as the most effective guides toward attaining this goal. The practices of the later Buddhist *tantra*s, broadly speaking, revolved around an elaborate set of preliminary initiation or consecration rites, followed by the rites associated with the "Stage of Generation" (*utpatti-krama*) and culminating in the rites of the "Stage of Completion" (*saṃpanna-krama*).

Stages of Tantric practice

Initiation rites are administered by the *guru* in order to consecrate the adept into the *guru*'s lineage, which is required before one is taught the esoteric rituals and yogic practices revealed in the texts and elaborated upon by the *guru*. The *guru* would typically determine which Buddha family the adept should join, a decision based largely on the particular adept's nature and tendencies. The implements of the ritual are gathered and arranged, and worship is offered to the Buddhas, *bodhisattva*s, other deities, and the *guru*. Rites of protection are performed by the *guru* to ensure safety and success in the upcoming ritual endeavor (Wallace 2005: 124). A pledge of secrecy is administered, whereby the initiate promises to guard the esoteric rituals that are about to be learned. A prolonged period of *mantra* recitation follows, as this practice forms the basis for undertaking the *sādhana* practice (English 2002: 29). The *guru* constructs a *maṇḍala*, which is used as a support for the visualization and meditation parts of the *sādhana*. Other higher initiations are administered in the two stages of Tantric yoga practice.

In the Stage of Generation, the practitioner undertakes rituals designed to effect one's full identification with a chosen deity. One engages in visualization and meditation practices to cultivate a non-dual relationship with a deity or deities, which would lead to the goal of self-empowerment for reasons varying from protection from enemy forces to spiritual Awakening (Wallace

2005: 126). The chanting of *mantra*s aids in the process of assimilating the identity of a deity into one's own. Different *yoginī tantra*s can contain different liturgies and, moreover, each sequence of rites could be subject to alteration or reinterpretation by a particular *guru*. The *Guhyasamāja Tantra* (Secret Assembly Tantra) includes several yogic practices and trance states in its Stage of Generation. These include: (1) the act of evoking a realm of emptiness within which the practitioner attains concentration by means of the *mantra* "*Oṃ* ... I am the intrinsic nature of the adamantine knowledge of emptiness," (2) visualizing within one's body three seed syllables such as *Oṃ*, *Āḥ*, and *Hūṃ* that are linked with various deities in the *maṇḍala* in use, (3) generating the bodies of the deities within one's own body, and (4) imagining one's chosen deity on the crown of the officiant's head and the other Buddhas on the heads of all the deities in their particular families (Wayman 1977: 156–60). Having generated the deity through visualizing seed syllables, which represent powerful *mantra*s, and then through visualizing the deity, the practitioner imagines that he or she acquires the identity of the deity, appropriating its divine powers in the process.

The Stage of Generation in the *Kālacakra Tantra* (Wheel of Time Tantra)—an *advaya* (non-dual) text—is also geared toward the identification of the yogin with the deity, albeit through different means. This *tantra*, likely the last such text to be composed in India, offers a clearer focus on the generation of an esoteric body consisting of a subtle physiology within which divine powers are generated and manipulated. The *Kālacakra Tantra* prescribes meditation on the *maṇḍala* with the deity Kālacakra in the center and his associated deities arrayed around his central realm (Wallace 2001: 190). Subsequent visualizations in the Stage of Generation are likewise focused on the *maṇḍala*. For instance, one proceeds to visualize oneself as the splendid Kālacakra deity, who represents bliss, in union with his consort Viśvamātā, who represents the wisdom of emptiness (Wallace 2001: 194). The union of male and female, bliss and emptiness, is treated as a metaphor for the experience of Awakening, wherein the metaphor serves to actualize what it represents. The *tantra*, moreover, states that the generation practices that rely on the contemplation of the *maṇḍala* can result only in the attainment of mundane powers (*siddhis*) to be used for worldly ends such as protection and pacification of malevolent forces (Wallace 2001: 199).

The Stage of Completion in Buddhist *tantra*s again varies in some details from one text to another. It can involve different levels of ritual practice within the same stage, but the primary rite involves the visualization and manipulation of energies or forces within one's subtle physiology through various yogic techniques. This subtle physiology, or "subtle body" was generally conceived of similarly to Hindu Tantric traditions. Three major channels (*nāḍī*) that run from the crown of the head down to the base of the spine are held to be the central conduits of the body's life force or subtle breath (*prāṇa*) within a system comprising 72,000 veins and four (or sometimes five) *cakra*s that function as energy centers where the channels intersect (Wayman 1977: 65–6). The yogic practice in the Stage of Completion basically involves manipulating the mind, the breath, and various red and white drops (*bindu*) that are linked with semen and uterine blood to generate the Awakening of Buddhahood in the practitioner (Jackson 2004: 33). Various practices, often involving sexual union or the visualization of union, were employed to purify the drops and force them either to ascend or descend along the central *nāḍī* to bring about one of four levels of bliss (*ānanda*) in the practitioner.

In the descending phase, when the white drop in the internal crown of the head is moved down to the throat *cakra* the first level of ordinary bliss is experienced; when it reaches the heart *cakra* utmost bliss (*paramānanda*) is attained; when it reaches the navel *cakra* the bliss of cessation (*viramānanda*) is attained; and when it reaches the tip of the sexual organ without being emitted one experiences innate bliss (*sahajānanda*) (Jackson 2004: 34). However, when the drop is drawn back up the central channel and one contemplates the truth of emptiness, the four types of bliss are experienced in a more profound way with innate bliss resulting from the purified drop reaching the crown of the head (Jackson 2004: 34). The Stage of Completion improves upon the previous stage by effecting the literal transformation of the practitioner's body into a divine vessel wherein bliss and wisdom are brought together in a non-dual state that mirrors the ultimate reality of existence and directly facilitates Awakening.

As detailed in various *yoginī tantra*s, sexual yoga and sexual symbolism are often included in various levels of the Stage of Completion. The use of sexuality as a means for empowerment and spiritual Awakening appears prominently in certain Hindu forms of Tantra as well, where intercourse and the drinking of sexual fluids are conceived to be transgressive means to power and wisdom (White 2003: 73–81). Tantric Buddhists who followed the ritual prescriptions of the *yoginī tantra*s similarly valued sexuality as that which, when properly controlled and sublimated, redirects the body's passions to transform it into the body of an Awakened One. Given the esoteric nature of Tantric texts and cults, it is impossible to know how prevalent sexual yoga was in medieval South Asia. Scholarly consensus seems to hold that the sexual rites described in *yoginī tantra*s were likely practiced to some degree when those texts first appeared. At the same time, there is evidence suggesting that when Indian monastics later attempted to appropriate these texts, they tended to proffer symbolic interpretations of the descriptions of sexual union and sexual fluids as found in the texts. In this way, for example, the union of male and female could refer instead to the internal yogic practice that combines the male and female channels of energy in the body. And, further, the consort with which one engages in a *sādhana* to produce bliss may be conceived as an imagined consort. Commentaries on the *yoginī tantra*s written by monks often de-emphasized their transgressive aspects and substituted the visualization of one's subtle physiology in place of the sexual practices intimated by the texts (Gray 2005: 441). The esoteric language of such texts always permitted different levels of interpretation. When sexuality was taken as only a symbolic feature of the *tantra*s, the celibacy and status of monastics could be preserved.

Nevertheless, the *yoginī tantra*s are often quite explicit about the use of actual sexual practices as the skillful means to gain power and wisdom into the true nature of reality. The *Cakrasaṃvara Tantra*, for its part, reveals more focus on the sacramental consumption of sexual fluids—such as semen mixed with uterine blood—than on the act of intercourse used to produce them (Gray 2007: 104–6). Seen alternatively as sources of impurity and sources of power, sexual fluids were understood by some *tantra*s to be the most efficient means to attaining the non-dual wisdom that transcends conventional dualities of "pure" and "impure," "male" and "female," and the like. Thus, there are *yoginī tantra*s that speak of a "secret" consecration wherein the drop of the *guru*'s semen is retaken from the vagina of the consort and placed in the pupil's mouth as a kind of sacrament representing the *bodhicitta* derived from the union of the feminine principle of wisdom with the masculine principle of skillful means (Snellgrove 1987: 289–90).

Beyond this higher consecration that takes place in the Stage of Completion, there are other ways in which sexuality is used to effect the non-dual state of Awakening. The pupil may be instructed to generate the bliss that comes from the union of skillful means and wisdom, that is to say the male and female sexual organs, in real or imagined intercourse with a consort. Sexual bliss, in this way, comes to represent and to bring about the highest stages of bliss when the practitioner's semen is retained without emission and when emptiness is made the focus of one's meditation (Wallace 2001: 189). Tantric *maṇḍala*s wherein a deity and his consort are depicted in a passionate embrace in the center become models for visualization and for actual practice. With a mind fixed upon emptiness, the union of wisdom and skillful means leads to a non-dual state of innate bliss (*sahajānanda*) that is identified with the experience of Awakening itself. The *yoginī tantra*s maintain that the visualization or ritual recreation of this union brings the practitioner to the highest spiritual state of Buddhahood more quickly and conclusively than practices available to non-Tantric Buddhists.

Figure 4.2 Paramasukha-Chakrasamvara Mandala, ca. 1100, Nepal (reproduced courtesy of The Metropolitan Museum of Art, Rogers Fund, 1995 (1995.233) Image © The Metropolitan Museum of Art).

Legacies of Buddhist Tantra

The manifold texts and practices of Buddhist Tantra in South Asia left their marks on the tradition in this region and beyond. The era in which Vajrayāna Buddhism grew in prominence along with the rise of *siddha* cults and empowerment rituals that appealed to regional kings and generals coincided with the growth of Buddhist monasteries in northeast India, as well as the incursions of Muslim armies across northern India. Some earlier scholars held that the development of Tantra represented a debasement of Buddhism and contributed to its ultimate downfall in India. The reasons that might explain why Buddhism receded in India are complex and will be taken up in the next chapter. Suffice it to say here that the legacies of Buddhist Tantra in India are quite diffuse. The unconventional messages and the rejection of cultural norms and elite religious institutions found in the poetic couplets of Buddhist Tantric practitioners like Saraha (ca. 1000 CE) came to influence the vernacular works of later North Indian devotional poets like Kabīr, Nānak, and Caitanya who were revered by Hindu and Sikh communities (Jackson 2004: 42).

For the most part, Buddhist Tantra became relocated around the periphery of South Asia, particularly in the Himalayan mountain regions where Muslim armies did not reach. Vajrayāna texts and practices were adopted by Buddhists in countries now called Nepal and Bhutan, where empowerment rituals and devotional worship to deities became prominent religious expressions still practiced today. The more esoteric yogic practices, especially those of a sexual nature, were likely devalued in these different cultural and political contexts. To the south, Sri Lanka seems to have received some Tantric texts, but no evidence of Tantric cults and practices has been found. A number of Indian Tantric Buddhists such as Naropa, Padmasambhava, and Atiśa are credited with having transmitted the Vajrayāna path to the Tibetan region, where it came to be recognized as the dominant Buddhist tradition.

Beyond South Asia and the Himalayan region, Buddhist *tantra*s were introduced into China and Japan as early as the eighth century. Although Buddhist Tantra in East Asia was never so popular as to displace other Mahāyāna traditions, its claims to provide access to supramundane power through ritual consecrations led them to become appealing to royal courts at different periods of history. Amoghavajra (705–774) popularized Buddhist Tantra around the western Chinese city of Chang'an in the eighth century, and Kukai (774–835) founded his esoteric Buddhist school called Shingon in the courts of Japan.

5

Reappraisals:

Later developments in the South Asian Buddhist world

Buddhism in Sri Lanka
Monastic institutions
Buddhist rituals in Sri Lanka
Sinhala Buddhist literature
Buddhism in Nepal
Buddhist literature in Nepal
Buddhism in Bhutan
Colonialism and Christianity
Buddhist responses to Christian missions
Colonial-era scholarship on Buddhism
Reinterpreting Buddhism in Nepal and India

Many scholars maintain that sometime around the twelfth and thirteenth centuries the Buddhist religion disappeared from the Indian subcontinent. Various theories seek to explain how the Buddhist religion could virtually disappear from the land of its birth. However, when considering the alleged disappearance of Buddhism from India, there are at least two points to keep in mind. First, there are signs that Buddhism continued to be practiced in particular locales in parts of India long after the thirteenth century. And second, even if Buddhism ceased to be an active presence in much of India, the religion persisted in Sri Lanka, Nepal, and some other Himalayan regions. Thus, in addition to rehearsing the theories for the disappearance of Buddhism in India, it is necessary to describe how the tradition was maintained and developed throughout the second millennium in other parts of South Asia.

As we have seen, a number of socio-economic and political changes in the first millennium of the Common Era weakened Buddhism in the subcontinent. Commercial trade and artisan guilds, which had been early and consistent supporters of the Saṅgha, lost much of their wealth and influence to the activities of medieval kings and Arab traders (Davidson 2002: 79–80). The diminution of the guilds resulted in a decrease in financial support for Buddhist monks and monasteries. Meanwhile, many of the medieval Indian kings also threw more support to Śaiva institutions, in part because Śaivas possessed a religious system that claimed access to divine power, which was appealing to military-minded kings. Moreover, much of medieval India became organized around a feudal model wherein "vassal" states were brought under the authority of a regional overlord in exchange for gifts of land. Buddhist communities gradually adopted Śaiva models of religious practice and feudal models of governance, leading to an embrace of esoteric Tantric traditions and a land tenure system whereupon monasteries collected rents and taxes. In short, from around the seventh century onward, we see evidence of less financial support for Indian Buddhism and a greater assimilation of practices and symbols associated with Tantric *siddhas*.

While esoteric forms of Buddhism would remain strong and vibrant for several more centuries in north and northeastern India, the fortunes of Buddhism in the rest of the country began to experience a general decline. The reasons offered by scholars for the decline of Buddhism in late medieval India include the withdrawal of royal patronage, hostility and persecution by Hindu Brahmins, the destruction of monasteries by invading Muslim armies, internal schisms and moral laxity within Buddhist monasticism, suppression by Hindu kings, absorption into Hinduism, and estrangement from the laity (Jaini 1980: 81; Hazra 1995: 377–95). Many such theories contribute plausible factors in the decline of Buddhism's vitality in late medieval India, although no single factor can account for the collapse of the religion by the early thirteenth century.

More often than not, the medieval fragmentation of power into regional kingdoms had a negative effect on Buddhist institutions. Although they flourished under the patronage of Indian kings like Aśoka, Kaṇiṣka, Harṣa, and the rulers of the Sātavāhana, Pallava, and Pāla dynasties, the Buddhists suffered setbacks when other rulers withheld their support and patronized Hindu or Jain communities instead. The dependency of monasteries on the donations of lay supporters made the Saṅgha particularly vulnerable to shifts in royal patronage. And outside of the Pālas in northeast India, who nevertheless regularly patronized Hindu Brahmins as well, there were few royal houses that reliably promoted Buddhism after the eighth century in India. Furthermore, some kings went so far as to persecute Buddhism, as seen in the actions of the sixth-century king Mihirikula who demolished *stūpas* and *vihāras* in Punjab and Kashmir, and in those of the seventh-century King Śaśāṅka from Bengal who, among other things, destroyed the Bodhi Tree at Bodh Gaya (Hazra 1995: 390–1). Over time, the loss of patronage and occasional persecution came to exert a debilitating effect.

Muslim incursions into northern India also took a heavy toll on the fortunes of Buddhism. Turkish armies conquered and converted Buddhist communities in what is now Afghanistan and Pakistan by the beginning of the tenth century. In time, they pushed further to expand their empire into northeastern India, sacking and destroying the Buddhist temples and monasteries they encountered along the way. The destruction of the universities at Nālandā in 1197 and Vikramaśīla in 1203 were particularly damaging to Buddhism in the subcontinent. Since these and other large monastic complexes functioned as the repositories of Buddhist texts and traditions, the acts of Muslim armies in plundering their wealth, killing their inhabitants, and burning their libraries dealt a mortal blow to an already weakened Indian Buddhist tradition (Robinson *et al.* 2005: 138). While some Muslim rulers in greater India sought merely to tax local Buddhists, others embraced a mission to destroy a religion that appeared to them as idolatry. However, had Buddhist institutions been more vital and well supported, they could have been expected to recover from these attacks. The fact is that following a period of gradual decline, late medieval Buddhism was simply too weak and lacking in support to regain a foothold in much of India.

Another important factor in the disappearance of much of Indian Buddhism was the effect that a more vigorous Hindu tradition had in both discrediting Buddhist ideas on the one hand and absorbing other ideas and images on the other. Some medieval Hindu thinkers such as Kumārila and Śāṅkara wrote strident critiques of such Buddhist philosophical positions as momentariness, No-Self, and emptiness. Jain polemicists too attacked Buddhism for its comparatively less stringent monastic code and its rejection of a permanent Self, which to them destroyed the ethical and soteriological validity of any religious path (Dundas 1992: 207). But it was the widespread reassertion of Hindu Brahmanical codes—the stability from which appealed to medieval kings—and the popular growth of Hindu devotionalism (*bhakti*) that did more to undermine the position of Buddhism in the subcontinent. The popularity of the *bhakti* cults associated with the gods Rāma and Kṛṣṇa, together with the depiction of the Buddha as an incarnation (*avatāra*) of the god Viṣṇu in texts like the *Mahābhārata*, certain *Purāṇa*s, and the *Gītagovinda*, have been cited as reasons why many Buddhist laypersons turned to Hinduism (Jaini 1980: 85). And rather than contesting these external challenges, it is generally held that Buddhism continued to adopt more elements from Hinduism—particularly Tantric deities and practices in the case of Vajrayāna. A related view, however, attributes the absorption of Buddhism into a Hinduism to the rise of Heavenly Bodhisattvas, figures to whom popular devotion was offered and who could more easily become identified with Hindu deities (Jaini 1980: 86–7). The absorption theory also presupposes that the Buddhist laity had limited interactions with scholastic and Tantric Buddhist monks, and without strong ties it was easy for the laity to drift away and support Hindu institutions.

Multiple factors lie behind the alleged disappearance of Buddhism from the Indian subcontinent by around the thirteenth century. Weakened by political and economic changes that accompanied the rise of feudalistic regional kingdoms in the medieval period, Buddhist institutions were unable to counter the challenges of a resurgent Hindu *bhakti* movement, the popularity of Hindu ideologies of kingship, and the destructive effects of Muslim armies. It appears that a Buddhist tradition already weakened from within by a general lack of popular and royal support was largely unable to resist the assimilative effects of Hinduism in its devotional and Tantric forms, nor was it able to be revived after the setbacks it experienced.

Nevertheless, contrary to conventional wisdom, Buddhism did not wholly die out in the Indian subcontinent by the thirteenth century, and it certainly remained a vigorous presence in other parts of South Asia. Buddhism continued to be practiced in many parts of the Himalayas, in parts of East Bengal, and in isolated communities in South India, which were places that largely escaped the destruction of Muslim armies. In Tamil Nadu, for instance, there are signs of a Buddhist presence that lasted up until the seventeenth century. The discovery of Buddhist bronzes in the southeastern coastal town of Nagapattinam, including images of Buddhas and Bodhisattvas, indicates that Buddhism persisted there for centuries later than in most other parts of India (Dehejia 1987: 60–2). Although not as vibrant as Hindu and Jain communities in South India, Buddhists made their presence felt in coastal towns where they depended mainly on the commercial economy rather than on royal land grants given to Hindus and Jains (Champakalakshmi 1998: 82). Sustained by ties with Buddhists in Sri Lanka and Southeast Asia, some Tamil communities maintained Buddhist traditions in southern India long after it had virtually disappeared elsewhere. Eventually, however, a living Tamil Buddhist tradition came to an end before the modern period, leaving isolated pockets in East Bengal as the only locations where Buddhism persisted in India below the Himalayan region.

Buddhism in Sri Lanka

Monastic institutions

As we have seen, Buddhism was established in Sri Lanka by the third century BCE. Embraced by King Devānampiyatissa, who initiated the custom of royal support for the Saṅgha in the forms of *vihāra*s, *stūpa*s, and other requisites for the monastic order, Buddhism spread quickly and became the dominant religion of the island. Sri Lanka became an important Buddhist center for the production and study of texts associated with what would later be called the Theravāda School. Much of the island became dotted with ancient monasteries and monuments, such as the large Mahāthūpa (Great Stūpa) relic shrine in Anurādhapura, which was built by King Duṭṭhagāmaṇī (2nd c. BCE) to store a large portion of the Buddha's cremated remains for veneration. The order associated with the Mahāvihāra (Great Monastery) became the guardians of a particularly conservative vision of Buddhism, forming a closed canon of Buddhist scriptures and rejecting later Mahāyāna texts as inauthentic. The residents of the Mahāvihāra traced their lineage back to the Buddha's original disciples. They enjoyed the patronage of most kings, and an ascetic forest-dwelling segment of their ranks called Āraññikas ("Those of the Forest") earned considerable respect and prestige for their discipline and scholarship. The Mahāvihāra did not, however, remain without monastic rivals.

The Abhayagiri-vihāra and Jetavana-vihāra arose as two competing orders in ancient Sri Lanka, supported by the patronage of various kings. The Abhayagiri monks, also called "Dhammarucis" after one of their leaders, formed a distinctive community in the first century BCE but began to flourish in the fourth century CE. Their willingness to accommodate a wide variety of Buddhist teachings allowed for the introduction of other Buddhist texts and ideas from India in later centuries. At times denigrated by Mahāvihāra authors as "Expansionists" for admitting newer Sanskrit texts into the Canon, the Abhayagiri monks were more receptive to certain Mahāyāna and Vajrayāna teachings. They apparently retained their identity as "*sthaviravāda*" monks, however, and were recognized as such by Indian and Chinese Buddhists. The relative success of the Abhayagiri-vihāra is measured by the sizable endowments they received from local kings between the fourth and tenth centuries, including custodianship of the Buddha's Tooth Relic (Panabokke 1993: 113–15). The properties and the royal patronage they received indicate that the Abhayagiri-vihāra rivaled the Mahāvihāra in terms of popularity and influence in early medieval Sri Lanka. However, scarcely any of their writings survived the late medieval period, which was marked by frequent invasions by foreign armies.

In contrast, the Jetavana-vihāra experienced less growth after being founded by a group of monks who broke away from the Abhayagiri-vihāra in the fourth century CE. Sometimes referred to as "Sāgalikas" after an early leader named Sāgala, the monks of the Jetavana-vihāra apparently remained doctrinally close to the Mahāvihāra order. Although they had their own Canon and interpretations of the Vinaya rules, the Jetavana monks held many of the same doctrinal tenets as the Mahāvihārins. Their existence as competitors in efforts to receive patronage may have been the main reason for enmity between Jetavana and Mahāvihāra monks.

The three traditional Sri Lankan *nikāya*s (sects) were all in existence by the time Buddhaghosa prepared his Pāli commentaries in the fifth century.

Monks and nuns enjoyed wide support from most Sri Lankan kings and laypersons, as the veneration of the Three Jewels remained the dominant form of religious expression. Central to the growth and development of the Sri Lankan Buddhist Saṅgha was the support of kings. Mindful of Sri Lanka's historic relationship with Buddhism, the laity came to expect that their kings be devout Buddhists as well, and the kings' fitness to rule depended on their participation in the cult of relics and their identification as *bodhisattva*s (Gunawardana 1979: 171–2). Royal legitimacy was thus a function of the support given to the Saṅgha in the form of endowments and monastic requisites such as robes, food, medicines and residences. The Buddha's Tooth Relic came to be recognized as a distinctive symbol of a righteous Buddhist king, and thus royal patronage flowed toward it and its custodians. In general, royal displays of piety and morality helped to earn kings the respect and loyalty of their Buddhist subjects.

A relationship of mutual support and dependence arose between the Saṅgha and the State in Sri Lanka. The monastic orders came to depend on royal patronage in the forms of gifts and endowments of land and irrigation works. Large monasteries tended to acquire extensive tracts of land granted by kings for their upkeep. Villages granted to monasteries often included the labor of the residents who lived on those lands, which developed into a feudal system whereby villagers gave part of the fruits of their labor to their monastic landlords. Crops were grown for consumption and sale, and irrigation works could accompany the gifts of land to assist in growing rice (Gunawardana 1979: 72–3). The privileged status of monastic lands resulted in royal declarations that they were exempt from taxes and seizure of their properties. The fact that larger Sri Lankan monasteries became the locus for the production and accumulation of wealth is consistent with what took place in India, as larger monasteries in both lands came to acquire land, cattle, buffalo, and servants to ensure a steady supply of food and income (Panabokke 1993: 134). Such wealth helped to insulate the monasteries from decreases and interruptions in lay support due to wars and other disturbances.

The Saṅgha also came to depend upon kings for the maintenance of peace and political stability that would enable monastics and laypersons to thrive. Warfare threatened the supply of food and other monastic requisites, as did the looting of monasteries by non-Buddhist invaders. Occasionally, some kings also intervened in monastic disputes and used their authority to mediate the disputes and to arrange for the "purification" of the order by expelling monks who were morally lax and who adhered to allegedly "false" teachings. The support of strong and pious kings who fashioned themselves after King Aśoka was thought necessary to maintain the integrity of the Saṅgha, and the assembly of monks periodically called upon their royal authority to assist in weeding out unsuitable persons from the monkhood.

At the same time, Sri Lankan kings came to depend on the Saṅgha for public support of their reigns. The moral righteousness to rule over the island was confirmed by monks, who recognized the worthiness of kings by accepting their gifts and by praising them for their virtues. To the extent that Sri Lankan kings could wield political authority, they depended on the sanction of the Saṅgha who alone could testify to the righteousness of kings (Gunawardana 1979: 176). The king's participation in public rituals that were administered by monks served to confer a status of righteousness upon him. As long as the Saṅgha expressed its favor upon the king, the Buddhist laity was expected to do the same.

The acquisition of land and wealth from endowments certainly assisted in the growth of Buddhism in early medieval Sri Lanka. Additional wealth, however, came with a price. For those monasteries that sought and received large endowments of land to bolster their supply of food and revenue, the resident monks necessarily found themselves increasingly involved in the worldly affairs of business and the management of temple resources. The original ideal of Buddhist monks renouncing all forms of wealth was circumvented early on in South Asia by the granting of unrestricted gifts and endowments to the "Saṅgha of the Four Quarters," or the collective body of Buddhist monastics wherein ownership was shared by all (Panabokke 1993: 129). Aside from a few personal requisites including robes and a bowl, the private ownership of goods by monastics was generally discouraged by the Pāli *Vinaya*. However, publicly held property—termed "immovables" (*garubhāṇḍa*) to denote articles that could not be taken away by individuals—could be accumulated and used to benefit the entire Saṅgha (Panabokke 1993: 129). Over time in both India and Sri Lanka, grants of land and other forms of wealth were directed to specific schools and particular monasteries for their more immediate use. In this way, some Buddhist monasteries became centers of considerable wealth by attracting gifts by devout laypersons eager to earn merit.

Furthermore, gifts given to the Saṅgha in Sri Lanka were generally assumed to be irrevocable and immune from taxation. While history shows that a handful of usually non-Buddhist rulers occasionally reclaimed or attempted to annex monastic lands, most were loathe to do so given the strenuous objections of the Saṅgha that would follow. As long as Sri Lankan kings were expected to be not only pious Buddhists but also *bodhisattva*s, it was clearly preferable to avoid alienating the Saṅgha. These factors enabled certain monasteries to obtain great economic wealth to go along with their political influence and their unparalleled religious status. At the same time, the accumulation of properties and wealth made Buddhist monasteries more vulnerable to charges of immorality and greed. Aware of the Buddha's teachings about renunciation and desire, Buddhist laypersons in early medieval Sri Lanka tended to redirect their attention and support away from the wealthiest monasteries and toward ascetic groups of monks such as the Paṃsukūlikas (Those with Robes from Dust Heaps) and forest-dwelling Āraññikas (Gunawardana 1979: 40–6). Those monks who refrained more from worldly comforts became seen as more virtuous and worthy of reverence. The Paṃsukūlikas, with their robes made out of discarded rags, and the Āraññikas, with their simple wilderness dwellings, distinguished themselves in the Saṅgha from the seventh century onward.

The division of the Sri Lankan Saṅgha into three *nikāya*s characterized the monastic community for much of the first millennium of the Common Era. The Mahāvihāra, Abhayagiri-vihāra, and Jetavana-vihāra had some disagreements in terms of their interpretations of the Dharma and the Vinaya, but they were generally minor. The Mahāvihāra was more insistent about doctrinal purity, while the other two *nikāya*s adopted a more liberal attitude toward Buddhist teachings and texts outside of the "Sthavira" tradition. The three communities were differentiated as much if not more by the fact that they developed into corporate bodies that owned vast amounts of land through their associated monasteries spread over many parts of the island (Gunawardana 1979: 86). However, with the onset of periodic foreign invasions from South India and the political and economic disturbances caused by warfare, the *nikāya*s began to cooperate more with each other. There is evidence of joint ritual performances and instances of communal residences for members of the three *nikāya*s beginning around the ninth century, a situation that lent itself to the eventual unification of the three *nikāya*s in the twelfth century (Panabokke 1993: 158).

After the fall of the ancient capital of Anurādhapura to South Indian invaders at the end of the tenth century, a new medieval Buddhist kingdom was built in the city of Polonnaruwa. Coḷa rule in the capital of Anurādhapura lasted from around the late tenth century to the middle of the eleventh. The Coḷas from South India were patrons of Śaivism and tended to loot Buddhist monasteries, destroy relic shrines, and drive monks to more remote parts of the island or abroad (Paranavitana 1960: 563). It was also during this period that the order of Buddhist nuns likely died out in Sri Lanka. The Saṅgha as a whole was weakened until King Vijāyabāhu I (1070–1110) recaptured the north and expelled the Coḷa forces. In an effort to restore the Saṅgha, he invited monks from Burma to come to Sri Lanka and initiate a new monastic ordination. Since there is little evidence to demonstrate that this order was a Burmese one, some scholars believe that the monks invited from Burma were either Sri Lankans who had fled there or their pupils (Paranavitana 1960: 564; Gunawardana 1979: 271–3). Notably, there is no evidence of attempts to revive the *bhikkhunī* order despite the survival of Burmese nuns into the twelfth and thirteenth centuries.

The organizational structure of the three *nikāya*s eventually was replaced by a system of eight *mūla*s (or *muḷa*s, "groups"), also called *āyatana*s ("spheres," "relations"), which represented different fraternities of monks. Some of the more prominent fraternities in this period include the Uttaromūla and Kapārāmūla, which were among the fraternities that formed out of the Abhayagiri-vihāra. The Uttaromūla enjoyed considerable patronage and was appointed as the official custodians of the Buddha's Tooth and Bowl Relics, which were sacred objects linked to the throne (Gunawardana 1979: 288). Another group called the Vilgammuḷa was linked with the Jetavana-vihāra and distinguished itself in literary and scholarly fields. Alongside the eight *mūla*s were other institutions of monastics, and it is unlikely that the eight fraternities together accounted for all monks. For instance, the Āraññikas maintained their identity as a distinctive monastic community that was primarily associated with the Mahāvihāra.

The system of the eight *mūla*s flourished from the eleventh to the thirteenth century while the capital was in Polonnaruwa. A landmark effort to purify and unify the Saṅgha was made by King Parākramabāhu I (1153–86). Parākramabāhu ruled over a period of prosperity in Sri Lanka, wherein he repelled foreign invaders and engaged in major restoration and building projects to benefit the Saṅgha and the agricultural economy. Literary accounts of a monastic council held during Parākramabāhu's reign depict the event as motivated by the king and resulting in the banishment or incorporation of heterodox Abhayagiri and Jetavana monks into the dominant Mahāvihāra. The fact that these reports were written by Mahāvihāra monks should give us pause about their accuracy. Instead it appears that leading members of the Saṅgha realized the need to be unified and led these efforts under the auspices of the king (Gunawardana 1979: 315). Led by the Thera Mahākassapa, a leader of the Āraññika community and a resident of a monastery located far away from the capital, the monastic council implemented reforms that had three major outcomes (see Panabokke 1993: 152). First, monks deemed impure by the strict standards of Mahākassapa and his colleagues were either expelled from the Saṅgha or demoted to novices in order to be re-trained. Second, the remaining monks were reconciled and sectarian divisions were diminished. Third, a code of disciplinary injunctions called the *Katikāvata* were issued and implemented to guide monastic conduct.

Historical sources indicate that the reforms of this Buddhist council were geared more towards purifying the Saṅgha from immoral and undisciplined monks than creating a single monastic body under the Mahāvihāra. Monks called before the council and expelled for exploiting monastic lands and keeping wives and children included members of all three *nikāya*s (Panabokke 1993: 154). And since the *nikāya*s themselves were fairly irrelevant by the twelfth century, the attempts to remove factionalism would have been directed more toward the *mūla*s. Nevertheless, the *Katikāvata* issued from this council indicates that monastic conduct, not doctrinal views, formed the basis of the Saṅgha reforms. And despite the fact that monks found wanting in monastic discipline were forced to become novices and re-ordained in the Mahāvihāra lineage, there is evidence that some Abhayagiri and Jetavana teachings persisted long after the council (Gunawardana 1979: 320–1). The discipline endorsed by the council emphasized strictness and a conservative view of the monastic code.

Subsequently, the standards of a more ascetic leaning branch of the Mahāvihāra became normative for the Saṅgha in Sri Lanka. Occasional political disturbances and warfare harmed the Saṅgha in later centuries, necessitating the issuing of new *Katikāvata* guidelines to reform the *sāsana* up through the seventeenth century. But the emphasis on adhering to strict standards of monastic discipline continued to function as the ideal against which the failings of contemporary monks were measured. Moreover, a new method of categorizing Sri Lankan monastics developed after the reforms of Parākramabāhu. Beginning in the twelfth century, the distinction between "village monks" (*gāmavāsin*) and "forest monks" (*āraññavāsin*) became more salient and represented two different monastic orientations. Village monks living close to settlements mainly served the ritual needs of the laity, whereas forest monks living in the wilderness were expected to devote more time to meditation. Monks of both types, however, had contact with laypersons and worked with religious texts.

Buddhist rituals in Sri Lanka

Buddhist monks were chiefly responsible for maintaining Buddhism in medieval Sri Lanka. Monks conducted and oversaw many rituals, preached sermons, and received gifts from lay donors. However, Buddhist practice in medieval Sri Lanka was not limited to monks. While monks in the Theravāda tradition were seen as following an advanced religious path compared with those who remained laypersons, there were numerous opportunities for lay Buddhists to engage in practices such as venerating images of the Buddha, which were conducive to auspicious rebirths and *nirvāṇa*. Moreover, many Buddhist monks evidently shared similar concerns about obtaining good rebirths and transferring merit to living and deceased family members. Monks therefore also participated in popular religious cults in Sri Lanka. Conversely, some laypersons even possessed the knowledge and skills to compose Buddhist texts during the late medieval period. As such, monks

Figure 5.1 Reclining Buddha image from Buduruwayāya, Sri Lanka (photo courtesy of Imali Berkwitz)

and laypersons participated in similar kinds of religious activities in medieval Sri Lanka.

Many of the popular Buddhist practices in medieval Sri Lanka had their roots in earlier centuries. The veneration of relics was foremost among these, as relic shrines holding deposits of the Buddha's corporeal remains were constructed and worshipped shortly after Buddhism was formally established in Sri Lanka around the third century BCE. However, many of the oldest *stūpa*s were located in the ancient capital of Anurādhapura, and these fell into varying states of disrepair and damage due to South Indian armies that periodically conquered the northern part of the island. In their place, popular relic cults developed around the Tooth Relic and the Footprint Relic, which were located in areas controlled by Sinhala Buddhist kings. The Tooth Relic became especially important for medieval Buddhist devotion. Tradition holds that a tooth taken from the Buddha's cremation pyre was eventually brought to Sri Lanka in the fourth century CE, where it was received with great veneration and safeguarded by the country's Buddhist kings. The Tooth Relic's importance grew in the medieval period, when it became a symbol of the king's authority and was kept in shrines near the palaces of kings (Ilangasinha 1992: 183–4). Among the several works composed about the Tooth Relic, the fourteenth-century *Daḷadā Sirita* (Story of the Tooth Relic) describes not only the legendary history of how it was brought over from India but also the rites of devotion shown by kings and others.

> When going to the Tooth Relic House once a day, [the king] leaving his entire retinue outside, purifying himself, entering the House with

> affection and reverence, taking brooms and sweeping the House, washing his hands, making offerings of such things as precious objects and flowers, reflecting on the nine virtuous qualities of the Buddha that start with "worthy," worshipping and venerating [the Tooth Relic], let the Five Precepts be observed by great kings who are endowed with righteousness and who have become the king of Sri Lanka.
>
> (Sorata 1950: 50)

Large public ceremonies were regularly held to honor and make offerings to the Tooth Relic. Kings assumed prominent places in the worship of this relic, as this lent legitimacy to their reigns. On certain occasions, the Tooth Relic was taken in ceremonious processions around the capital to receive veneration. Similar to other relics, veneration to the Buddha's Tooth could yield merit and, in a belief distinctive to this relic, ensure regular rainfall for crops.

The veneration of the Buddha's Footprint Relic, located on top of a mountain called Samantakūṭa or Śrī Pāda in the southern highlands of Sri Lanka, also became a popular practice in the medieval period. Tradition holds that the Buddha left his footprint on this mountain on one of his three legendary visits to Sri Lanka after his Awakening. Local Tamils interpreted and honored the mark as belonging to Śiva, while Muslims and later Christians viewed it as the footprint of Adam after he was cast out of the Garden of Eden. It is unclear when Buddhists began to climb the mountain in order to venerate this relic. However, there is evidence that renewed steps to support the worship of this holy site began around the beginning of the twelfth century, and it is mentioned in numerous medieval texts (Ilangasinha 1992: 186).

Another form of Buddhist practice popular in medieval Sri Lanka—again, with much older roots—is the chanting of protective Pāli verses or *paritta*. Its importance in this period is evidenced by the twelfth-century construction of a permanent building wherein monks could chant *paritta* to bestow blessings of protection and auspiciousness (De Silva 1980: 20–2). Canonical Pāli *sutta*s contain references to instances where the Buddha enjoined his followers to chant verses to alleviate illness, spirit-possession, and drought. *Paritta* developed as a popular ritual to bestow the protective powers deriving from the truthfulness of the Word of the Buddha. The recitation of certain Pāli *sutta*s by monks over a thread with one end placed in a jug of water was thought to infuse these objects with some of the potency of the Buddha's speech. At the conclusion of the ceremony, the water could be sprinkled as a blessing on the attendees and the thread would be worn as a temporary source of protection (Gunawardana 1979: 225–6). The affirmation of truth in the Dharma and the extension of loving-kindness to other beings became the primary sources of power behind the *paritta* ritual (De Silva 1980: 14). As such, the recitation of verses from the Buddha assumed the status of protective *mantra*s that could substitute for older Hindu ritual formulas, yet bring about similar worldly benefits of protection, health, and good fortune.

Worship of deities and Bodhisattvas

Among the popular Buddhist practices in late medieval Sri Lanka, there was a marked increase in the worship of deities from the Hindu pantheon and the worship of Heavenly Bodhisattvas from Mahāyāna literature. The frequent invasions from South India resulted in periods where part of the island was ruled by Hindu kings. Hindu Brahmins began to find a ceremonial place in royal courts, and temples were built in honor of Hindu deities. Beginning around the fourteenth century, shrines for Hindu gods were constructed in Buddhist temples, allowing laypersons and even monks to venerate the Buddha who had shown them the path to liberation and then worship gods who could bestow worldly blessings in the present (Ilangasinha 1992: 190). The incorporation of Hindu deities into the Buddhist fold rendered them inferior to the Buddha, as they were held to be un-awakened, subject to death, and of little or no assistance in attaining *nirvāṇa*. The gods were assigned to the category of the worldly (*laukika*), while the Buddha and *arahant*s were seen as transcendent (*lōkōttara*) for having put an end to rebirth. Nevertheless, the cultural assimilation of Hindu deities into medieval Sri Lankan Buddhism offered Buddhists not only a way to obtain worldly aims but also a means whereby good health and prosperity in the current life could prepare one for the attainment of *nirvāṇa* in a future life (Holt 1991: 24).

The assimilation of the deities into a Buddhist worldview entailed locating them in the Sri Lankan terrain and subordinating them to the Buddha and other more spiritually developed beings like *arahant*s. In ancient times, Hindu deities made appearances in Buddhist texts and on Buddhist *stūpa*s as devoted servants to the Buddha. During the medieval period, however, there is evidence for the development of discrete cults of the gods who occupied shrines (*devale*) and temples (*kovil*) dedicated to them. Four guardian deities, namely Upulvan, Saman, Vibhīṣaṇa, and Skandakumāra, became identified as the divine protectors of the island and of the *sāsana* established by the Buddha. Upulvan, who was later identified with Viṣṇu, had a large shrine at Devinuvara along the southern coast that was the site of large, elaborate rites until its destruction by a Portuguese force in the sixteenth century (Ilangasinha 1992: 197–8). Saman was the divine custodian of the Footprint Relic, and was popularly worshipped in the southern highlands around Śrī Pāda. Vibhīṣaṇa was identified as the brother of the demon Rāvaṇa, but who helped Rāma slay his brother and who was given the throne of Laṅkā in the Hindu epic *Rāmāyaṇa*. Vibhīṣaṇa was deified at some point in Sri Lanka and located in the western city of Kelaṇiya where devotees traveled to seek his assistance in giving birth to a child (Ilangasinha 1992: 209). Lastly, Skandakumāra was identified with Kārttikeyya (Tamil: Murugan), the son of Śiva, and a shrine dedicated to him was established in the southeastern town of Kataragama.

The apparent popularity of Hindu gods did not reduce the veneration or position of the Buddha in medieval Sri Lanka. The Buddha, the Dharma, and the Saṅgha retained their privileged position as being most worthy of veneration and most effective for spiritual progress. But in addition to venerating the Three Jewels, many medieval Sri Lankan Buddhists worshipped deities for divine assistance in obtaining more immediate aims. This worship, however, was not readily accepted or condoned by all Buddhists. The fifteenth-century monastic author Vīdāgama Maitreya criticized and parodied the worship of Hindu deities in a verse work entitled *Buduguṇālaṅkāraya* (Ornament of the Buddha's Virtues). Therein, he argues that the limitless power and majesty of the Buddha eclipses that of gods such as Śiva, who rides around on a decrepit old ox, and Viṣṇu, who in the form of Rāma needed the help of a monkey to build a bridge to cross over to Laṅkā (Ilangasinha 1992: 215).

Many medieval Buddhists worshipped and petitioned not only Hindu gods for divine assistance but also Heavenly Bodhisattvas adopted from the Mahāyāna pantheon. Among the early Sthavira schools, the Bodhisattva Maitreya was recognized as a highly developed spiritual being destined to become the next Buddha. Aside from him, however, the early Theravāda School in Sri Lanka did not embrace other *bodhisattva*s found in Mahāyāna texts. Over time, due mainly to the inclusive orientation of the Abhayagiri-vihāra, elements of the Mahāyāna were incorporated into Sri Lankan Buddhist practice. Numerous bronze images of *bodhisattva*s dating from the eighth to the tenth centuries have been found in the island, suggesting that this period coincided with a wave of Mahāyāna influence (Gunawardana 1979: 224). This same period roughly marks when Avalokiteśvara started to receive devotion in the island. His cult grew in influence during the fourteenth century, when he became reinterpreted as the local guardian deity Nātha, and he later came to serve as a source for sustaining the political power of local kings (Holt 1991: 91). Images of Nātha and his female consort Tārā proliferated in the late medieval period, suggesting the presence of vibrant cults of worship. Significantly, Heavenly Bodhisattvas like Nātha possessed both worldly and transcendent aspects (Holt 1991: 113). Unlike the Buddha whom Sri Lankans believed attained *parinirvāṇa* and was no longer in contact with the world, Nātha represented a benevolent power that could assist people with their worldly needs and work to bring them closer to *nirvāṇa*. The popularity of Nātha extended beyond the sixteenth century, but his identity has been reinterpreted again in modern times into the Bodhisattva Maitreya.

Sinhala Buddhist literature

The picture of medieval Sri Lankan Buddhism is brought into greater focus by the numerous texts composed between the tenth and fifteenth centuries in literary forms of the vernacular Sinhala language. An archaic form of Sinhala was apparently used in some of the ancient commentaries on the Pāli Canon, but these texts were rendered superfluous by the Pāli commentaries written by Buddhaghosa and others between the fifth and seventh centuries. Pāli texts and scholarship received more attention in Sri Lanka during the first millennium of the Common Era. However, Sri Lankans became active participants in the broader vernacularization of literature in South Asia, which occurred roughly between the tenth and fifteenth centuries when local languages were used to express literary themes and aesthetic ideals that previously appeared in Sanskrit (Pollock 2006: 28). After around the ninth or tenth century in Sri Lanka, authors increasingly turned to a literary form of Sinhala to compose Buddhist texts. The study of Sanskrit literature and literary values flourished, while Pāli compositions generally declined apart from some Abhidhamma manuals and works of poetry.

Significantly, the decline of Buddhism in much of India probably reinforced the sense among Sri Lankan Buddhists that the Buddha's *sāsana* was being preserved first and foremost in their island. The increased use of Sinhala in writing texts coincided with an era wherein Sinhala kings struggled to establish strong, unified kingdoms, and when there was scarcely any creative influx of Buddhist literature and thought from India. Contacts with Southeast Asian Buddhist communities helped to sustain some role for Pāli works, but by the twelfth and thirteenth centuries Sri Lankan Buddhist authors made Sinhala the primary vehicle for literary expression in the island. These Sinhala Buddhist texts reveal a widespread interest in devotional themes such as extolling and reflecting upon the virtues of the Buddha. There were efforts also to translate and adapt older Pāli historical narratives into Sinhala works detailing the history of Buddhism in the island and, in particular, the events whereby relics of the Buddha—including his collar bone, forehead bone, hair, tooth, footprint, Bodhi Tree, and a large portion of his cremated ashes—were brought to Sri Lanka and deposited for Buddhist devotees to venerate and to earn merit (Berkwitz 2004: 197–8). Some Sri Lankan authors also composed poetic works in Sinhala, often using particular *Jātaka* stories as their themes, and adopting the highly figurative and aesthetically rich style of Sanskrit court poetry (*kāvya*).

Among the notable Sinhala texts from this period, many served to edify and encourage Buddhists to engage in practices to augment their present lives, future rebirths, and progress toward liberation. Although literary Sinhala likely deviated from everyday colloquial usage, Sinhala works were still more accessible to the broader laity, including those who were illiterate. Using texts inscribed on dried palm leaves, monks and lay scholars read portions of Sinhala texts aloud to audiences in order to convey the messages contained therein. Such works are called *baṇapot*, or "preaching texts," and were widely disseminated. One influential example of this genre is the thirteenth-century Sinhala prose work *Butsaraṇa* (Buddha-Refuge) written by Vidyacakravarti. This work details with great esteem and devotion the wondrous qualities of the Buddha. As such, Vidyacakravarti presents numerous reasons for embracing the Buddha whose marvelous attainments and qualities were directed toward liberating all beings.

> Because of such things as the heavenly, divine, and noble abidings; the detachments from the body, the mind, and the substrata of existence; the [three] liberations by means of emptiness [of selfhood], the signless [nature of impermanence], and the desireless; one should go to the Buddha-Refuge, saying 'I go to the refuge of the Buddha,' who gives shelter with his knowledge due to the exhausted nature of his remaining worldly and transcendent factors [i.e. *dharmas*].
>
> Moreover, one should go to the Buddha-Refuge, saying 'I go to the refuge of the Buddha,' who has put an end to the journey in *saṃsāra*.
>
> And moreover, as many virtues of the Buddha that I express are like the water in a small boat that has sunk in the great ocean. Whereas the virtues that are found in the Buddha are vast like the rest of the water in the great ocean. The virtues of the Buddha that I express are small like a mustard seed, but the virtues found in the Buddha are enormous like the Great Cosmic Mountain. Leaving aside one like me, even if an [ordinary] god, or a *brahmā*-deity, or a *māra*-deity, or a *śakra*-deity, or a recluse, or a Brahmin, or a disciple, or even a world-transcending Buddha himself were to express them throughout an eon, they could not finish while reciting them over even a lac or a crore [of eons]. So one should go to the Buddha-Refuge saying, 'I go to the refuge of the Buddha,' who has infinite virtues.
>
> (Sorata 1966: 216)

Numerous other Sinhala prose works from the medieval period emphasize devotion to the Buddha in expressive ways. Some of them include the twelfth-century *Amāvatura* (Liquid of Ambrosia) and the thirteenth-century *Pūjāvaliya* (Garland of Offerings). Other works, such as the thirteenth-century *Sinhala Thūpavaṃsa* (History of the Relic Shrine) incorporate feelings of reverence and gratitude toward the Buddha through a focus on the relics he allegedly left behind for worship (Berkwitz 2007: 24–7). Although the *Pūjāvaliya* was written by a monk, the *Amāvatura* and *Sinhala Thūpavaṃsa* are the works of lay authors. This indicates that laypersons were also involved in crafting a medieval Buddhist discourse that emphasized the Buddha's transcendent and marvelous qualities, through which spiritual attainments were possible.

Sinhala poetic works from the medieval period differ substantially from prose texts in terms of style and language. The somewhat rarefied language and the metrical constraints found in Sinhala poetry were likely directed toward smaller audiences. Nevertheless, Sinhala poetic works represented important markers for erudition, power, and aesthetic taste in royal courts in fifteenth- and sixteenth-century Sri Lanka. The works of the monk Toṭagamuve Śrī Rāhula from the fifteenth century exemplify a poetic literary culture wherein authors exulted in their own prestige as persons who can compose poetry that yields affective experiences for refined connoisseurs—such as kings (Hallisey 2003: 715). Śrī Rāhula's epic poem entitled *Kāvyaśēkhara* (Crest Jewel of Poetry) illustrates the conjunction of Buddhist admonition and aesthetic aims in Sinhala poetry from this era. Using a particular *Jātaka* story as its central theme, the *Kāvyaśēkhara* instructs its readers and listeners in the finer points of Buddhist doctrine while delighting them with its fine poetic qualities and aesthetic sentiments (*rasas*). Śrī Rāhula's poems also acknowledge the benevolent powers of gods that are available to grant boons to people who petition them. In contrast, the poems of the monk Vīdagama Maitreya, also from the fifteenth century, tend to eschew the esteem for deities and the more ornate poetic features found in Śrī Rāhula's works. His *Buduguṇālaṅkāraya* and *Lō Väḍa Saṅgarāva* (Treatise on the Welfare of the World) represent poetic works written to deliver sermons on the Buddha's qualities and the importance of doing merit.

Sinhala works in prose and poetry helped to augment the island's Buddhist traditions up till the onset of colonial rule in the sixteenth century. They convey a general picture of a society wherein devotion to the Buddha, the Dharma, and the Saṅgha was expressed in the form of narratives, ritualized offerings of worship (*pūja*), and alms to renunciants and the poor. Deities and *bodhisattva*s were worshipped by many, as people sought to enlist many sources of aid in order to improve their lives at present and in the future.

Buddhism in Nepal

The modern state of Nepal lies on the southern slopes of the Himalayas between India and the Tibetan region. Historically, it comprised a smaller territory in the Kathmandu Valley marked off from other lands by the mountain ranges surrounding it. Its location resulted in the development of a distinctive cultural sphere, yet it received strong cultural influences from India and Tibet. Most scholars locate the Buddha's birthplace of Lumbini within the modern state of Nepal. It appears, however, that the Buddha traveled south to the Gangetic Plains, where he gained his Awakening and established his *sāsana*. Although wandering monks could have traveled to the Kathmandu Valley preaching the Dharma at an earlier point in history, the first historical evidence of Buddhism in Nepal is found during the Licchavi period, named after the dynasty that ruled over the Valley between the fifth and eighth centuries CE. Large numbers of *vihāra*s and *stūpa*s were built by the Licchavis, although it appears that these rulers encouraged a broad range of religious traditions including Hinduism and different forms of Buddhism (Slusser 1982: 274). The most notable monument built in this period is the Svayambhū *stūpa*, the large relic shrine that was built in the city of Kathmandu in the first part of the fifth century. It appears that Mainstream Buddhist schools maintained a presence early on, and these were joined by adherents of the Mahāyāna in the sixth century and the Vajrayāna by the seventh century (Slusser 1982: 271–2). The Mahāsāṃghikā order was among the most popular at first.

As a multi-ethnic country, Nepal is home to various communities where Buddhism is practiced by particular ethnic groups. Several of these groups practice a form of Buddhism influenced by Tibetan traditions. This is true for the Sherpa, who live mainly in the northeastern mountain region; the Tamang, who live mainly in the north and in areas surrounding the Valley; and the Gurung from the central region of the country. These communities are not homogeneous, and even those who practice Buddhism also typically embrace other local, shamanic practices. The focus here, however, will be on the Buddhism of the Newar community, which is based in the Kathmandu Valley and reflects Indic traditions more than Tibetan ones.

Buddhism developed in the Kathmandu Valley alongside Hinduism, albeit with lesser influence and smaller numbers of adherents. Licchavi patronage to Buddhist and Hindu institutions ensured that the Valley contained large numbers of temples and monasteries to serve the adherents of both religions. Buddhas and deities were venerated, at times probably by some of the same devotees. Many in the Newar ethnic group, especially those who engaged in trade and related businesses, were among the most ardent supporters of Buddhism in the Valley. For those Newars and other communities who worshipped Buddhas, *stūpas* became important sites of religious practice at an early period. They were the centers of much devotional and economic activity, attracting pilgrims who contributed to the local trade and patrons who built monasteries nearby (Lewis 2000: 40). Four major *stūpas* received the most veneration during the Licchavi period. The Svayambhū *stūpa* received much worship after being built, and retains great religious importance in the present day. Secondly, the Dharmadeva, or Chabahil, *stūpa*, built in the middle of the fifth century by another Licchavi ruler attracted other smaller shrines, monasteries, and devotional images that were founded to support the devotional activity of the site (Slusser 1982: 276–7). Thirdly, the Bodhnātha *stūpa* appears to have been built by the Licchavi king Mānadeva I. The fourth major ancient *stūpa* in the Valley is called Bandegaon and is located south of the city of Lalitpur. Other *stūpas*, including the four so-called Aśokan *stūpas* surrounding Lalitpur, were built elsewhere in the Valley. Such evidence suggests that the *stūpa* was the primary cult object of Buddhists who lived in Licchavi Nepal, and that successive kings and other patrons continued to build new shrines or enlarge older ones in later centuries (Slusser 1982: 280).

Aside from *stūpas*, Buddhists in ancient Nepal worshipped Heavenly Bodhisattvas in the form of images. These images appeared with figures of

Figure 5.2 Svayambhunath Stūpa, Kathmandu, Nepal (photo courtesy of Dina Bangdel).

the Buddha as his attendants, but also individually as objects of devotion in their own right. Images of Avalokiteśvara and Vajrapāṇī predominate in the Licchavi period, and the number of sculptures and epigraphic references suggest that Avalokiteśvara was the most beloved Bodhisattva at this time (Slusser 1982: 280). Traces of an ancient *bodhisattva* cult indicate that the worship of powerful, spiritually advanced Buddhist deities has been a fairly consistent feature of Buddhism in Nepal. Even today, many Newar adherents of the Mahāyāna express strong devotion to Heavenly Bodhisattvas and make regular offerings to them, especially Avalokiteśvara and Mahākāla, at temples and shrines in the Valley (Lewis 2000: 13).

The period between the ninth through the twelfth centuries in Nepal represented something of a transitional period between the fall of the Licchavis and the rise of the Malla dynasty. Buddhist monasteries in the Kathmandu Valley may have lost some of the patronage they enjoyed from the Licchavi kings, but the religion continued to expand its influence. Scholarship became a focus among the numerous *vihāra*s in the city of Lalitpur, and there the teachings of Indian monks and *siddha*s contributed to a tremendous increase in manuscript texts and the acceptance of Vajrayāna as the dominant form of Buddhism in the Valley (Slusser 1982: 281). The worship of older *stūpa*s continued unabated, but increased emphasis was given to devotional expressions to various spiritual beings. Images of Avalokiteśvara continued to be featured in this period, and his popularity as the Buddhist deity of compassion who was also known as Lokeśvara (Lord of the World) and Karuṇāmaya (Compassionate) may be in part due to the conflation of his identity with Śiva and a deified Nātha yogin named Macchendra (Slusser 1982: 283). Also popular in the Valley during this period was the Bodhisattva Vajrapāṇī, the Buddhist version of the Vedic god Indra, who was portrayed as a guardian of the Buddha and a bringer of rain (Slusser 1982: 283–4).

Aside from the ongoing cults devoted to particular *bodhisattva*s, numerous Tantric deities assimilated from Vajrayāna texts gained importance around the tenth century. Wrathful images of Hevajra and Heruka proliferated during this period, and they were often joined by various female deities. Tantric goddesses such as Tārā, the savior goddess, Vasudhārā, the goddess of good fortune, and Prajñāpāramitā, the deification of the *Aṣṭasāhasrikā-prajñāpāramitā* text who personified wisdom were among those worshipped in the Valley (Slusser 1982: 282). As representatives of the feminine principle, which came to be highly esteemed in Buddhist Tantric thought, these female deities came to occupy prominent places in Nepalese Buddhist society.

During the Malla period, which lasted from around the early thirteenth century to the middle of the eighteenth century, Buddhism in the Kathmandu Valley underwent significant social changes even while its emphasis on devotional displays to various deities remained constant. Pressures from the surrounding Hindu-dominated society and occasional restrictions placed on Buddhist institutions by unfriendly kings led to the transformation of Buddhism in the Valley toward greater imitation of existing Hindu institutions. One of the most important changes was the disappearance of the celibate Buddhist monkhood in Nepal. The influences of the Hindu, caste-oriented society together with the value attributed to *siddha*s and Tantric lineages in the Vajrayāna brought celibate monasticism to an end. In its place arose a hierarchy of specifically Buddhist castes led by a community of Tantric ritual specialists called *vajrācārya*s and ordinary "monks" called *śākyabhikṣu*s, both of whom began to take wives like Hindu Brahmins (Slusser 1982: 287). With their caste identities established, Vajrācāryas and Śākyas assumed their place in the broader society within a Buddhist social hierarchy that co-existed with the Hindu caste structure. People assumed these identities and social positions by birth and heredity. Vajrācāryas occupied the higher rank as the Buddhist counterparts of Hindu Brahmins. They assumed responsibility for performing the fire sacrifices needed for major life-cycle rituals, and for worshipping Buddhist Tantric deities. The Śākyas retained a nominal identity as *bhikṣu*s, and qualified to perform day-to-day domestic rites, including the worship of conventional Buddhist deities.

The shift from a celibate monkhood to a community of caste-based, lay religious specialists occurred over the long period of Malla rule. This change may be partly explained by the cultural forces of an ascendant Hindu community that received strong support from Malla kings. At the same time, political forces such as the social reforms implemented by King Jayasthiti Malla in the fourteenth century compelled Buddhists to occupy places in the caste system that was reorganized by the king, and they also had to abide by the land reforms established by Brahmins in accordance with Hindu legal codes (Ram 1978: 200–1). The Vajrācāryas and Śākyabhikṣus thus gradually became endogamous caste groups, wherein admission into their communities was determined by birth. In time, a mixed celibate and married clergy gradually gave way to a closed caste group of married religious specialists (Tuladhar-Douglas 2006: 150). There is little evidence that the study of scripture and doctrine was of pre-eminent concern among the emergent married clergy in Nepal. Instead, the chief roles within this Newar household Saṅgha consisted of the performance of rites for the worship of the Five Vajrayāna Buddhas and the host of other deities in an expanded Tantric pantheon.

Avalokiteśvara maintained his popularity as the compassionate *bodhisattva* who offers assistance to his devotees. And during this same period, the Bodhisattva Mañjuśrī became a new recipient of Buddhist devotion. Many other Buddhas and *bodhisattva*s continued to be worshipped and honored with elaborate rites. A new cult arose in devotion to the Buddha Dīpaṅkara, a Buddha held to have preceded Gautama by innumerable eons, and who, as the protector of merchants, was popular among Newar Buddhist traders (Slusser 1982: 292–3). As for the array of benign and terrifying Tantric deities that were worshipped in tandem with the older figures of Buddhas and Heavenly Bodhisattvas, a cult devoted to Mahākāla, the Defender of the Law and a guardian deity historically linked to Śiva's wrathful manifestation as Bhairava, grew in popularity during the Malla period (Slusser 1982: 291). The great powers attributed to Mahākāla and other Tantric deities meant that Buddhists often approached them and petitioned them for assistance with worldly and otherworldly aims.

In addition, numerous Buddhist rites in the Kathmandu Valley have involved life-cycle rites and festivals held during specific times. Often employing the ritual knowledge of *vajrācārya*s, these events lend structure to the collection of everyday offerings and devotion to *stūpa*s and deities. Many of the life-cycle rites still observed by Newar Buddhists are adapted from parallel Hindu life-cycle rites. The specific rites and their performances may vary by caste and gender, but carrying out the life-cycle rites for one's family has traditionally been the duty of each Newar Buddhist householder (Gellner 1992: 200–1). Some important life-cycle rites include Birth Purification shortly after the birth of a child, the First Rice-Feeding after about six months of age, the First Head-Shaving at around five years, Marriage, and Death. These rites fall under the category of exoteric rituals, which are performed publicly and typically involve the worship of deities. Two other important life-cycle rites held primarily for those of the Vajrācārya caste are the Tantric Initiation (*dīkṣā*) and the Consecration of the Vajra-Master (*vajrācārya-abhiṣeka*). The former initiation rite is open to other high castes, and it enables them to participate in the cult of esoteric Tantric deities. The Consecration of the Vajra-Master, however, is reserved solely for the sons of Vajrācāryas, who undergo this rite in order to perform the fire sacrifice (*homa*) and act as priests to conduct a variety of domestic rituals for parishioners (Gellner 1992: 266).

Buddhist literature in Nepal

During the Malla period, there were important efforts to preserve and augment the collections of Buddhist texts held in libraries and homes in the Kathmandu Valley. Buddhism in this region had already embraced the Vajrayāna as the primary and superior form of the tradition. Sanskrit texts were singled out for special attention, and significantly it was in Nepal that a Sanskrit-based Buddhist tradition survived after the demise of a similar tradition in India. The old customs of copying Sanskrit Buddhist manuscripts as an act of merit and a pedagogical exercise continued. And yet there are clear signs that Newar Buddhists did more than just copy and preserve Sanskrit texts from India. A significant number of Sanskrit Buddhist texts were composed in Nepal as original works, albeit based on Indian precursors that were often cited to lend authority to the newer texts. From the thirteenth century onward, significant numbers of works containing popular narratives (*avadāna*s), hymns of praise to divine beings (*stotra*s), works on *bodhisattva* conduct (*caryā*s), ritual texts, historiographical works, performance songs (*caryāgīti*), and other handbooks were composed in a form of Sanskrit marked by phonetic and grammatical changes under the influence of the local Newari language (Tuladhar-Douglas 2006: 28–33, 42–4).

In the fifteenth century there emerged a fairly coherent genre of narrative literature written in Newar Sanskrit. These works consisted mainly of collections of stories about specific past or present *bodhisattva*s. Often having titles containing the word *mālā*, or "garland," these verse works were often composed as verse recensions of earlier Indian Sanskrit texts conventionally framed within a narrative between a Nepalese king named Jinaśrī and his *guru* Jayaśrī (Tuladhar-Douglas 2006: 44–5). This Garland literature in general promoted the practice of *vrata*s, or "lay vows." Such vows often orient lay religious practice in the Valley, as they are made with the assistance of priests to Buddhist deities such as Avalokiteśvara, Mahākāla, Svayambhū, and Tārā who, in return, are thought to grant specific boons, general good fortune, heavenly rebirths, supernatural powers, and even the possibility of attaining Awakening (Lewis 2000: 116). *Vrata*s consist mainly of offerings and petitions made to a particular deity, often while fasting. The devotional relationships and pragmatic concerns revealed by *vrata*s are illustrated by the following excerpt from the fifteenth-century *Guṇakāraṇḍavyūha* (Array of Baskets of Virtues).

> Those with faith in him (Avalokiteśvara), constantly recollect (him), concentratedly meditate upon him, chant his name, take refuge in him and are devoted to him: because of that, they will not have a bad rebirth, anywhere, ever! They will always arise in good rebirths, with wealth and good qualities. As they have done good deeds on behalf of sentient beings, they will always experience delightful things, and maintaining the Bodhisattva vow, they will eventually arrive in Sukhāvatī. Endlessly quaffing the Dharma nectar of the teacher Amitabha, they will attain the threefold awareness and arrive at the stage of Nirvāṇa.
>
> (Tuladhar-Douglas 2006: 51)

In this sense, the *Guṇakāraṇḍavyūha* succinctly explains the benefits of making vows and honoring the Bodhisattva Avalokiteśvara. In works such as these, lay Buddhist practice is promoted due to its alleged practical benefits, while the intricacies of doctrinal speculation scarcely appear.

The fifteenth-century Garland texts mark the beginning of an important transition in the production of Buddhist literature in the Kathmandu Valley. While the Malla rulers usually promoted local Hindu institutions over Buddhist ones, and the vibrant condition of Hindu practice came to exert even more influence over Buddhist rites, some Nepalese Buddhist authors sought to reassert the integrity and value of their practices. *Vajrācārya*s composed Garland texts in Newari Buddhist Sanskrit to compete with Hindu Brahmins for prestige and patronage (Tuladhar-Douglas 2006: 199). By offering a system of lay religious practice dependent upon their ritual expertise, the *vajrācārya*s encouraged Newar Buddhists to maintain their devotion of Buddhist deities like Avalokiteśvara in rites under their direction. Buddhist authors in the Valley showed creativity and initiative by writing such works under the less than favorable conditions of Malla rule. Their literary output in the fifteenth century marks the final stage of significant new Sanskrit composition of Buddhist literature. Older Sanskrit texts continued to be copied, preserved, and worshipped. However, from the sixteenth century on, Buddhist authors begin to rely more on the vernacular Newari language for composing new texts.

Newari Buddhist texts employ a literary version of the vernacular to communicate more effectively with local language speakers. Buddhist pandits continued to study and use Sanskrit, and certain *dhāraṇī*s and other ritual texts in Sanskrit were used in certain ceremonial settings. Moreover, the older Sanskrit texts were incorporated into the working canon of Nepalese Buddhist texts. In everyday practice, however, Buddhist texts in Newari were used to communicate the basic ritual and devotional knowledge to members of the community. Newari Buddhist narratives assumed critical roles in the expansion of Buddhism as a tradition that came to express a more local flavor in terms of its values and the people and places mentioned therein. This process has continued up to the modern day through public readings of ancient tales retold by Newari Buddhist texts (Lewis 2000: 6). Devotional narratives and ritual manuals predominate in this corpus of texts. Equally important among Newari Buddhist texts included works such as the *Aṣṭamī Vrata* and *Tārā Vrata* that blend directions for purifying oneself and making offerings to Heavenly Bodhisattvas such as Avalokiteśvara and Tārā (Lewis 2000: 91–5). Newari collections of *mantra*s and *dhāraṇī*s recited for blessing and protection also comprised an important genre. The *Pañcarakṣa* (Five Protectors) is perhaps the most well-known example. Containing stories, *dhāraṇī*s, and descriptions connected with five protective deities, the *Pañcarakṣa* became used in rituals designed to protect people from misfortune and harm.

Buddhism in Bhutan

The traditional isolation of the eastern Himalayan kingdom of Bhutan has effectively limited the scholarship done on its Buddhist traditions. Bhutan is formally considered to be part of South Asia. Its history and culture have been profoundly shaped by Vajrayāna Buddhist traditions from Tibet more so than from Nepal. The early history of the people living in what is now recognized as the state of Bhutan is largely unknown. Buddhism had likely been introduced to this land from about the seventh century, although its growth accelerated in the eighth century. Tradition holds that in the latter part of the eighth century an Indian refugee prince invited the Indian Tantric saint Padmasambhava to come to this land from his mission in Tibet, whereupon he established several monasteries and the Nyingma Buddhist tradition in a principality of this territory. At this time, several minor kingdoms comprised the land that would later be unified by the Shabdrung (also Zhabdrung) in the seventeenth century. In the region of Bhutan, Padmasambhava was credited—as he was in Tibet—with taming local demons and spirits who were seen as chaotic and malevolent, enabling the widespread acceptance of Buddhism in the land (Kowalewski 1994: 125). Padmasmabhava's influence in the region was so great that he quickly became a revered *lama* who has been deeply venerated by the Bhutanese up to the present.

Other adherents from Tibetan Buddhist orders came to this region and founded monasteries that maintained ties with Tibet. Adherents of the Sakya order followed the Nyingma, and in the eleventh century the Kagyü order arrived. A branch of the Kagyü called the Drukpa came to dominate the land following the efforts of the scholar Padmakarpo (1527–92) to systematize the Drukpa teachings (Olschak 1979: 19). Equally important were the political maneuvers of the married Drukpa nobility who expanded their influence through building monasteries and contracting marriages with other important families. The Gelug order's rise to dominance in sixteenth-century Tibet, assisted by the support of their Mongol patrons, drove numerous Tibetan *lama*s belonging to other orders south into Bhutan. This process whereby Buddhist exiles from Tibet and India sought refuge from political strife in Bhutan made up a recurrent theme in the history of the country (Kowalewski 1994: 131).

Followers of the Nyinmga co-existed peacefully with the Drukpa Kagyü sect, and among the former the tradition of *tertöns*, or discoverers of treasure-texts (*terma*), became influential in this region. According to Nyingma teachings, the guru Padmasambhava hid certain texts within the memories of his original disciples. Later on, their reincarnations would discover and teach these texts, which had been hidden away in their subconsciousness. Some discoverers like Dorjelingpa (1346–1405) were active in both Tibet and Bhutan. Pemalingpa (1450–1521) was a native of Bhutan and a renowned discoverer of treasure texts. He contributed much to the Bhutanese Nyingma tradition, including a number of visionary writings, a reputation as a fine metal craftsman, a large number of spiritual disciples, and wealth that he spent on constructing or refurbishing temples throughout eastern Bhutan (Aris 1979: 160–1). Another influential Nyingma *lama* who spent time in exile in Bhutan was Longchenpa (1308–63), an adherent of the Great Perfection (Dzogchen) branch, and who founded eight monasteries and wrote several treatises while in this region (Aris 1979: 155).

Similarly, the influence of the Drukpa Kagyü order in Bhutan was realized largely by the efforts of some charismatic Buddhist *lama*s. Among them was the so-called "holy madman" Drukpa Kunley (1455–1529), whose unorthodox conduct and skill in taming local demons earned him the status of an enduring cultural hero. Although Drukpa Kunley left his mark by contributing various songs and dances that were embraced by his immediate descendents as well as others in the region, other Drukpa *lama*s operated more in the realm of politics. Chief among them is Shabdrung Ngawang Namgyal (1594–1651?), a Tibetan *lama* who had a disputed claim to being the reincarnation of the leading Drukpa scholar Padmakarpo. Educated to assume the leadership of this school, Namgyal was driven into exile in Bhutan by hostile rivals in 1616. This flight has been memorialized by an account of a vision experienced by the young *lama*. In this vision, he went flying after a raven to a place to the south, in which the raven represented the Tantric deity Mahākāla and the place was an old monastery in western Bhutan (Aris 1979: 209). Once in Bhutan he assumed the spiritual leadership of the Drukpa order in exile, and inaugurated a lineage of reincarnated *lama*s called the "Shabdrung" to head the Drukpa community. He brought the various kingdoms under his command as the first spiritual and secular ruler of a newly unified Bhutan, building a network of fortress monasteries called *dzong*s that housed administrative offices and monastic chambers within their imposing walls (Olschak 1979: 137–9). Each *dzong* served as a district headquarters to assist in the imposition of the Shabdrung's authority across the land. They also functioned as fortifications that were employed during a series of invasions by Tibetan armies in the seventeenth century.

The first Shabdrung succeeded not only in unifying Bhutan but also in establishing Drukpa Kagyü Buddhism as the state religion. Other sects originating in Tibet, with the exception of the Gelug order, continued to exist within the country. After receiving a male heir, the Shabdrung left his status as a married *lama* behind to become a fully ordained monk in 1632 (Aris 1979: 219). While continuing his rule as the leader of the country, the Shabdrung built more fortresses, fended off Tibetan invaders, and worked to regulate the monastic rituals in Bhutan. At the end of the Shabdrung's reign, it was rumored that he went off into a secret retreat, and his death was not officially recognized for several more decades. In the interim, other regents ruled in his name to stave off succession disputes. The theocracy established by the first Shabdrung succeeded in imposing a uniform set of institutions and a system of Buddhist-inspired laws for Bhutan. Buddhist monks from the Kagyü, Nyingma, and Sakya orders were housed in *dzong*s and involved themselves in politics, scholarship, and occasional meditation retreats (Aris 1979: 265–6). In time, a series of reincarnated Shabdrungs were recognized and guided Bhutan with the assistance of appointed lay officials. This dual monastic and lay system of administration remained normative for Bhutan, even after the establishment of a new hereditary monarchy in 1907.

Nurtured by a steady stream of exiled or visiting Tibetan *lama*s, Buddhism developed in Bhutan in close imitation of select Tibetan forms. Kagyü and Nyingma traditions exerted the most influence over local forms of Buddhism, while the Gelug order that had become predominant in neighboring Tibet was largely rejected in Bhutan. Rituals performed are centered on the three great *lama*s, namely the Buddha, Padmasambhava, and the first Shabdrung, although other *lama*s and deities may be venerated as well (Kowalewski 1994: 127). While Bhutan has taken steps to incorporate more democratic politics, it remains a fairly isolated Buddhist kingdom that preserves its local Tibetan-inspired forms of the religion as a major part of its cultural heritage.

Colonialism and Christianity

In the second millennium of the Common Era, people in Sri Lanka, Nepal, and to a lesser extent Bhutan developed more localized Buddhist traditions. The scarce traces of Buddhism in India had little to offer in terms of support. However, beginning in the sixteenth century, Buddhists in South Asia were confronted with new challenges. European colonial powers began to make their presence felt among South Asian Buddhist communities. Elsewhere in the region, new political systems and laws forced Buddhists to accommodate and at times respond to unfavorable conditions. New forms of religious competition challenged South Asian Buddhists to maintain their traditions in the face of initiatives undertaken to weaken and even eliminate Buddhism.

European colonialism had a greater and more sustained impact on Buddhist communities in Sri Lanka than elsewhere in South Asia. Colonial powers tended to re-order the local political and economic systems, and these changes had profound effects on the Buddhist Saṅgha, which had long been dependent upon the support of kings. Often linked with colonialism were Christian missions and attempts to convert local inhabitants. In time, colonial powers took a greater interest in developing knowledge about local religions and customs, and these initiatives helped to spur new projects to investigate the history and the doctrines of the Buddhist religion. Some local colonial officials and civil servants in Sri Lanka, Nepal, and India learned Sanskrit, Pāli, and local vernaculars in order to study Buddhist texts, while others conducted archaeological excavations in order to reconstruct Buddhist history. These efforts were part of a larger trend called "Orientalism," whereby cultures across the Middle East and Asia were subjected to the scrutiny, study, judgment, discipline, and ultimately the governance of western peoples (Said 1979: 41). For our purposes, what is relevant here is that the very idea of "Buddhism" as a distinctive world religion originating in South Asia but spreading far beyond the region took shape largely as a result of the scholarly investigations that accompanied efforts to extend colonial knowledge and authority over South Asian lands.

In the case of Sri Lanka, Portuguese trading interests in Asia brought this expansive empire to the island in 1506. Initially attracted to the island's valuable commodities in cinnamon, elephants, precious gems, and so forth, the Portuguese crown sanctioned the construction of a fort in Colombo and ongoing negotiations with the local king of Koṭṭe in the southwest to establish favorable trading terms. In the middle of the sixteenth century, the Portuguese began dispatching Franciscan missionaries to the island as part of a broader effort to convert the "heathens" in the Portuguese *Estado da Índia* (State of India) that included Goa, Sri Lanka, and other coastal regions in southern India. Catholic missionaries had some success in converting people from lower-caste fishing communities but found most other Sinhala Buddhists, including local kings, to be resistant to their efforts. More aggressive proselytizing took place in the later sixteenth and early seventeenth centuries. The Council of Goa, first held in 1567, approved a policy to destroy "pagan" temples in Portuguese-held territories, which led to the destruction of many Buddhist and Hindu temples, including the famous Upulvan shrine in Devinuvara, Sri Lanka (Strathern 2007: 197). Moreover, the ongoing battles fought between Portuguese-led armies from the Koṭṭe Kingdom in the southeast and the armies of Sinhala kings in the interior effectively depopulated and destroyed numerous villages, making it nearly impossible to feed monks or to sustain the monasteries and shrines in the coastal and lowland regions.

By the time the Portuguese were forced out of Sri Lanka by the Dutch in 1658, many Buddhist institutions and forms of public practice had been relocated to the independent Kingdom of Kandy in the central highlands. Although the Dutch Calvinists were more interested in eradicating Catholicism, they still took steps to convert Buddhists and suppress the religion. Dutch rule of the coastal regions was fully supplanted by the British in 1796. The British Empire valued Sri Lanka for its naval operations in the Indian Ocean, and the British eventually developed plantation crops such as tea to bolster its trade and economy. An effort by the British to subjugate the highland kingdom of Kandy succeeded in 1815, and they gained control of the entire island. A treaty called the Kandyan Convention was signed that same year, and it obliged the British to continue government support of the Saṅgha. In fact, the British colonialists did little to assist the monastic establishment, while their efforts to build schools and hospitals made the laity less dependent on monks for their education and health.

Notably, efforts were made to reintroduce the *upasampadā* ordination ceremonies of Theravāda lineages from Thailand and Burma earlier in the eighteenth century. The status of monastics had declined under several generations of colonial rule to the point where by 1730 no fully ordained monks remained in Sri Lanka. The Siyam Nikāya was established in 1753 by visiting Thai monks, and this new monastic order served to revive Buddhist monastic and educational institutions. Led by Ven. Väliviṭa Saraṇaṃkara, the Siyam Nikāya instituted monastic reforms that not only reintroduced higher ordination, but also came to stress Pāli study and the texts of the Tipiṭaka as marks of distinction in monastic learning (Blackburn 2001: 198–9). The Siyam Nikāya was based in Kandy, and it restricted its membership to those of the highest caste. Subsequently, some lower-caste Sinhala Buddhists in the coastal regions, while continuing to profess Christianity to please their European rulers, began to make arrangements to establish another monastic order that was not restricted by caste (Malalgoda 1976: 96–8). Hence, in 1803, the Amarapura Nikāya was founded with the help of Burmese monks, and it grew to incorporate a wide range of lowland monks from different caste backgrounds. Later, in 1864, a group of Amarapura monks established a new order called the Ramañña Nikāya after the site in Burma where they had renewed their ordination earlier. The Ramañña Nikāya was a smaller, reform-minded sect that sought to distinguish themselves through stricter adherence to monastic discipline.

Buddhist responses to Christian missions

Although the British rulers tolerated efforts to revive Buddhism in Sri Lanka, the Christian missionaries who arrived in the nineteenth century were more intent on converting Buddhists to Christianity. Earlier reports by British authors on Buddhism in Sri Lanka were fairly charitable, containing positive assessments of the religion's ethical ideals. However, in the middle decades of the nineteenth century, British missionaries in Sri Lanka adopted more hostile attitudes toward Buddhism. Missionary scholars such as Daniel John Gogerly and Robert Spence Hardy studied Buddhist texts in order to condemn Buddhism for its denial of God and its alleged nihilistic teachings associated with *nirvāṇa* and *anattā* (Harris 2006: 69–71). In the eyes of missionaries who believed that only Christianity held the truth that leads to salvation, Buddhism was a false religion to be refuted. As such, many missionaries began publishing pamphlets and treatises in both English and Sinhala to attack the Buddhist religion and to "reclaim the deluded victim of Idolatrous superstition" (Malalgoda 1976: 204). Along with their written refutations of Buddhist teachings, Christian missionaries sought out public debates with Buddhist monks to demonstrate the superiority of their own religion. At first, Buddhist monks were reluctant to contest the missionaries. As time wore on and the attacks on Buddhism intensified, a number of monks accepted the challenge and agreed to a series of public debates with a group of Sinhala converts to Christianity. Beginning in 1865 and culminating in the two famous Panadura Debates on August 26 and 28, 1873, Buddhist monks responded to the critiques of the missionaries with a defense of Buddhism and their own objections to Christian teachings. Ven. Mohoṭṭivattē Guṇānanda, a Buddhist monk who adopted the more animated speaking style of Christian evangelical preachers, was a particularly persuasive orator who captivated the crowds of between five and ten thousand who gathered to watch the Panadura Debates (Malalgoda 1976: 225–6).

The forceful response of the monks and the strong support of the Sinhala crowds caught the missionaries by surprise. Having previously thought that Buddhism in Sri Lanka was dying out, the debates demonstrated that the majority of Sinhalas continued to embrace their traditional religion despite missionary efforts to convert them. From the 1860s onward, Sinhala Buddhist monks and laypersons engaged in energetic efforts to defend and revive the religion that had languished under foreign rule. A number of charismatic, learned monks such as Ven. Hikkaḍuwe Śrī Sumaṅgala (1827–1911) led these efforts, and they received the support and assistance from some sympathetic westerners. Among these supporters was the American Theosophist Col. Henry Steele Olcott (1832–1907) who, with the help of local Sri Lankans, encouraged Buddhists to found schools, celebrate public holidays, and create a catechism to instruct children in the basic points of Buddhist doctrine. One of the Sinhala leaders of the late nineteenth-century revival of Buddhism in Sri Lanka was the Anagārika Dharmapāla (1864–1933), a layman who organized efforts to promote a moralistic interpretation of Buddhism led by monks who would be socially active like Christian missionaries (Seneviratne 1999: 55). Dharmapāla urged his fellow Sri Lankan Buddhists to adopt a this-worldly form of lay asceticism combined with a rejection of folk rituals to create a vibrant, ethical society more conducive to attaining *nirvāṇa*.

Dharmapala redefined Buddhism in his writings and speeches as a religion fully compatible with modern values and scientific thought. He was a key proponent in what has been called "Protestant Buddhism" or "Buddhist Modernism," although to him he simply espoused what was taught by the

Buddha in canonical texts. The work of Dharmapāla to revive Buddhism in Sri Lanka was closely linked to his efforts to promote Buddhism abroad and to rouse his fellow citizens to reject Christianity along with western customs and tastes. The "Protestant Buddhism" for which he is credited with founding entailed the dissemination of Victorian–Protestant ethical ideals in urban Buddhist culture, resulting in a form of religion that at once imitated yet also rejected Protestant Christianity (Obeyesekere 1972: 61–2). Although its similarities to Protestantism should not be overstated, Dharmapala's vision of Buddhism highlighted monks engaging in social service and laypersons involved in the practice of meditation and the study of Buddhist scriptures. His work and impact continued well into the twentieth century.

Colonial-era scholarship on Buddhism

Dharmapala was not alone in reinterpreting South Asian Buddhism in the latter part of the nineteenth century. A number of western scholars pursuing what was known as "Oriental Studies" also contributed new perspectives on the Buddhist religion. Seeking to understand the alleged foundations of the religion, scholars generally ignored contemporary expressions and living informants in favor of ancient texts and monuments to uncover what Buddhism was like in its so-called pristine purity. In Sri Lanka, the research of T.W. Rhys Davids (1843–1922) typifies an early generation of scholars who emphasized the study of ancient Pāli texts as central to understanding Buddhism as taught by the Buddha. Davids argued that the Pāli Canon of the Theravāda alone conveyed the Buddha's unadulterated teachings, while later innovations by the Mahāyāna and Vajrayāna schools of Buddhism on the one hand, and contemporary Sri Lankan Buddhist practice on the other, were inauthentic and contradicted the Buddha's original message (Harris 2006: 137). The Orientalists' view of Buddhism extolled the ancient heritage of Theravāda in Sri Lanka while dismissing its contemporary, vernacular forms. Davids and other scholars of his generation typically defined Buddhism in terms of its earliest manifestations. It thus appeared as a rationalist, ethical movement that was free of ritual, and Davids arrived at this view not only from the Pāli texts that he read but also with the encouragement of scholarly monks who shared an interest in adapting Buddhism to modern tastes and values (Hallisey 1995: 45–7).

Meanwhile, in nineteenth- and twentieth-century Nepal, the reinterpretation and study of Buddhism were being undertaken in ways that resembled some of the efforts under way in Sri Lanka. Brian Houghton Hodgson (1801–94), the British Resident in Kathmandu during the first half of the nineteenth century, collected large numbers of Sanskrit Buddhist texts and sent them back to Europe for further study. Like Davids, Hodgson valued the depiction of Buddhism in ancient texts over what could be seen in the contemporary society. And he, too, relied on local scholars for assistance.

Reinterpreting Buddhism in Nepal and India

Unlike Sri Lanka, Nepal was a Hindu-dominated state with much less direct British intervention in local affairs. Christian missionaries in the Kathmandu Valley had been expelled in the latter part of the eighteenth century, but the state support given to Hinduism effectively diminished the standing of Buddhism in the region. The conquest of 1769 by Prithvi Narayan Shah and the Gorkhali ruling class unified the various kingdoms into one kingdom of Nepal where Hinduism was promoted and protected over other religions. In the north, far away from the Valley, the Thakali and other ethnic communities preserved their Tibetan-influenced form of Vajrayāna Buddhism.

Closer to the major cities in the Valley, however, Newar Buddhists experienced increased pressure to adopt Hindu identities. Under the rule of the Rana aristocracy, which began in 1846, Valley Buddhists were encouraged to imitate the Hindu customs of their rulers and employ Hindu Brahmins to perform their domestic rites instead of Buddhist *vajrācārya* priests (Gellner 2005: 767). The conversion of Hindus was prohibited, but Buddhists and members of other minority religions could be persuaded to adopt Hinduism. The Rana Prime Ministers who ruled the country consolidated their power by following a policy of isolationism and by incorporating all religious and ethnic communities under a single legal system called the National Code in 1854 (Leve 2002: 838). This code assigned all citizens, including non-Hindus, into a network of caste-based relations. In effect, the Rana's National Code forced Buddhists and other non-Hindus to be subsumed within the caste-based legal code. The resulting political and legal pressures encouraged many Buddhists to adopt more Hindu customs and embrace the state religion to a greater extent than before. Beginning in the twentieth century, some Newar Buddhists began to resist these trends and sought to carve out a specifically Buddhist identity in opposition to the Hindu hegemony supported by the Ranas. The adoption of Buddhist Modernism in twentieth-century Nepal will be examined in the next chapter.

As for India, leaving aside the small communities of Indian Buddhists in East Bengal and some southern Himalayan territories, there were few remnants of the Buddhist religion by the end of the nineteenth century. British scholars in India had begun to decipher the historical traces of the religion through textual and archaeological inquiries. Having been previously led to conclude by their Hindu Brahmin informants that the Buddha was an *avatāra* or incarnation of Viṣṇu, British scholars eventually understood the Buddha to be the founder of a separate religion in India. Research by

James Prinsep (1799–1840), who deciphered the Brāhmi script on the pillars commissioned by King Aśoka, and by Sir Alexander Cunningham (1814–93), who participated in the excavations of ancient Buddhist sites including the Bhārhut Stūpa, the shrine at Sārnāth, the Sañchi Stūpa, and the Mahābodhi Temple at Bodh Gayā, launched the modern discovery of India's ancient Buddhist past. Dharmapāla, the Sri Lankan reformer, became keenly aware of the sorry state of Buddhism's ancient sites in the land of its birth. After a visit in 1891 to the temple marking the Buddha's Awakening in Bodh Gayā, Dharmapāla bemoaned the neglect of the site, which had been under the custodianship of Hindus for several centuries. He founded the MahāBodhi Society in Calcutta that same year as an organization to lead the restoration of Buddhist sites and a revival of Buddhism in India.

Dharmapāla's efforts to reclaim Bodh Gayā for the Buddhists took several decades to be even partly realized. He made efforts to install a Buddha image in the temple and to settle a number of monks in a nearby rest house, only to have them opposed by the Hindu custodian of the site. Buddhist revivalists turned their attention to the restoration of other ancient sites. And numerous societies were founded and joined the Mahābodhi Society in efforts to preach, propagate, and preserve the Buddha's Dharma in India (Ahir 1995: 596). Monks from various Buddhist countries established monasteries at Bodh Gayā and other Buddhist sites in India, while a small number of Indians converted to become monks. Although the numbers of Indian Buddhists were quite small compared with Hindus and other religious communities in modern India, the Buddhist revival in India was well under way prior to the country's Independence in 1947. After centuries of near absence, Buddhism began to have a presence in the land of its birth once again.

6

Revivals:

Buddhism and modernity in South Asia

Modern Buddhist revivals
Buddhist nationalism in Sri Lanka
The Buddhist revival in Nepal
The Buddhist revival in Bangladesh
Buddhist nuns
The revival of the *Bhikkhunī* order in Sri Lanka
The revival of Buddhist nuns in Nepal
Buddhist activism
Ambedkar Buddhism
Buddhist development in Sri Lanka
Tibetan Buddhism in South Asia
Lay Buddhist practice

By the beginning of the twentieth century, many Buddhists in South Asia were confronting the modernizing forces of science and western political ideologies that colonial powers had introduced into their cultures. In Sri Lanka, where the colonial intrusion had been intensive since the late sixteenth century, Buddhists such as the Anagārika Dharmapāla responded by seeking to revive the religion along modern lines. This Buddhist revival, which had started in the latter part of the nineteenth century, gained steam in the twentieth century. Dharmapāla and other like-minded reformers sought to promote Buddhism as a uniquely rational and appropriate religion for the modern age. Such a message was appealing to an emerging urban middle class, which had received a western education and had been exposed to western values and religion. In a manner that imitated certain aspects of Protestant Christianity, yet also protested against the influence of its missionaries, this form of Buddhist Modernism (or "Protestant Buddhism") encouraged the laypeople to permeate their lives with Buddhism, and to make Buddhism permeate their society (Gombrich and Obeyesekere 1988: 216).

This new ethos, whereby daily life became more infused with Buddhist practices and symbols, was an important aspect of the modernization of Buddhism. Laypersons were encouraged to participate actively in the religion through textual study and meditation. Whereas in earlier centuries most Buddhist laypersons did little of either, focusing instead on giving offerings to shrines and alms to monks, from the twentieth century onward a diffuse movement arose to encourage the laity to pattern their lives and their society after Buddhist moral values. Some of these values, however, appear to have been modeled more after certain characteristics of Protestant Christianity—e.g., thrift, hard work, social welfare activity—than those traditionally highlighted in premodern Buddhist contexts (Gombrich and Obeyesekere 1988: 231–2). Theravāda texts from the Pāli Canon were identified as the primary sources for knowledge about Buddhism. And English translations of Buddhist scriptures became highly valued, since the laity trained in British-style schools obtained access to what was held to be the authoritative word of the Buddha. And with knowledge of the Dharma, even laypeople could aspire to attain the highest goal of *nirvāṇa* in this very life.

Buddhist Modernism developed along different lines according to where and when it arose. Broadly speaking, however, the introduction of modern values and technologies through encounters between Asian Buddhists and westerners spurred efforts to adopt such values and technologies for the sake of strengthening and spreading Buddhism. Some westerners made positive contributions to the Buddhist religion. For instance, Colonel Olcott, the American Theosophist, assisted in the Buddhist revival by founding Buddhist schools and proposing a *Buddhist Catechism* to instruct the laity in Buddhist doctrine. Other westerners, particularly missionaries, often expressed unfavorable views of Buddhism. A common strategy among western scholars and observers in the nineteenth century was to draw a sharp contrast between the simple, rational Buddhism that appears in texts and the idolatrous and corrupt Buddhism as practiced by contemporary Asians (Harris 2006: 114–15). This dichotomy, which favored ancient texts over contemporary practices, came to influence modern Buddhist reformers as well. Dharmapāla, for one, decried the rural superstitions of Buddhist villagers in favor of preaching sermons on the Dharma (*dharmadēśanā*) and moral development (Seneviratne 1999: 47). Ancient texts came to typify the models for daily Buddhist practice, whereas popular village rituals and the worship of deities were denigrated as superstitious and extraneous to the rational core of the Buddha's teachings.

Positive assessments of early Buddhist literature by western scholars left a strong mark on South Asian Buddhists. At the level of doctrine, Buddhists could argue that their texts were equally if not more rational and consistent with scientific thought than the texts of Christians. Dharmapāla sought to rehabilitate the status and legitimacy of Buddhism by stressing its rational, scientific nature, which he claimed made it perfectly suited for the modern age (McMahan 2004: 907–8). While Sri Lankans and other Buddhists could not compete with western military and economic power, they could still lay claims to moral and intellectual superiority as adherents of a religion that rejects alcohol, beef-eating, violence, and irrational faith in supernatural powers. Buddhist modernists thus argued that ancient Buddhist texts were actually compatible with modern scientific thought, implying that Buddhists stress the rational and empirical verification of truth, unlike the adherents of religions that relied on "blind faith" and "superstitions" derived from allegedly divinely revealed texts. The rhetorical move to argue for the rational superiority of Buddhism had the effect of flipping charges of superstition that were once leveled at Buddhists back on to the foreigners who initially leveled them. Buddhism was represented as a rational, this-worldly religion directed toward attaining *nirvāṇa* in this life, while privileging personal spiritual attainments over collective merit-making rituals (Harris 2006: 168). This reinterpretation of Buddhism, in turn, set the stage for numerous revivals of the religion in twentieth-century South Asia.

Modern Buddhist revivals

Buddhist nationalism in Sri Lanka

A crucial aspect of Dharmapāla's project was the combination of religious reform and cultural reaffirmation. According to Dharmapāla, by giving more emphasis to the modernist roots of the Buddhist religion, Sinhala Buddhists could develop the basis for a strong, independent nation alongside other modern nations. In Dharmapāla's view, European colonialism had diminished the vitality of the Buddha's *sāsana* and undermined Sinhala culture. Writing on the virtues of Buddhism and the Sinhala people around 1897, Dharmapāla explicitly linked the survival of both over against colonial rule.

> A people who had created a literature, whose history dates back 2,400 years, whose accounts have been verified and corroborated to the very letter two thousand years later by the researches of European orientalists and archaeologists in deciphering Asoka inscriptions; who had made known their civilization by sending their embassies to China, Rome, and Egypt, who sent their women to Tibet to establish the order of Nuns; who had never been drunkards or murderers, are now, under British rule, a slavish people, victims of drunkenness and many western vices. But Buddhism still survives and it is due to her influence alone that the Sinhalese have not met with the fate of the Tasmanian, the African savage, or the North American Indian. When the day of reckoning arrives, England will have to answer for the many unjust things that she has done

in destroying the independence of a people who had maintained a noble and peaceful independence for 2,300 years.

(Guruge 1991: 207–8)

From the perspective of Dharmapāla, the European colonialists undermined the moral character of Sinhala Buddhists, since they robbed them of their political independence. The Buddha's *sāsana* appears here as the source of Sinhala pride and civilization. With Buddhism, the Sinhalas could feel confident of their capacity for self-rule. And to the extent that the British weakened Buddhism and the morality of the Sinhalas, colonial rule appeared increasingly unjust and immoral.

In between his travels to India and other parts of the globe, Dharmapāla also wrote articles and spoke out at public gatherings around the island of Sri Lanka during the early twentieth century. His calls for reforming Buddhism were accompanied by appeals to restore national pride and denunications of western influences in Sri Lanka. Dharmapāla's critique of colonial rule typically included a rejection of British moral authority. In the eyes of early Buddhist nationalists, the British fell short of demonstrating that they were fit to govern the island, since they failed to provide adequate support to Buddhist institutions and since they condoned selling alcohol and eating beef. Moreover, nationalist claims about the innate "rationality" of the Buddha's original teachings and the "scientific" orientation of the religion as a whole reinforced their position that Sinhala Buddhists were fit to govern a modern state by themselves (Gokhale 1999: 39). This line of argumentation is significant since it connected political and economic agendas with moral and religious ones. Nationalist calls for independence and cultural revival were thus linked to calls for reforming and reviving the Buddhist religion.

Dharmapāla was instrumental in developing Buddhist nationalism in Sri Lanka. He called on Buddhist monks to lead a twofold program of economic and cultural regeneration that would uplift both Buddhism and the nation. In his vision, monks should go outside of the monasteries and preach a form of Buddhism that emphasized moral restraint while rejecting theism and ritual superstition. Specifically, monks should tell villagers how to follow proper Buddhist conduct, which would lead to a higher morality and a higher standard of life for all (Seneviratne 1999: 37). Abiding by Buddhist norms, in other words, would make Sinhalas more energetic in work and thrifty in their spending, giving rise to increased wealth and less poverty in the country. Dharmapāla, and numerous Sinhala nationalists after him, equated colonialism with efforts to undermine Buddhist morality. This, it was feared, would make the Sinhalas more accepting of western culture and more dependent on British rule. Dharmapāla and others decried the tendencies of some Sinhalas to "ape" British customs by wearing western dress, adopting western names, and devaluing their traditional language and religion.

The Buddhist nationalist program relied on new, more vigorous forms of communication to mobilize people in a religious and cultural revival. For example, a novel method of preaching was developed. These new sermons on the Dharma (*dharmadēśanā*) were initially pitched to the urban middle class, a group that sought more instruction in Buddhist doctrine in response to the attention given to doctrine by Christian missionaries. A new temple in Colombo called Vajirārāma" was founded with the aim of promoting Buddhist doctrine and practice to the urban laity. A monk called Palane Vajiragñāna (1878–1955) was named the chief incumbent of the temple, and he put many of Dharmapāla's ideas into action by preaching concise sermons that related Buddhism to people's daily lives (Seneviratne 1999: 53). Whereas most other monks continued to preach in traditional ways, emphasizing the importance of earning merit to attain good rebirths, the Vajirārama monks sought to show how Buddhism could be adopted to fit the needs and interests of modern life. The focus on what Buddhism has to offer in the present world reflected a response to Christian missionary critiques that the religion was unresponsive to people's immediate needs.

Subsequent generations of monks in the twentieth century tended to pick up different aspects of Dharmapāla's program for national and religious revival. In the 1930s, while the country was still under British colonial rule, monks associated with the Vidyodaya *pirivena*, or monastic college, spearheaded a village development program that combined Buddhist morality with economic assistance. Ven. Kalukondayave Paññasekhara (1896–1977) was particularly instrumental in leading the efforts to revive village life, calling for monks like him to guide the economic and religious development in the countryside. Kalukondayave developed a program that revolved around economic development, crime eradication, and abstinence from alcohol to create a harmonious and prosperous village community (Seneviratne 1999: 71). The goal of economic regeneration formed one plank in Dharmapāla's program for national and religious revival. Kalukondayave and his monastic colleagues dedicated themselves to the uplift of the villagers' current lives, as they felt that the Saṅgha must serve society and alleviate social ills in the present world rather than focus exclusively on facilitating a positive rebirth in the next world (Seneviratne 1999: 66–7). This call for monks to serve Sri Lankan society in both material and spiritual ways paved the way for the reinterpretation of the monastic vocation along more worldly lines.

While leading monks associated with Vidyodaya focused their efforts on the economic regeneration of village life, the monks affiliated with the Vidyālaṅkāra *pirivena*, which was another large monastic college near Colombo, came to emphasize Dharmapāla's program for cultural revival. In the 1940s, the Vidyālaṅkāra monks began to assert the need for monks to lead a national revival of Sinhala culture and religion. From this perspective, centuries of colonial rule had weakened the vitality of Buddhism and traditional Sinhala culture. These monks were swept up in the nationalist opposition to colonial rule, and they expressed their frustration with the British and the conservative Sinhala elites who began to assume political leadership in the years prior to Independence in 1948. Notable leaders of the move by some monks to claim a prominent place in political discourse include Walpola Rāhula (1907–97), a scholar-monk who did a Ph.D. in Sri Lanka and post-doctoral work at the University of Paris-Sorbonne. Rāhula published the renowned modernist Buddhist treatise *What the Buddha Taught* in 1959, but his earlier works would be more influential in Sri Lanka for arguing that Buddhist monks have traditionally engaged in social service to protect Sri Lanka and Buddhism.

Rāhula published *The Heritage of the Bhikkhu* (*Bhikṣuvagē Urumaya*) in Sinhala in 1946, just as the nationalist movement had picked up steam in Sri Lanka. This particular text argued for the restoration of the monk's social role prior to the colonial era wherein he allegedly occupied a critical role in ensuring a righteous society in partnership with a just Buddhist king (Seneviratne 1999: 136). Taken together with a number of other works published by him and other monks such as Yakkaduve Pragnārama, *The Heritage of the Bhikkhu* presented an image of the Sinhala Buddhist monk as a tireless advocate for the Buddha *sāsana* and for the maintenance of the customs and wellbeing of the Sinhala people. Rāhula argued that prior to foreign domination, monks were always active in protecting the country and the religion, even advising kings on how to rule effectively and righteously (Rāhula 1974: 50–1). In Rāhula's view, Buddhist monks should be equipped with a modern education in order to best serve efforts to revive Sinhala Buddhism, Sinhala culture, and the Sinhala language.

According to Rāhula and other Buddhist nationalists, centuries of foreign domination threatened to displace and erase traditional Sinhala life as lived in the home, at the temple, and in the paddy fields. He accused missionaries of not only displacing monks in their traditional social and welfare activities in society, but also of teaching Sinhala children in their schools to despise Buddhist culture (Rāhula 1974: 90–1). Herein lay a critique of Sinhala elites who abandoned Sinhala culture in the rush to adopt Western dress and customs. Speaking English and adopting Christianity were seen as two striking instances of the rejection of Sinhala culture. Thus, in a manner similar to Dharmapāla's calls to resist foreign influences and to revive Sinhala Buddhist culture, Rāhula and other Buddhist nationalists linked the Buddhist revival to the creation of a prosperous and morally righteous state in the years immediately preceding and following Independence in 1948.

This vision of the new Sri Lankan state, which was called "Ceylon" up to 1972, depended on efforts to restore the privileged position of Buddhism and the Sinhala people as the majority religion and community. Boosted by texts such as the *Mahāvaṃsa*, which long ago asserted that the island was destined to be where the Buddha's Dharma and *sāsana* would be preserved, Buddhist nationalists argued that the country had the utmost duty to protect and promote the religion. Many politicians from 1956 onwards reiterated this ideological stance by offering their public support for Buddhism and the Saṅgha in speeches and in visible displays of ritual offerings.

While not everyone in Sri Lanka was—or still is—comfortable with the monkhood assuming the mantle of political activism, nationalist calls for promoting Buddhism and for governing the state in accordance with Buddhist principles appeal to many Sinhalas. In response, some centrist politicians have portrayed "political monks" as unethical and undisciplined, constructing instead an image of "apolitical Buddhism" as the only legitimate form of religious expression (Abeysekara 2002: 97–102). This tension over the proper roles of Buddhist monks in Sri Lanka amounts to an ongoing contest to define what is "Buddhist" and what is not in society. And while the status and conduct of so-called "political monks" remains controversial in Sri Lanka, there have been numerous monks following Rāhula who advocate on behalf of Buddhism and the Sinhala people in the political sphere. The main problem with this activity is that it has also marginalized the country's religious and ethnic minorities. When Sinhala-dominated parties began to assert their collective strength over parties formed to represent the Tamil minority, more extremist elements in the Tamil community began to call for solutions ranging from federalism to a separate Tamil state. Militant groups, most notably the separatist rebels called the Liberation Tigers of Tamil Eelam (LTTE), formed to fight for an independent Tamil state in the north and the east of the island. Buddhist nationalists (including monks) have led the opposition to the separatist claims, often rejecting peace negotiations and various political compromises designed to bring an end to a devastating civil war that began in 1983.

Sinhala Buddhist nationalism has been fomented by the writings and speeches of nationalistic monks beginning from the 1940s and continuing up to the present. Their grievances about the harm suffered by the religion and the monkhood under colonial rule and foreign missionary activity have some basis in fact. Nevertheless, the politicization of the Saṅgha in Sri Lanka has also led to some negative effects in public perceptions of monks and in the efforts to promote cultural and religious harmony in a modern democratic state. The more pernicious forms of Buddhist nationalist ideology hold that Sri Lanka should only be for Sinhala Buddhists, and that foreign non-governmental organizations (NGOs) and missionaries are complicit with the

Figure 6.1 Sri Lankan Buddhist monks take part in a peaceful protest (Lakruwan Wanniarachchl/ AFP/Getty Images).

LTTE in trying to break up and divide the state (DeVotta 2007: 3). Activist monks who have inherited the cultural revivalist programs of Dharmapāla and Rāhula have been known to advocate their positions in sermons, public speeches, and protest marches in Sri Lanka. Such nationalists continue to link Buddhism and the Sinhala nation as inseparable entities that form the basis for the Sri Lankan state. Their support for this notion led the government to declare in its Constitution that Buddhism has the foremost place among religions recognized in Sri Lanka.

The country's inconsistent economy and partisan disputes have at times overshadowed nationalist calls to strengthen Buddhism in the island. At other times, however, the voices of Sinhala Buddhist nationalists have had an influential effect on the country's politics and public debates. Ven. Gangodawila Soma (1948–2003), for example, emerged in the late 1990s as a prominent critic of Tamil separatism and foreign influences in the forms of NGOs and missionaries in Sri Lankan society. Soma continued many of the cultural revivalist themes of his Buddhist nationalist predecessors. He was renowned for his television programs and newspaper columns advocating the values and practices of the "pure" Buddhist Dharma in order to reverse generations of cultural and religious decline in the island (Berkwitz 2008: 77–8). His writings and sermons in Sinhala often contained harsh critiques of the country's politicians.

> Since the national leaders have no understanding about *karma* and the fruits of *karma*, having wicked thoughts on account of their lust for political power, they engage in an evil course of action and cause the decline of the state and of the welfare of everyone. The Buddha preached a sermon saying that when the king is unrighteous, the entire kingdom and its inhabitants arrive at suffering. He spoke thus for the sake of showing how disasters arise due to the false views of national rulers.
>
> We know well the results of the action taken by the government. However powerful a king may be, if one accounts for the fruits of the unwholesome actions he has done, that power is worthless.
>
> (Soma 2002: 40–1)

Soma's denunciation of Sri Lanka's political leaders was a bold use of his moral authority as a monk to speak out against powerful laypersons who failed to govern the state righteously and in accordance with Buddhist principles.

Aided by his exceptional reputation for monastic discipline and knowledge of the Dharma, Soma called upon Sinhala Buddhists to strengthen their commitment to Buddhist morality as the basis for protecting the nation and regenerating the island's economy. His Buddhist nationalist discourse blamed "false views" and "wicked conduct" among Sinhala Buddhists, including the use of alcohol and cigarettes, as the chief cause for moral and national decline, as evidenced by increasing poverty, rising divorce rates, and smaller families among Sinhalas (Berkwitz 2008: 94–5). He used humor and sarcasm to great effect, attempting to persuade Buddhists to work together in creating a righteous state. His efforts to recombine the economic and cultural agendas in Dharmapāla's nationalist program involved founding the Janavijaya Foundation to engage in social welfare and rural development work, as well as impassioned political critiques and even hints that he might one day run for President.

Soma's sudden death in 2003, reportedly due to a heart attack but subject to rumors of foul play, made him into a kind of martyr for the Buddhist nationalist cause. His history of denouncing Christian missionary work in Sri Lanka led some of his sympathizers to vandalize churches and issue threats to pastors and parishioners in various parts of the island following his death. Meanwhile, in the spring of 2004, a number of nationalist-minded monks formed a new political party called Jathika Hela Urumaya (National Sinhala Heritage) to campaign formally against alleged "unethical conversions" arranged by missionaries, to oppose a peace settlement with the LTTE as mediated by the Norwegian government, to combat widespread corruption in politics and society, and to revive the Sinhala Buddhist heritage of the country (DeVotta and Stone 2008: 37). The efforts by the JHU to nominate over 260 candidates for the local parliamentary election in April 2004 represented a stunning, unprecedented step for Sri Lankan monks in politics. The substantial number of votes received by the JHU surprised many observers. For the first time, nine monks representing an all-monk political party were elected to the country's parliament. Specific party aims involving the passing of legislation to criminalize "unethical conversions," to pressure the government to promote Buddhist principles and to monitor closely the activities of various NGOs in the island were presented as steps toward the formation of a "righteous state" (*dharmarājya*) (Deegalle 2004: 94–5). Whether the JHU can preserve party unity and maintain the respect of a Buddhist laity that remains unaccustomed to seeing monks participate in the often immoral realm of politics remains to be seen.

Despite the vocal calls of some Buddhist monks for the government to promote the interests of the religion and the Sinhala community, there remains a wide spectrum of opinion on the validity of Buddhist nationalism and the role of monks within it. Contrary to media reports and the claims of the LTTE separatists, not all monks support the ethnic exclusivism found in some of the more extreme examples of Sinhala Buddhist nationalism. Some monks have openly criticized their monastic brethren in the JHU, while others avoid partisan politics by focusing either on social welfare projects or on their religious duties. In short, there is a plurality of ideas among monks regarding "political Buddhism" as advocated by Rāhula, with numerous monks opposed to the ideology that legitimates political action among monks and that extols a military solution to the ethnic conflict (De Silva 1998: 61–8).

The Buddhist revival in Nepal

Meanwhile, in twentieth-century Nepal, there have been similar efforts to revive the Buddhist religion, albeit without government support. As seen in the previous chapter, the restrictions on the practice and spread of Buddhism by the ruling Rana dynasty limited the opportunities for the growth and development of the religion. Much like the Gorkhali rulers that they succeeded, the Ranas envisioned Nepal as a Hindu state, and they promoted conceptions of citizenship based on the observance of Hindu moral statutes that reinforced loyalty to the king and stability in society. Tamangs and other ethnic groups that practiced Tibetan forms of Buddhism continued to do so through the Rana period. However, Newar Buddhists living in the Kathmandu Valley in cities like Lalitpur and Kathmandu experienced pressure to submit to state demands and take up the performance of certain Hindu rituals while conforming, at least in theory, to the view that since the Buddha was an incarnation of Viṣṇu, Buddhism was a Hindu sect.

Nevertheless, Newar Buddhists continued to employ *vajrācārya* family priests to perform life-cycle and protective rituals. And the complex patterns of Buddhist Tantric and devotional rituals were largely sustained among Newars, even if many of them also participated concurrently in Hindu rites. A Newar cultural renaissance began in the early twentieth century, which included public readings in Nepali of the ancient Buddha-biography called *Lalitavistara*. Increased interest in Lumbini, the site of the Buddha's birth in Nepal, contributed to efforts to revive Buddhism in the country. At the same time, however, several events in the early twentieth century combined to undermine Newar support for the traditional practices of Vajrayāna Buddhism. A Tibetan teacher named Kyangtse Lama came to the Kathmandu Valley on a pilgrimage in 1925, and his teachings were translated into Nepali before huge crowds who were interested and impressed with this pious and knowledgeable monk (LeVine and Gellner 2005: 38–9). Resentment toward this foreign monk among local *vajrācārya* priests led the latter to reproach and punish the Newar Buddhist laity for supporting Kyangtse Lama. The subsequent refusal of *vajrācārya* priests to accept rice in the homes of Uday caste families caused some members of the Buddhist laity to become disenchanted with the *vajrācārya*s and more interested in patronizing the first generations of Newar Theravāda monks (LeVine and Gellner 2005: 39–40).

The ordination of the Newar novices Mahapragya and Pragyananda by the Burmese monk Candramaṇi at Kuśinagara in India was the first step toward a Theravāda revival in Nepal. These two monks eventually returned to Kathmandu and appeared as a new type of Buddhist monastic for the Newar community. A year later in 1931, three Newar widows from the Uday caste walked from Kathmandu to Kuśinagara to seek ordination from Chandramaṇi. Unable to ordain nuns without the presence of ordained *bhikkhunī*s, he in turn administered the Ten Precepts to them, enabling them to adopt the status of female renunciants in the Theravāda tradition (LeVine and Gellner 2005: 45–6). Most of the early monks, novices, and nuns from Nepal were initiated by him, although they were also encouraged to continue their studies in Burma or Sri Lanka (Kloppenborg 1977: 305). Growth in Theravāda was slow in Nepal, and it suffered a reversal when the few monks were expelled by the Rana government in 1944. Among the exiles, the Newar monk Amritānanda enlisted the help of Ven. Nārada of the Vajirārāma temple in Sri Lanka to arrange for the Newar monks to be permitted to return to Nepal (LeVine and Gellner 2005: 48). Nārada persuaded the Ranas that the Theravāda monks were pursuing religious rather than political aims, and thus the Newar monks were allowed to return in 1946. On their return, the Theravāda monks set out to establish their community in the Valley, requesting their supporters to build them a dwelling called Ananda Kuti. Nārada visited in 1947, bringing a Buddha relic and a sapling from the Bodhi Tree to help establish the Ananda Kuti as the new headquarters of Theravāda in Nepal (LeVine and Gellner 2005: 50).

Theravāda in Nepal, like Newar Vajrayāna and the Tibetan forms practiced by other ethnic communities outside the Valley, was constrained by restrictions that prohibited the conversion of Hindus. In addition, Theravāda received little state support and had to rely almost exclusively on their patrons among the Newar laity. In their favor was the fact that the Newar monks had been exposed to the modernist strands of Theravāda from Dharmapāla's Maha Bodhi Society and from temples in Sri Lanka and Burma. The monks adopted the discourse that privileged the antiquity and the rationalism of Theravāda Buddhism. They were also trained to engage the laity in social service and to exhort them in moral conduct deemed relevant for modern life. The processes associated with modernity in Nepal during the latter half of the twentieth century have also resulted in a loss of prestige and support for traditional *vajrācārya* priests. In general, these family priests are called upon less frequently to perform domestic rites, the payments for their services are too meager to convince the sons of priests to take up their family's traditional occupation, and the introduction of modern education has exposed Newars to western scholarship that often associates Theravāda with the Buddha's original message (Gellner 1992: 333–5). The ritual demands and caste-consciousness of the *vajrācārya*s' religion has become less attractive next to what the modernist form of Theravāda offers.

Because Theravāda appears more "modern" and perhaps progressive to a growing number of Newar Buddhists, the traditional rites of Vajrayāna in Nepal have become more difficult to maintain. It is certain that most Newar Buddhists continue to seek out assistance from *vajrācārya* priests to perform obligatory rites and to offer the means to acquire merit and blessings for protection from harm. The ritual chanting of the *Pañcarakṣa* text by *vajrācārya* priests is a common example of how the traditional Vajrayāna religion is employed to protect one's homes from disasters, while the five protective deities associated with the text are frequently worshipped for divine aid (Lewis 2000: 154–5). At the same time, modern pressures appear to be undermining the traditions of Newar Vajrayāna Buddhism. This form of Buddhism appears more ritualistic and hierarchical, and its Sanskrit texts are in general less accessible to ordinary Newars than the Theravāda writings available in English, Nepali, and Newari (Gellner 1992: 335). Efforts to improve the education of *vajrācārya* priests are under way, but it remains to be seen how successful these will be in attracting young priests and in improving their abilities to understand and perform the rites.

Although Nepal remains known as a Hindu country, there is an undercurrent of a Buddhist revival, particularly with respect to Theravāda.

Political changes including the abolition of the monarchy in the spring of 2008 and the strength of the Communists may open up greater opportunities for the development of Buddhism in what may eventually become a more secular state. Improved Buddhist education and more opportunities for lay practice in the form of meditation centers and social activism promises to contribute to the growth of Buddhism in Nepal.

The Buddhist revival in Bangladesh

Buddhism has had a long history in the region of East Bengal, now known as the modern state of Bangladesh. Although the exact date of its introduction is unknown, there is evidence of thriving Buddhist communities in East Bengal in the early centuries of the Common Era. Chinese pilgrims in the seventh century noted the existence of monasteries with numerous monks in this region (Chaudhuri 1982: 5-7). The proximity of East Bengal to the center of the Pāla dynasty in northeast India meant that its Buddhist communities received patronage and were exposed to Tantric practices. Buddhists survived in East Bengal long after the religion virtually disappeared elsewhere in India, due to its location at the margins of Muslim rule and its proximity to the Buddhist kingdom of Arakan to the southeast. While most inhabitants were converted to Islam, some Hindus and Buddhists retained their religious identities, with Buddhists concentrated in the southeast Chittagong region and adjacent Chittagong Hill Tracts.

In the eighteenth century, when East Bengal came under British colonial rule, the Buddhists enjoyed more freedom to own land, earn money, and build temples. And in 1795, the kingdom of Arakan was annexed by the Burmese king Bodawpaya, initiating the first of a series of waves of Arakanese Buddhists who came to Chittagong to escape the violent subjugation of their kingdom by the Burmese.

Although Buddhists were more numerous and better off by the nineteenth century, many people felt that it was necessary to revive the tradition. Buddhism in East Bengal had become a heterogeneous collection of Tantric, Hindu, and Theravāda practices. A leading monk from Arakan, the Saṅgharaj Sāramedha Mahāthera (1801-82) was invited to Chittagong in 1856, whereupon he began preaching and encouraging Buddhists to give up worshipping Hindu deities and making animal sacrifices (Chaudhuri 1982: 32-3). He was invited into the Chakma kingdom in the Chittagong Hill Tracts, where he converted the local Queen and her subjects to this purer form of Theravāda. Sāramedha made a return visit to Chittagong in 1864, accompanied by other monks to administer the *upasampadā* ordination to those who sought it. Many monks were thus re-ordained under Sāramedha in a new monastic lineage called the Saṅgharaj Nikāya. His disciples undertook efforts to purify and spread Theravāda around the region, while some traveled to study in Sri Lanka and Burma.

Buddhists in contemporary Bangladesh generally fall into three communities, all of whom favor Theravāda. The Baruas make up the largest group and are the descendents of longstanding Buddhist communities from northern India and East Bengal. The Chakmas, who reside in the Hill Tracts, have also practiced Buddhism in the region for several centuries. The Marmas are mainly the descendents of later Arakanese refugees. Each community contributes monks to the Saṅgha, and the laity supports and venerates them along with the Buddha. As a religious minority of about 1% of the population, Buddhists in Bangladesh must coexist with the Muslim majority. The recent rise of local Islamist groups has led to increased harassment of Buddhists, Christians, and Hindus. Under pressure from economic hardship, religious intimidation, and the construction of the Kaptai dam that displaced around 100,000 Chakmas between 1957-1963, many Bangladeshi Buddhists have left the country. Some monks have relocated to parts of northern India, where they are establishing Theravāda temples and Buddhist communities anew.

Buddhist nuns

The revival of the *Bhikkhunī* order in Sri Lanka

A noteworthy aspect of Buddhist modernism in South Asia is the revival of Buddhist "nuns" in Sri Lanka and Nepal. As noted above, the *bhikkhunī* order appears to have died out in Sri Lanka around the eleventh century, and a different order of nuns in Nepal likely died out around the same time. The decline of Buddhism in India probably contributed to these events, although in the case of Sri Lanka, efforts to reintroduce Theravāda nuns from abroad were apparently not made. Thus, for the better part of a millennium, South Asian Buddhist women were prevented from adopting an institutionally recognized role as female renunciants. However, among the efforts made to revive Buddhism in the latter part of the nineteenth century there were endeavors to train women to assume roles as Buddhist teachers and "Ten Precept Mothers" (*dasa sil mātā*).

After centuries of the absence of Theravāda nuns in Sri Lanka, communities of female Buddhist renunciants begin to reappear in the island during the 1890s. The Anagārika Dharmapāla encouraged and organized women at this time to renounce lay life and to serve in reviving Buddhism (Bartholomeusz 1994: 10). He envisioned pious Buddhist women helping to lead efforts to preach the Dharma and to assist in promoting Buddhist morality. Significantly, such women were not encouraged to become full-fledged *bhikkhunīs*, as their disappearance in Theravāda lands made such a proposition appear unlikely if not impossible to Dharmapāla and other reformers. The women who adopted the status of female renunciants were encouraged to do so for the sake of social service rather than to obtain *nirvāṇa*. The first female Buddhist renunciants in Sri Lanka at the turn of the twentieth century were generally presumed to have the duty of educating Sinhala children in the Dharma. These women were ascribed with the status of a "lay nun" who lacks the formal, higher ordination into the monastic order. Nevertheless, such lay nuns observed the Ten Training Precepts of novice nuns, shaved their heads, and donned robes to signify their enhanced religious status. They renounced many of the normal features of lay life, and yet they remained somewhat ambiguously within this sphere since they could not (until recently) be ordained in an *upasampadā* ceremony.

Dharmapāla was assisted in his efforts to establish a community of female Buddhist renunciants by some sympathetic western women. He recruited an American woman named Countess Miranda de Souza Canavarro, a Theosophist who had been married to a Portuguese diplomat, to help him establish a cloister for female renunciants wherein meditation, service and the revival of Buddhism structured their daily activities (Bartholomeusz 1994: 10). The education of female lay nuns was held to prepare them to teach and distill Buddhist knowledge while promoting traditional culture. Although the "Countess" had numerous personality conflicts with Dharmapāla, the two combined to create a lay nunnery (*upāsikārāmaya*) out of the Saṅghamittā School for girls in 1898. The activities of the "sisters" at the Saṅghamittā Upāsikārāmaya reflected a "this-worldly" asceticism and included meditation, ministering to the needs of the laity, and taking counsel from learned teachers (Bartholomeusz 1994: 71). Among those teachers was Dharmapāla himself, as he made frequent visits to the nunnery and advised the sisters on moral discipline. However, internal conflicts and a general lack of support led to the closure of the Saṅghamittā Upāsikārāmaya soon after it was founded.

A few years later another, more successful attempt to establish a community of female renunciants took place. A Sinhala woman named Catherine de Alwis (1849–1939), a Christian convert to Buddhism after the death of her parents, was influenced by some lay Burmese nuns in Sri Lanka and traveled to Burma, where she received more instruction in the Dharma and was ordained as a lay nun by a female renunciant in Rangoon. When she returned to Sri Lanka in 1905, she partnered with some other lay supporters to acquire the land in Kandy where she established the Sudharmā Upāsikārāmaya around 1906. De Alwis had taken the name Sudharmā after her ordination as a lay nun, and she worked to establish a community of *upāsikās* who observed the Ten Precepts and contributed to the Buddhist education of women (Bartholomeusz 1994: 94). Her lay nunnery was later called Lady Blake's Upāsikārāmaya, after the generous support given by the wife of the British Governor at the time. Sudharmā's community succeeded where the Countess's had failed, due in large part to the support it received from social elites and the relative lack of infighting among its leaders. Lady Blake's Upāsikārāmaya in Kandy became home to young and old lay nuns, and originally there was no expressed interest in obtaining higher ordination as a *bhikkhunī*. This lay nunnery remains open in the twenty-first century, although its women today generally come from lower classes and lack the status and support once enjoyed by their predecessors (Bartholomeusz 1994: 107).

The Buddhist lay nuns in twentieth-century Sri Lanka generally occupied a paradoxical position between that of an ordinary pious laywoman and that of a full-fledged nun. The lack of certainty about their identity has resulted in different appellations and a lack of uniformity in terms of their moral practice. Described earlier as "sisters," "nuns," or "*upāsikā*s," these female renunciants gradually adopted the term "Ten Precept Mother" (*dasa sil mātā* or *dasa sil mäniyo*) for themselves (Bartholomeusz 1994: 142). This title represents a neologism that does not appear in older Buddhist literature or epigraphy. However, it connotes that some of these female renunciants have been ordained under the Ten Lay Precepts that are taken by some householders on Buddhist full-moon days, which comprise days of heightened religious significance and observance in Sri Lanka. Other female renunciants are ordained in the ten monastic precepts of a novice under the tutelage of senior *dasa sil mātā* (Salgado 2000: 32). Still, some other women are ordained as *upāsikā*s or are self-ordained. All female renunciants effectively adopt the status of a lay nun who observes moral precepts on a permanent rather than temporary basis, as other laypersons would do. They shave their heads and wear robes, often in a yellow color that differs from the common orange of the monks' robes. Until recently, many lay nuns expressed little interest in seeking higher ordination as *bhikkhunī*s, as this would subordinate them to the authority of monks (Bartholomeusz 1994: 136).

Since the late 1980s, however, women's attitudes toward receiving higher ordination have begun to change. Interest in reviving the Theravāda *bhikkhunī* order appeared after the country's Independence in 1948. Again, this support came mainly from progressive lay Buddhist leaders rather than monks, as many Theravāda monks objected to the resuscitation of the *bhikkhunī*s by means of an ordination performed by Mahāyāna nuns from East Asia. The more conservative view held that the re-establishment of the *bhikkhunī* order was impossible since there were no existing Theravāda *bhikkhunī*s who could administer the ceremony and confirm the ordination.

In theory, according to the dominant readings of the Theravāda monastic code, the ordination of new *bhikkhunī*s depended on the presence of older *bhikkhunī*s. The use of nuns from China and Taiwan to ordain Sinhala nuns into the Theravāda was controversial due to the formers' Mahāyāna associations. With their ordination lineage in doubt, the presence of fully ordained *bhikkhunī*s in saffron-colored robes caused controversy in some circles. But lay nuns, who were modeled after Christian nuns and expected to perform social service for the benefit of society and the religion, were broadly acceptable in Sri Lankan society. Equivalent to female novices, however, these women generally received less alms and lay support than monks, as the latter's higher status made them stronger fields of merit according to many lay donors.

Nevertheless, Sri Lankan women have increasingly been able to view the *bhikkhunī* higher ordination (*upasampadā*) as a realistic alternative to being a lay nun. In 1988, under the guidance of the Sri Lankan monk Havenpola Ratanasāra, five Sri Lankan women were ordained as *bhikkhunī*s in Los Angeles before a group of Theravāda and Mahāyāna monks and a group of Mahāyāna nuns from Taiwan. The Sri Lankan monks in America have more liberal views of female ordination than many of their co-religionists back in Sri Lanka. Believing that *bhikkhunī*s are necessary for the propagation of Buddhism in America, and that the continued refusal to ordain women would only harm the religion's reputation in the West, these expatriate monks decided to hold a new ordination ceremony in order to re-establish the order of Theravāda *bhikkhunī*s (Bartholomeusz 1994: 187–8). Moreover, the historical evidence suggesting that Chinese nuns were first ordained by Sri Lankan nuns in 434 CE is held by sympathetic monks to justify the use of Chinese nuns in the modern *bhikkhunī* higher ordination ceremony. As it turned out, however, the women ordained in America have not actively pursued efforts to live as *bhikkhunī*s or to ordain more women (Bartholomeusz 1994: 182–6).

Later, in 1996, several Sri Lankan *dasa sil mātā* traveled to Sarnath, India to be ordained in another *bhikkhunī upasampadā* ceremony conducted by Korean monks and nuns in cooperation with the Maha Bodhi Society in India. This event caused a great deal of controversy and protest back in Sri Lanka since the women were widely seen to have been ordained into a Korean Mahāyāna tradition (Bhadra 2001: 25–6). However, the ordained Sri Lankan nuns settled down in Sarnath, and so the controversy died down in Sri Lanka. This event motivated several female renunciants and monks to begin drafting plans to reintroduce the *bhikkhunī* lineage in Sri Lanka. An organization led by Ven. Inamaluwe Sumaṅgala, abbot of the Dambulla Golden Temple, was formed to educate female novices in an institute at the Dambulla Temple. Then on March 12, 1998, after welcoming the Sri

Lankan nuns who had been ordained the previous month in Bodh Gaya, India, Ven. Sumaṅgala hosted an *upasampadā* ceremony, in the presence of monks and nuns from Sri Lanka and Taiwan, for the female renunciants trained at his institute (Bhadra 2001: 27). Although there continue to be Sri Lankan monastics and laypersons who reject the legitimacy of that ceremony, those who support the new order of nuns recognize this event as the formal re-introduction of Theravāda *bhikkhunī*s in Sri Lanka. Since that time, the Dambulla Temple has held several higher ordination ceremonies for *bhikkhunī*s and other ceremonies to initiate novice nuns. The numbers of Sri Lankan *bhikkhunī*s continues to grow steadily, with around a few hundred *bhikkhunī*s recognized in Sri Lanka by the middle of the first decade of the twenty-first century.

The reasons behind female renunciation in Sri Lanka are diverse. Although the first *dasa sil mātā* embraced their ambiguous roles as lay nuns around the beginning of the twentieth century as part of the broader social effort to revive Buddhism, more recent female renunciants identify different reasons for their decisions to become "nuns." Two recurring motives behind female renunciation in Sri Lanka are power and autonomy, since renunciation allows women to be liberated from their traditional, socially restrictive

Figure 6.2 Newly ordained Buddhist nuns leaving the Dambulla Golden Temple in Sri Lanka (photo by Stephen C. Berkwitz, reproduced from *Buddhism in World Cultures: Comparative Perspectives,* ed. Stephen C. Berkwitz, Santa Barbara, CA: ABC-CLIO, 2006).

roles as daughters, wives, and mothers (Bartholomeusz 1994: 136). For some women, the decision to renounce was reinforced by domestic troubles connected with unhappy marriages (Bartholomeusz 1994: 134). Other women renounced the world after having experienced grief from losing a loved one. Moreover, now that Sri Lankan women have a viable option to be ordained as a *bhikkhunī* after completing a period of training as a novice, some may be motivated to pursue a religious vocation that affords them more recognition and a better opportunity to achieve higher religious goals.

The revival of Buddhist nuns in Nepal

Efforts to establish an order of nuns in Nepal took place soon after the first Newar monks became ordained in the Theravāda tradition and started to promote it among other Newars in the Kathmandu Valley. As noted above, the first Newar women were ordained in 1931 by the Burmese monk Candramaṇi as *anagārikā*, or "female homeless ones," which was equivalent to the "lay nun" status of the *dasa sil mātā* of Sri Lanka. A second group of Newar laywomen traveled to Kuśinagara for ordination in 1934, but Candramaṇi encouraged them to study in Burma first. Some months later the six women were pronounced ready and ordained in the Ten Precepts. One of these six lay nuns called Dhammachari was literate and had read widely on Buddhism for several years beforehand. Dhammachari and the others returned to Kathmandu and moved into the Kindo Baha residence founded by the three lay nuns before them (LeVine and Gellner 2005: 47). These female renunciants lived in accordance with the discipline demanded by the Ten Precepts. Recruitment of new nuns was slow, as most were uneducated and either divorced or widowed. Restrictions on Theravāda in Nepal were still in place, and donations to lay nuns were not easily obtained.

Later, in 1947, a young twelve-year-old girl named Ganesh Kumārī (b. 1935) was sent by her mother, a Theravāda convert, to study the Dharma with a Nepalese monk who had trained in Burma. Against the wishes of her father, she studied Pāli and resolved to go to Burma and learn more of the Dharma. After some time in Kuśinagara with Candramaṇi, she reached Rangoon and began a lengthy course of study at a residence for Burmese female renunciants. She was ordained as a lay nun and re-named Dhammavati. Over the course of about thirteen years of study, Dhammavati earned the "Dharmachariya," which was the highest level of Burmese monastic education, and returned to Nepal in 1963 to spread the Dharma while living in private residences of lay supporters (LeVine and Gellner 2005: 79–80). Dhammavati, who unlike the older lay nuns at Kindol Vihara had never been married, impressed the Newar laity with her deep knowledge. Eventually, she was able to buy land and build the Dharmakīrti Vihāra in Kathmandu with the help of her family.

Along with a Burmese nun named Daw Gunawati, Dhammavati established a new community of lay nuns that would preach sermons, receive *dāna*, and chant *paritrana sūtras* for the protection of their lay supporters (LeVine and Gellner 2005: 84–5). They also taught children, including young girls.

The development of Theravāda in Nepal after the overthrow of the Rana regime in 1950 enabled a steady number of females to join the community of lay nuns. Since that time, the nuns have entered the order at a young age, never having been married, and they reside either in nunneries or in private houses (Kloppenborg 1977: 311). While some in the newer cohort of nuns cite a desire to be free of family bonds or the experience of *dukkha* as the cause for their renunciation, an increasing number of young nuns specify individual spiritual aims as their primary motivation. The 1980s saw the introduction of *vipassanā* meditation into Nepal through visits by renowned teachers Mahasi Sayadaw in 1980 and S.N. Goenka in 1981. Some Newar laypeople, in addition to monks and nuns, took up *vipassanā* practice, and the International Buddhist Meditation Center was established in Kathmandu in 1988 to coordinate meditation courses and visits by foreign instructors (LeVine and Gellner 2005: 211–23). The rise in popularity of *vipassanā* meditation among Buddhists in the Kathmandu Valley coincided with interests in a form of Buddhism that seemed to resonate with modern thought and values. More recently, women entering the order of lay nuns have cited the opportunity to practice meditation without hindrances as a reason for their renunciation (LeVine 2000: 26–7).

Like in Sri Lanka, the Buddhist "nuns" in Nepal are the products of a modernist Buddhist revival motivated by similar interests and opportunities. Contemporary female renunciants in Nepal are typically younger and better educated than their predecessors. Their goals, moreover, include not only to serve Buddhism and society, but also to pursue higher spiritual aims on their own. Some Nepal nuns have also joined the international networks of women striving to develop the *bhikkhunī* order worldwide. A total of about forty nuns from Nepal have been ordained in *bhikkhunī upasampadā* ceremonies held in California, China, Bodh Gaya, and Taiwan up to 2002 (LeVine and Gellner 2005: 195). The ordination of Newar *bhikkhunī*s remains controversial and is not supported by more than a handful of Theravāda monks in Nepal. Nevertheless, the new opportunity for full ordination of female renunciants in Nepal offers women a new religious path and more opportunities to gain respect and support from the small but growing Theravāda community in Nepal.

Buddhist activism

It is widely noted that Buddhist Modernism is characterized by "this-worldly" practice and values. Modern South Asian Buddhists generally accept the idea that wisdom and action can guide people toward the reduction of *dukkha* in the world. While most modern Buddhists would not dispute the inevitability of suffering in *saṃsāra*, many of them recognize that people have the ability and the responsibility to act with compassion in order to reduce the suffering of others. While Buddhist Modernism has spurred nationalist and feminist movements, it has also given rise to other forms of activism related to human rights and the eradication of poverty. Buddhist activists in modern South Asia often blend religious values with social action. They illustrate some of the many different forms of "Engaged Buddhism," which is the name commonly given to modern movements that actively work to improve the lives of living beings, to campaign for political freedoms, and to help the environment. Buddhist activism in modern South Asia encompasses a wide range of oppositional and non-confrontational groups.

Ambedkar Buddhism

Among the largest and most influential South Asian Buddhist communities pursuing an activist agenda are the so-called "Ambedkar Buddhists" in India. As noted above, Buddhism receded from most of the Indian subcontinent in the late medieval period. In the twentieth century, however, a distinctly different Buddhist revival took place in India compared with those in Sri Lanka and Nepal. In the state of Maharashtra, a western-educated political leader from the "untouchable" Mahar caste endeavored to organize and uplift his fellow Mahars by leading them in a conversion from Hinduism to Buddhism. Bhimrao Ambedkar (1891–1956), the Mahar leader, protested the Hindu concept of untouchability and eventually led several thousands of his followers in a mass conversion to Buddhism. Despite his many talents and the excellent education he received at Columbia University and the University of London, Ambedkar experienced caste discrimination and physical intimidation in India. Angered by the injustices suffered by him and his fellow Mahars, he began to organize protests to gain access to water tanks and temples during the 1920s and early 1930s, even publicly burning the ancient treatise on Hindu Law called the *Manusmṛti* (Doyle 2003: 260). Ambedkar concluded that Hinduism would never reform itself and abandon caste discrimination. He believed that the ruling caste hierarchies of the Brahmin and intermediate castes had a vested interest in keeping the millions of untouchables in their "place" (Gokhale 1999: 42). As long as the Mahars and other untouchable castes remained in the

Hindu fold, Ambedkar reasoned, they would be subject to discrimination, poverty, and injustice.

Influenced by western ideas of equality and the dignity of all people, Ambedkar campaigned to uplift the plight of the lowest castes. He was involved in negotiations with the British government in India to secure greater political representation for the "Depressed Classes" of Indian society. Hindu reformers such as Mohandas K. Gandhi objected to Ambedkar's proposal for a separate electorate for untouchable castes, and thus Ambedkar finally agreed to a compromise wherein the untouchable castes would be awarded a number of reserved seats in the Indian parliament instead (Beltz 2005: 49). This protracted struggle convinced Ambedkar that only through conversion would untouchables gain greater happiness and emancipation in society. And having considered other religions for conversion, he decided upon Buddhism since it was originally an Indian tradition and seemed to lack the caste prejudices found in Indian Christian and Muslim communities. Moreover, since Buddhism lacked any existing institutional structure in India at the time, Ambedkar was free to fashion his own idealized version of Buddhism to fit the needs of the Mahar community (Beltz 2005: 53–4). He consulted western writings on Theravāda Buddhism, leading him to embrace many aspects of the modernist vision of Buddhism made popular in texts and by leaders such as Dharmapāla. Ambedkar borrowed selectively from these works and came to emphasize the notion that early Buddhism promoted rational and egalitarian values (Beltz 2005: 73).

Ambedkar studied Buddhism and met with Buddhist leaders at international gatherings. He stressed Buddhism's egalitarian values and its potential for achieving justice and liberation from the oppression that the Mahars experienced in Hindu society. He recognized the Buddha's Dharma to be a principle of morality and social justice, rejecting the idea of religion as a private affair and instead seeing the Dharma as a kind of social contract to guide human relations (Beltz 2005: 62). This fundamentally social interpretation of the Dharma required some reinterpretation of early Buddhist doctrines. Significantly, Ambedkar argued that the Buddha's Four Noble Truths had been distorted by later monks. Rather than accepting the idea that suffering was the product of one's own *karma* and thus admitting that the untouchables were somehow to blame for their own plight, Ambedkar maintained that suffering for the Buddha was equivalent to the material poverty and social exploitation forced upon certain communities by their high-caste oppressors, while the cessation of suffering was defined as the eradication of social and economic injustices (Doyle 2003: 260). Ambedkar's form of Buddhism was much more concerned with liberation from social ills leading to the creation of a just world than it was with liberation from the world itself.

In 1956, during the last year of his life, Ambedkar had prepared thousands of Mahars to join him in converting to Buddhism as a means of escaping the oppression and discrimination that they suffered. He had been attracted to Buddhism since the 1930s, worked to get the Buddhist *dharmacakra* symbol added to the new Indian flag after Independence, published writings on the religion, and participated in international meetings of Buddhists held in Sri Lanka and Burma in the 1950s (Beltz 2005: 54). In the early part of 1956, he published *The Buddha and His Gospel*, a work that conveyed his distinctive interpretations of Buddhism. And during this same year, one that was celebrated by Buddhists in other parts of Asia as the 2500th anniversary of the Buddha's *parinirvāṇa*, Ambedkar encouraged his Mahar followers to join him in converting to Buddhism in the city of Nāgpur. Several thousands of Mahars, dressed in white robes, came to this city in eastern Maharashtra. On October 14, 1956, the Burmese monk Candramaṇi converted Ambedkar to a type of Theravāda Buddhism by having him recite the Three Refuges and Five Precepts three times, and then having him throw rice on a statue of the Buddha and make offerings of white lotuses (Beltz 2005: 56).

Thereafter, at the same ceremony, Ambedkar converted the great crowd of Mahars by having them recite the Three Refuges and Five Precepts. He then administered to them a list of twenty-two vows that he compiled in order to guide the new converts in their Buddhist practice.

> I do not believe in Brahma, Vishnu and Mahesha (Shiva) and I shall not worship them.
> I do not believe in Rama and Krishna and I shall not worship them.
> I do not believe in any of the Hindu deities such as Gauri, Ganapati, etc., and I shall not worship them.
> I do not believe in divine *avatara*s.
> I believe that the idea that the Buddha is an *avatara* of Vishnu is false propaganda.
> I shall not worship my ancestors. I shall not make rice ball offerings to them.
> I shall abstain from doing anything that goes against Buddhism.
> I shall not ask a Brahman to perform any ritual.
> I believe in the equality of all human beings.
> I shall try to establish equality.
> I shall follow the Noble Eightfold Path laid down by the Buddha.
> I shall observe the Ten Principal Virtues [i.e. *pāramitās*] of the Lord [Buddha].
> I shall show compassion towards all living beings.
> I shall not steal.
> I shall not commit adultery.

I shall not lie.
I shall not drink liquor.
I shall lead my life according to the following three Buddhist principles: wisdom, morality and compassion.
I shall quit the Hindu *dharma* which hinders the progress of humanity, which creates inequality between human beings and makes them vile in nature. Thus I shall convert to the Buddhist *dhamma*.
I am totally convinced that only Buddhism is *saddharma* [i.e. the true or best religion].
I believe that I am reborn.
I henceforth resolve to act in accordance with the teachings of the Buddha.
(Beltz 2005: 57–8)

By taking these vows, the first group of Mahar converts to Buddhism were shown what was required to leave their Hindu affiliation behind and to adopt a new Buddhist identity, which would in theory entitle them to greater equality and happiness.

Ambedkar's death later in the year did not put an end to the new Mahar Buddhist community. More Mahars converted to Buddhism in subsequent years, and the community continues to hold occasional public ceremonies wherein thousands of untouchables formally convert to Buddhism. Ambedkar's Buddhist movement, however, did not spread much beyond the Mahars to other Dalit (i.e., "untouchable") communities in India. Many Mahars have become Buddhists, and they continue to honor Ambedkar as the one who led them to freedom from oppression. Accordingly, Ambedkar is widely seen as a *bodhisattva*, and his image or photograph is often venerated next to the Buddha's in Mahar Buddhist shrines (Beltz 2005: 136–7, 161–2). The Mahar converts, who are also sometimes called "Ambedkar Buddhists" or "Neo-Buddhists," celebrate festivals associated with key events in Ambdedkar's life, such as his birth on April 14, his conversion, and his death. Several *stūpa*s have been constructed, although without his relics, and statues of Ambedkar have been erected in numerous cities. On some occasions, these statues have been the targets of vandalism, setting off vigorous protests by his Mahar followers. Evidently, while many high-caste Indians continue to treat Mahar Buddhists as untouchables, the Buddhist converts have obtained more pride and self-respect due to their conversion (Beltz 2005: 133).

Ambedkar Buddhism represents a modern form of Buddhism that interprets some of the ancient teachings of the religion as a program for self-empowerment and social emancipation. Ambedkar taught that suffering is caused primarily by the social struggles between caste groups, and that the Noble Eightfold Path is more a path to "remove injustice and inhumanity that man does to man" than the means to *nirvāṇa* (Queen 1996: 57–61). The strong social concerns of this movement, as well as its modern origins, have resulted in a distinctive lay emphasis with less interest in developing a community of *bhikkhu*s and *bhikkhunī*s. While an estimated one thousand Mahar monks and several dozen Mahar nuns have taken up robes after being ordained by other monastics or by self-ordination, the broader social concerns of Mahar Buddhists make many of them feel less dependent on the Saṅgha. Nevertheless, in some cases, these Ambedkarite monks take leading roles in public protests and strikes, including a series of ongoing efforts to wrest control of the Mahabodhi Temple in Bodh Gaya away from Hindu authorities. Ambedkar Buddhists practice a socially engaged form of Buddhism inspired by their Mahar leader, who led them to embrace the religion to be liberated from societal oppression and economic deprivation.

Buddhist development in Sri Lanka

Other forms of Buddhist activism exist in Sri Lanka, where modernist concerns for reviving Buddhism continue to spur efforts to improve the lives of those who are impoverished and who lack the resources to develop their rural communities. As noted above, the Sri Lankan Buddhist revival that began in the late nineteenth century incorporated the goals of economic development and the alleviation of rural poverty. Early Buddhist modernists were also mindful of Christian missionary critiques that cast Buddhism as an otherworldly religion that ignores people's everyday needs. As time went on, individuals and organizations launched social welfare and economic development programs that were motivated by Buddhist values of compassion, generosity, and loving-kindness. Even today, many Sri Lankan Buddhists are reluctant to cede all welfare and development efforts to foreign missionary and non-governmental organizations.

One of the oldest and best-known "Buddhist" organizations devoted to promoting social and economic welfare is Sarvodaya, a Sri Lankan based NGO that has carried out projects in the areas of rural and spiritual development since it was founded by the Buddhist layman A.T. Ariyaratne in 1958. Sarvodaya emphasizes the idea of self-realization through voluntary labor for the benefit of others, combining the Gandhian ideals of spiritual and economic development through village-based service with Buddhist ideals of spiritual awakening and the alleviation of suffering by reducing egoistic desire (Berkwitz 2006: 65). As a result, Sarvodaya supports projects that, in theory, benefit their volunteers just as much as the impoverished recipients of their work. It pursues a wide range of projects in Sri Lanka including teacher training, volunteer training, health clinics, children's camps, *shramadana* (voluntary labor) camps, relief assistance, technology training, village banks, biodiversity programs, and the construction of homes, wells, and latrines. Added to its rural development programs, Sarvodaya has also sponsored peace demonstrations calling for an end to war in the island. It has held large-scale peace meditations as a first step toward building up a culture of peace and reconciliation between Sinhala and Tamil communities (Bond 2004: 41). These events have drawn hundreds and even thousands of people, although they have at times also attracted counter-protestors who reject the idea of granting territorial concessions to Tamil separatists in the name of peace.

The Buddhist roots of Sarvodaya are conspicuous, even if they are played down by the organization. Ariyaratne has cited the group's inclusiveness and its ecumenical stance on integrating ideas from different sources to form its core philosophy. And yet, Sarvodaya also emphasizes that its practical programs are the instruments through which volunteers develop insight into the nature of reality and reduce the craving and suffering in oneself while working toward the spiritual and economic regeneration of Sri Lanka in accordance with Buddhist values and principles (Kantowsky 1980: 43–4). Buddhist principles guide the development program of Sarvodaya and the ethos that motivates its work in the island. Buddhist ideas of interdependence and the alleviation of suffering are among the cornerstones of the organization's activities (Berkwitz 2006: 66).

Sarvodaya does not, however, limit its development programs to the Sinhala Buddhist community. It also recruits local Tamils, Christians, and Muslims to assist in its projects, and it maintains offices and programs throughout much of the island to benefit people of all religious and ethnic backgrounds. Despite the inclusive nature of some of its discourse, Sarvodaya continues to articulate its goals in terms of Buddhist spirituality. It translates *sarvodaya* as the "Awakening of all," a goal that combines social service with spiritual enlightenment. Buddhist notions of loving-kindness and compassion are generalized and extended to encompass other religions in a vision of spiritual unity (Bond 2004: 13–14). Clearly, however, Sarvodaya owes most of its principles to Buddhism. It includes among its activities a "Bhikkhu Services Programme" that endeavors to train monks to organize local community development projects. Although it has been criticized for having an overly romantic image of village life that is outdated and impractical in a world of globalized markets and trade, Sarvodaya remains a respected and largely effective NGO for village development and disaster relief.

Although Sarvodaya is the best-known example of Buddhist activism in modern Sri Lanka, it is not alone. Many other groups and individuals also draw on Buddhist notions and values in activist work. Unlike Sarvodaya, which receives much of its financial support from international donor organizations, countless smaller Buddhist activists draw primarily upon local resources and Sinhala Buddhist communities abroad to assist in such efforts as alleviating poverty, educating rural youth, and caring for the blind and the elderly. Such groups may be motivated by their compassion for others who suffer disproportionately, while others see social welfare activities as a form of national service. One example of a Sri Lankan based Buddhist activist organization is Janavijaya (Victory of the People), an organization founded by the late Ven. Gangodawila Soma to engage in social work and to promote a Buddhist lifestyle. Janavijaya asserts that by adhering to the Five Precepts of Buddhist morality, Sri Lankans will strengthen their commitment to wholesome conduct and contribute to the social and economic development of the nation (Berkwitz 2008: 86). Janavijaya's motto: "Righteousness Enhances the Prosperity of the Nation," speaks to its twin concerns for developing morality and developing the nation.

Associated with Soma's temple in Maharagama, Sri Lanka as well as the affiliated Washington Buddhist Vihara in Washington, DC, Janavijaya's activities include building preschools in rural communities and providing relief supplies and medical care to people living in areas affected by the Indian Ocean Tsunami of December 26, 2004. Janavijaya responds to other natural disasters such as floods by collecting and distributing food and other supplies for victims. And in keeping with its humanitarian focus, Janavijaya also maintains a small temple at the Colombo National Hospital to assist the ill, the injured, and their families with spiritual comfort and material needs such as clothing. Large numbers of lay supporters provide the financial and material resources utilized by this monastic-run organization.

Another activist group motivated by a Buddhist social philosophy is the Damrivi Foundation. Founded in 2004 by a group of lay Buddhist academics and professionals, Damrivi (Sunshine of the Dharma) has embarked on an ambitious plan to integrate social welfare projects with Buddhist practice and education. The projects that are run out of its center in Colombo include rural development programs, irrigation projects, scholarship programs for youth, relief work in Tsunami-affected areas, computer training, and a free counseling center. Damrivi's interests in providing counseling to families, cancer patients, inmates, and others in need of guidance and comfort has led the organization to create Diploma and Certificate Courses in Buddhist Psychology and Psychological Counseling, whereby individuals are trained to meet contemporary mental health needs with insights gleaned from the Buddha's Dharma. Like many other Buddhist activist organizations, Damrivi seeks to facilitate the spiritual, social, and economic needs of Sri Lankans by engaging in welfare projects that are inspired and guided by Buddhist principles of loving-kindness and generosity. Moreover, Damrivi also sponsors Buddhist activities such as meditation programs and classes to educate children in the Dharma. Sri Lanka is home to countless Buddhist activist organizations like Sarvodaya, Janavijaya, and Damrivi that are engaged in social welfare projects and seek to practice the Buddha's Dharma for the benefit of the many. They embody the distinctively modern application of Buddhist values in social work for the wider society, and utilize modern technologies such as websites to promote their activities.

Tibetan Buddhism in South Asia

We can also consider the establishment of Tibetan refugee communities in India and Nepal as, in part, another form of Buddhist activism in South Asia. In the roughly four-dozen Tibetan settlements in South Asia, Tibetan Buddhists strive to support themselves economically and to preserve their religion and culture while in exile from Tibet. Some one million Tibetans were internally displaced during the Chinese expansion into Tibet between 1949 and 1959, and tens of thousands of them left Tibet for India, Nepal, and Bhutan to escape political and religious persecution (Moynihan 2003: 313). The Fourteenth Dalai Lama, Tenzin Gyatso (b. 1935), fled Tibet ahead of advancing Chinese troops in March 1959 and received refuge in India up to the present day. In 1960, the Dalai Lama and a large number of his followers were invited to establish a settlement in the hill station of Dharamsāla in Himachal Pradesh, India. Other settlement camps were set up around India with the permission and support of the Indian government. The Tibetan Government in Exile was set up and based in Dharamsāla, which has become the residence of the Dalai Lama and the headquarters of the Tibetan diaspora community.

From 1960 onwards, under the leadership of the Dalai Lama, the Tibetans in exile have sought to establish a modern, independent political structure while preserving their traditional religious and cultural heritage. Earlier generations of Tibetans migrated voluntarily to places like Sikkim, Ladakh, and Bhutan and have maintained a presence in these lands for centuries. However, the mass migration of Tibetan refugees in the 1960s produced a wholly new situation. Tibetan Buddhists were often compelled to settle in camps located in unfamiliar, warmer climates. Orphanages and schools had to be built and staffed. The Tibetan exile community undertook steps to ensure the survival of their members and their religion abroad. Aside from agricultural and economic endeavors, Tibetan Buddhists living in exile in India and Nepal sought to maintain their monastic traditions and the educational institutes needed to support them. Tibetan monasteries founded in South Asia vary widely in size and in orientation. Certain monasteries tend to emphasize education, ritual, or meditation, while some of the largest ones—associated with the Gelug School of Tibetan Buddhism—may have populations ranging from 2,500 to 4,700 monks (Gyatso 2003: 219–21).

In spite of numerous challenges, Tibetan monks have tried to recreate traditional monastic settings in their new locations. The influence of Buddhism over the Tibetan exile community has become weaker, however, as younger traditions apparently prefer political work over religious duties, and some even blame the monks for contributing to the loss of Tibet to China (Avedon 1984: 100–1). Refugees experience pressure to assimilate to their new surroundings. At the same time, the Dalai Lama and the Tibetan Government in Exile devote considerable energy to conserving traditional Tibetan religion and culture in refugee communities, as well as promoting their heritage abroad to spread awareness of the challenges facing Tibetans at home and in exile. Monks who escape Tibet often find their way to these monasteries in South Asia. Meanwhile, lay Tibetans who are able to leave their native land sometimes become ordained in exile due to the monasteries' opportunities for education, the reassertion of their cultural identity, and the financial security that comes with being a monk (Gyatso 2003: 222–3). Monks in Indian monasteries generally pursue the same types of activities that they would in Tibet. Philosophical debates and scriptural studies make up the largest part of their training. And although youths living in exile have been less likely to join monasteries, the steady stream of refugees sustains the population of Tibetan monks in exile (Gyatso 2003: 214–15).

The influx of Tibetan *lama*s in South Asia has allowed the exile community to maintain its traditional reverence for spiritual leaders. Distinguished from ordinary monks by their higher spiritual attainments and authority, these *lama*s guide the religious affairs of the Tibetan exiles and offer counsel to individuals who seek their advice and help. They may lead or witness public rituals wherein the merit earned is dedicated to alleviate the suffering of their countrymen in Tibet. Some Tibetan *lama*s have toured outside of South Asia, teaching and speaking to sympathetic audiences in the West and other parts of Asia, and gaining more financial support for their monasteries (Gyatso 2003: 232). The *lama*s' responsibilities to serve the laity and to raise funds for their monasteries and communities often cut into the time that might otherwise be spent in educational pursuits. Some monks, like their lay brethren, devote substantial time and energy to the causes of preserving Tibetan culture and protesting China's occupation of Tibet. Tibetan *lama*s and monks are thus challenged to maintain traditional standards of learning and discipline in their South Asian settings. The Tibetan Government in Exile makes efforts in the name of religious and cultural preservation to facilitate the education of monks, and there are still some Tibetan *lama*s in exile who possess impressive levels of knowledge.

Due to the political events of the mid-twentieth century, Tibetan Buddhism has been spread across many lands and cultures in South Asia and beyond. Wherever substantial populations of Tibetans are found, for example in

Dharamsāla, India and Bodhanath, Nepal, Buddhist monasteries and monks form crucial aspects of these communities in exile. The construction of monasteries, schools, and *chorten* (i.e. *stūpa*s) are visible signs of Tibetan Buddhist culture in South Asian locales. Monasteries are well populated by monks, but there are signs of liberalization in terms of, for instance, greater acceptance for those who decide to leave the monkhood (Gyatso 2003: 241–2). The spread of Tibetan Buddhist communities outside of Tibet has brought the tradition into greater contact with other cultures and systems of knowledge that force the Dalai Lama and other Buddhist leaders to accommodate these newer influences. Science, democracy, and ecumenical dialogue with other Buddhist and non-Buddhist communities—all of which are topics that appear in the Dalai Lama's writings—affect how Tibetan Buddhism in South Asia and elsewhere becomes expressed.

Consequently, one can discern two distinct forms of activism among Tibetan Buddhists living in exile across parts of South Asia. One form involves the propagation of a more rational, less ritualistic type of Buddhism that is more palatable to people in the modern world. Thus, the Dalai Lama has become a leading proponent of contemporary Buddhist Modernism, wherein traditional rituals and cosmologies are abandoned in favor of depicting Buddhism as a religion of reason that is dedicated to relieving suffering and is compatible with scientific thought (Lopez 1998: 185–6). This modern re-casting of Buddhism is often prepared to devalue and discard traditional religious theories and practices if they appear too irrational. As such, under this modernizing agenda, Tibetan *lama*s sometimes seek to suppress practices associated with the worship of certain deities and other shamanic rites.

The other type of activism is concerned with promoting Tibetan religion, culture, and its political aspirations ranging from autonomy within China to outright independence. Tibetans living in exile in South Asia affirm that the practice of Buddhism is a critical component of Tibetan culture. And thus, in efforts to promote awareness and support of their cause, many leading Buddhist *lama*s and activists seek to make Tibetan culture—with Buddhism as its alleged mainstay—visible to the world (Moran 2004: 46). Foreign tours of Buddhist *lamas* serve the twin purposes of reminding the world about the plight of Tibetans both inside and outside of Tibet, and of raising political and financial support. In places like Bodhanath, a neighborhood of Kathmandu that has become home to a large population of Tibetan exiles in Nepal, Buddhist monks are perceived by Tibetans and tourists to embody the cultural "essence" of Tibet, the vessels through which Buddhist traditions and values are transmitted to younger generations of exiles and western pilgrims (Moran 2004: 87). The representation of Buddhism by monks, monasteries, and rituals in exile also functions to represent what is allegedly most authentic about Tibet. In a sense, the "real" Tibet—as seen in the figure of the Dalai Lama and the unhindered expression of Buddhist and other cultural expressions—exists now in South Asia rather than in the Tibetan Autonomous Region of the People's Republic of China. The practice of Buddhism by Tibetan exile communities thus manifests the political aims of preserving and promoting Tibetan culture, which is otherwise in danger of disappearing inside Tibet under Chinese rule.

Lay Buddhist practice

In the midst of modern trends of revival, women's ordination, and social and political activism, most Buddhists in contemporary South Asia continue to practice their religion in accordance with the needs and interests of everyday life. These Buddhists are thus likely to expend most of their religious activity in acts of merit that are expected to yield good fortune. Individual and communal acts of giving (*dāna*) are among the most common practices that are performed to earn merit. Giving alms and other requisites to the Saṅgha is perhaps the most common form of *dāna* in Theravāda communities. Other forms of charitable giving to people in need and even to benefit animals, such as purchasing and releasing cows from slaughterhouses, also qualify as *dāna*. In general, all acts of merit involve shunning wicked deeds and directing one's mind to the performance of morally good actions, the consequences of which are held to result in benefits received in this life and happiness in future lives (Karunatillake 1979: 22–3). The worldly benefits of merit make the practices that are designed to earn it quite popular across South Asia.

Related to acts of merit are expressions of devotion. The worship of *stūpa*s in Sri Lanka, Nepal, India, and Bhutan represents enduring modes to display Buddhist devotion. In Sri Lanka, offerings made to the Buddha in the form of his relics or his image (which is a type of relic) are understood to be *pūjā*, or devotional gestures that signal one's faith and commitment to the Buddha and his *sāsana*. Offerings of flowers, incense, food, water, and oil lamps in honor of the Buddha along with symbolic gestures of devotion such as bowing, circumambulating, and holding one's palms together at one's chest and head are formal methods of showing reverence and respect to the Buddha (Karunatillake 1979: 28). Such gestures, when undertaken with a wholesome state of mind, are held to generate merit and to facilitate progress along the Buddhist path. The worship of *stūpa*s in Nepal is just as popular. Such monuments have attracted pilgrims, widows, and other devotees seeking to honor the Buddha and gain blessings, while others create hundreds and thousands of miniature shrines out of sand at riverbanks to earn merit (Lewis 2000: 38–40). Meanwhile, *stūpa*s associated with Ambedkar attract Mahar pilgrims and devotees to certain sites in India. Another contemporary form of Buddhist devotion is the singing of hymns in Nepal. Called *gyanmala* (garlands of knowledge), these vernacular hymns are patterned after Hindu devotional hymns (*bhajans*) but impart knowledge of the Dharma and serve to consolidate the support of Theravāda in the Kathmandu Valley (LeVine and Gellner 2005: 124–5).

Protective rituals also remain influential in most forms of contemporary South Asian Buddhism. The recital of protective *mantras* and *dhāraṇīs* in Newar Buddhist communities in Nepal typifies the perceived need to allay malevolent forces and to gain the protection of Vajrayāna deities who may assist their devotees. Likewise, among Theravāda communities in Sri Lanka and Nepal, the recitation of *paritta* or protective verses associated with the Buddha's Word are held to offer blessings and protection to those who hear it. Although conceived differently, these Vajrayāna and Theravāda protective recitations are believed to accomplish the same purpose in bestowing the listeners with supernatural forces of protection animated by verbalizing inherently powerful speech.

Buddhist education continues to be an important facet of contemporary South Asian Buddhism as well. Monasteries and other Buddhist schools typically attempt to provide some form of religious education to young people. This may involve retreats, programs, or "Dharma School" with classes held on Sunday in imitation of Christian Sunday Schools. In Sri Lanka, "Dharma School" is taught by monks and laypersons to inculcate more knowledge and more discipline to young Buddhists. Theravādins in Nepal have pursued comparable educational efforts, and the Newar Buddhists who wish to revive Vajrayāna have also founded schools to train young priests. Furthermore, South Asian Buddhists often publish books and newspapers on Buddhist subjects in vernacular languages to edify general lay audiences.

Lastly, an increasingly important aspect of lay Buddhist practice in South Asia is meditation. Long associated mainly with monks and nuns, meditation now enjoys a broader popularity in Sri Lanka and Nepal. This is particularly seen in the case of *vipassanā*, or "insight" meditation, as developed and popularized by Burmese meditation teachers from the mid-twentieth century and by the Indian layman S.N. Goenka, who has offered *vipassanā* instruction in Sri Lanka and Nepal. Modern *vipassanā* differs from older Theravāda traditions on meditation in that it involves deep breathing, an internal focus on the stomach moving with the breathing, and an assumption that meditation is useful for promoting good health and success in this life (Gombrich and Obeyesekere 1988: 237–9). In other words, one may meditate without developing the traditional *jhānas*, or trance-states, to pursue this-worldly goals along with liberation. Advocates for *vipassanā* typically stress that one can meditate without having to renounce the world or engage in systematic study of the Dharma (Bond 1988: 186). Rather, the modern Buddhist outlook accepts meditation as a practice open to everyone, and it is commonly thought that laypersons can obtain mental purity, peace of mind, and even progress toward *nirvāṇa* by practicing *vipassanā*. In Sri Lanka, increasing numbers of laypersons are taking up *vipassanā* meditation, either at certain temples where such practices are led by monks or at recently founded meditation centers with lay or monastic instructors. It is still the case that most Sri Lankan lay Buddhists do not meditate regularly, but there have been clear signs of increasing numbers of laypersons practicing *vipassanā* meditation in both urban and rural settings (Bond 1988: 197).

Similarly, Buddhists in Nepal have begun to embrace *vipassanā* as a beneficial and fulfilling form of Buddhist practice. Monks and nuns who studied in Burma have returned to Nepal and teach the methods of meditation associated with the late Burmese master Mahāsī Sayādaw. In addition, periodic visits by Goenka to Kathmandu in the 1980s laid the foundation for more widespread meditation practice among laypersons (LeVine and Gellner 2005: 216–17). A number of meditation centers have been established since the 1980s, the most notable of which is the International Buddhist Meditation Center (IBMC), which was built in Kathmandu in 1988 with funds collected from Thailand, Burma, and the local Newar business community (LeVine and Gellner 2005: 212). Although the meditation groups and centers in Nepal do not typically maintain close relations with their counterparts in Sri Lanka, the practitioners of *vipassanā* in both countries typically share similar techniques and attitudes toward the practice as a method for the laity to improve their lives in this world and the next.

However, some of the reasons for the growing popularity of *vipassanā* in Nepal differ from those in Sri Lanka with its long history of Theravāda Buddhism. In Nepal, *vipassanā* seems to have broad appeal since it is perceived to be older and more "pure" than other Buddhist practices, it is relatively simple to do and is available to everyone irrespective of caste background, it could be introduced without resistance from conservative monks who are in short supply in Nepal, and it appears to blend Buddhist practices with scientific ideas and modern values (LeVine and Gellner 2005: 229). Furthermore, the *vipassanā* methods of close observation of one's bodily movements and sensations represents an individualistic practice that departs from the communal Hindu and Vajrayāna rituals that structure social relationships and norms in Nepali society (Leve 2002: 852). As such, the value assigned to *vipassanā* represents a subtle critique and rejection of the traditional socio-moral norms associated with the dominant Hindu society in Nepal.

In sum, lay Buddhist practices in South Asian countries combine traditional practices with modern values that assign a greater role to the laity in their pursuit of Buddhist goals. Age-old practices of selfless giving take on new significance when people sponsor the building of meditation centers or the publication of vernacular texts to help the laity learn more about the Dharma. Devotional acts of showing reverence for the Three Jewels are sustained, while new ones such as the *gyanmala* hymns are being created. And the popularization of meditation enables more South Asian Buddhists to take up respected practices and to participate more fully in the religious values and institutions of Buddhism. All of these examples illustrate that contemporary South Asian Buddhists follow a range of practices, from the political to the socially aware, and from the ethical and devotional to the therapeutic. Challenges persist, but Buddhism maintains a robust presence in twenty-first-century South Asia.

Appendix

Numerical lists of Buddhist concepts (in Pāli and Sanskrit)

Two kinds of *nirvāṇa*:

1. Extinction of defilements (*kleśanirvāṇa*) with substratum remaining
2. Extinction of aggregates (*skandhanirvāṇa*) without substratum remaining

Two Truths:

1. Conventional Truth (*samvṛti-satya*)
2. Ultimate Truth (*paramārtha-satya*)

Three Baskets of Buddhist scriptures (Tripiṭaka):

1. Vinaya
2. Sūtra
3. Abhidharma

Three Bodies of the Buddha (*trikāya*):

1. Truth Body (*dharmakāya*)
2. Enjoyment Body (*saṃbhogakāya*)
3. Apparition Body (*nirmāṇakāya*)

Three channels (*nāḍī*) of the subtle body:

1. Right (*rasanā*)
2. Middle (*avadhūti*)
3. Left (*lalanā*)

Three Detachments:

1. Bodily Detachment (*kāya-viveka*)
2. Mental Detachment (*citta-viveka*)
3. Detachment from the Substrata of Existence (*upadhi-viveka*)

Three doors of action (*karmamukha*):
1. Body (*kāya*)
2. Speech (*vāk*)
3. Mind (*citta*)

Three gateways to liberation:
1. Signless (*animitta*)
2. Desireless (*apraṇihita*)
3. Emptiness (*śūnyatā*)

Three Jewels (refuges) (*triratna*):
1. Buddha
2. Dharma
3. Saṅgha

Threefold knowledge:
1. Knowledge of remembering one's previous existences
2. Knowledge of deaths and rebirths of all beings
3. Knowledge of having destroyed the defilements

Three Marks of existence:
1. Impermanence (*anicca*)
2. Dissatisfaction (*dukkha*)
3. No-Self (*anattā*)

Three Natures (*trisvabhāva*):
1. Constructed Nature (*parikalpita-svabhāva*)
2. Dependent Nature (*paratantra-svabhāva*)
3. Perfected Nature (*pariniṣpanna-svabhāva*)

Three realms of the universe:
1. Realm of Sense-Desires (*kāma-dhātu*)
2. Realm of Form (*rūpa-dhātu*)
3. Realm of Formlessness (*arūpa-dhātu*)

Three Tantric seals:
1. Sexual yoga with flesh-and-blood partner (*karmamudrā*)
2. Imagined engagement with a visualized partner (*jñānamudrā*)
3. Non-dual contemplation of ultimate reality (*mahāmudrā*)

Three temptations:
1. Desire, Greed (*lobha*)
2. Discontent, Ill-will (*dosa*)
3. Delusion (*moha*)

Three vehicles:
1. Vehicle of the Disciples (*śrāvakayāna*)
2. Vehicle of the Solitary Buddhas (*pratyekabuddhayāna*)
3. Vehicle of the Bodhisattvas (*bodhisattvayāna*)

Fourfold assembly:
1. Monks (*bhikṣu*)
2. Nuns (*bhikṣuṇi*)
3. Male Lay Devotees (*upāsaka*)
4. Female Lay Devotees (*upāsikā*)

Four Divine Abidings (*brahmāvihāra*):
1. Universal Friendliness (*maitri*)
2. Compassion (*karuṇā*)
3. Sympathetic Joy (*muditā*)
4. Equanimity (*upekṣā*)

Four ethical practices of purity (*catuparisuddhisīla*):
1. *Paṭimokkha* Rules
2. Restraint of the Senses
3. Purity of Livelihood
4. Correct Use of Requisites

Four foundations of mindfulness (*satipaṭṭhāna*):
1. Mindfulness of the body
2. Mindfulness of feeling
3. Mindfulness of mental states
4. Mindfulness of objective factors (*dhammas*)

Fourfold Higher Reality (*catudhāparamattha*):
1. Physical matter (*rūpa*)
2. Mental factors (*cetasika*)
3. Consciousness (*citta*)
4. Ultimate reality (*nirvāṇa*)

Four levels of bliss:
1. Bliss (*ānanda*)
2. Utmost Bliss (*paramānanda*)
3. Bliss of Cessation (*viramānanda*)
4. Innate Bliss (*sahajānanda*)

Four mental intoxicants (*āsava*):
1. Desire (*kāma*)
2. Existence (*bhava*)
3. False Views (*dṛṣṭi*)
4. Ignorance (*avidyā*)

Four Noble Truths:
1. There is suffering (*dukkha*)
2. There is a cause to suffering (*samudaya*)
3. There is cessation of suffering (*nirodha*)
4. The path leading to the cessation of suffering (*magga*)

Four paths:
1. Stream-winner (*sotapatti*)
2. Once-returner (*sakadāgāmī*)
3. Non-returner (*anāgāmī*)
4. Worthy One (*arahant*)

Four perverted views:
1. Seeing permanence where there is impermanence (*nitya*)
2. Seeing purity where there is impurity (*śuci*)
3. Seeing pleasure where there is suffering (*sukha*)
4. Seeing a Self where there is No-Self (*ātman*)

Four signs:
1. Old Man
2. Sick Man
3. Dead Man
4. Recluse

Five Aggregates (*skandha*):
1. Material Form (*rūpa*)
2. Feeling (*vedanā*)
3. Perception (*saṃjñā*)
4. Karmic Dispositions (*saṃskāra*)
5. Consciousness (*vijñāna*)

Five deadly sins leading to rebirth in hell:
1. Killing one's mother
2. Killing one's father
3. Killing an *arhat*
4. Splitting the Saṅgha
5. Causing a Buddha to bleed

Five energy centers (*cakra*):
1. Crown *cakra*
2. Throat *cakra*
3. Heart *cakra*
4. Navel *cakra*
5. Sexual organ *cakra*

Five Eyes of the Buddha:
1. Bodily Eye (*maṃsacakkhu*)
2. Divine Eye (*dibbacakkhu*)
3. Eye of Wisdom (*paññacakkhu*)
4. Buddha Eye (*buddhacakkhu*)
5. Universal Eye (*samantacakkhu*)

Five higher knowledges (*abhijñā*):
1. Supernormal powers
2. Divine Ear
3. Knowing the thoughts of others
4. Remembering one's previous existences
5. Divine Eye

Five hindrances to meditation:
1. Desire for Sense-Pleasures (*kāmacchanda*)
2. Ill-Will (*vyāpāda*)
3. Sloth and Torpor (*thīna-middha*)
4. Distractedness and Worry (*uddhaccha-kukkucca*)
5. Doubt (*vicikicchā*)

Six-colored Buddha rays:
1. Blue
2. Yellow
3. Red
4. White
5. Copper
6. Radiant Mixture

Six heavens in realm of sense-desires (*kāmabhava*):
1. Heaven of the Four Guardian Kings (*catummaharājika*)
2. Heaven of the Thirty-three gods (*tāvatiṃsa*)
3. Heaven of those that have attained divine bliss (*yāmā*)
4. Heaven of the delighted (*tusita*)
5. Heaven of those who delight in their own creations (*nimmāna-ratin*)
6. Heaven of those who delight in the creations of others (*paranimmita-vasavattin*)

Six perfections (*pāramitā*):
1. Giving (*dāna*)
2. Morality (*śīla*)
3. Patience (*kṣānti*)
4. Effort (*vīrya*)
5. Meditation (*dhyāna*)
6. Wisdom (*prajñā*)

Six realms of rebirth:
1. Gods
2. Humans
3. Jealous Gods (*asura*)
4. Animals
5. Hungry Ghosts
6. Hell-dwellers

Six sense fields:
1. Seeing
2. Hearing
3. Smelling
4. Tasting
5. Touching
6. Thinking

Six Tantric Buddha families:
1. Vairocana
2. Amitābha
3. Akṣobhya
4. Ratnasambhava
5. Amoghasiddhi
6. Vajrasattva

Seven limbs of enlightenment (*sattabhojjhaṅga*):
1. Mindfulness (*sati*)
2. Investigating the Dharma (*dhammavicaya*)
3. Effort (*viriya*)
4. Joy (*pīti*)
5. Tranquility (*passadhi*)
6. Concentration (*samādhi*)
7. Equanimity (*upekkhā*)

Eight great Hells (*mahāniraya*):
1. *Saṃjīva* (Reviving Hell) – Beings are cut to pieces then come back to life repeatedly
2. *Kālasūtra* (Black Thread Hell) – Bodies are marked with black thread and chopped with adzes
3. *Saṃghāta* (Crushing Hell) – Beings are constantly crushed by a huge fiery rock
4. *Raurava* (Weeping Hell) – Beings cry incessantly from fire entering their nine orifices
5. *Mahāraurava* (Great Weeping Hell) – Beings baked in a huge mass of flames
6. *Tāpana* (Heating Hell) – Beings strung on fiery crossbars and unable to move
7. *Pratāpana* (Greatly Heating Hell) – Beings forced to repeatedly climb a fiery mountain
8. *Avīci* (Unceasing Hell) – Beings attacked unceasingly by the most intense fire and heat

Eight higher attainments (*samāpatti*):
1. Path of a Stream-winner
2. Fruit of a Stream-winner
3. Path of a Once-returner
4. Fruit of a Once-returner
5. Path of a Non-returner
6. Fruit of a Non-returner
7. Path of an *arhat*
8. Fruit of an *arhat*

Eight levels of trance (*dhyānas*):
1. Without sense desires – with discursive thought; detached, rapturous, joyful
2. Rapture and Joy – free of discursive thinking, seeing constituent *dharmas*
3. Joy – subject–object dichotomy drops away
4. Equanimity – total mindfulness, beyond happiness or unhappiness
5. Infinite Space – beyond all perception of form
6. Infinite Consciousness – consciousness no longer limited to own body
7. Nothingness – no objective content to awareness, beyond space and mind
8. Neither Perception nor Non-perception – *dharmas* fall away, beyond nothingness

Eightfold Path:

1. Right View (*sammā-diṭṭhi*)
2. Right Intention (*sammā-saṅkappa*)
3. Right Speech (*sammā-vācā*)
4. Right Action (*sammā-kammanta*)
5. Right Livelihood (*sammā-ājīva*)
6. Right Effort (*sammā-vāyāma*)
7. Right Mindfulness (*sammā-sati*)
8. Right Concentration (*sammā-samādhi*)

Nine aesthetic sentiments (*rasa*s):

1. Erotic (*śṛṅgāra*)
2. Heroic (*vīra*)
3. Disgust (*bibhatsa*)
4. Anger (*raudra*)
5. Humor (*hāsya*)
6. Terrifying (*bhāyāṅkara*)
7. Compassionate (*karuṇā*)
8. Surprise (*adbhūta*)
9. Tranquility (*śānta*)

Ten Bodhisattva stages (*bhūmi*):

1. Joyful Stage
2. Free from Defilements Stage
3. Light-giving Stage
4. Glorious Wisdom Stage
5. Very Hard to Conquer Stage
6. Face-to-face Stage
7. Proceeding Afar Stage
8. Immovable Stage
9. Good Insight Stage
10. Dharma-cloud Stage

Ten fetters (*saṁyoga*):

1. False View of Self
2. Doubt
3. Belief in purification by external rites
4. Sensual lust
5. Ill-Will
6. Attachment to pure form-existence
7. Attachment to formless existence
8. Conceit

9. Distraction
10. Ignorance

Ten foul objects of meditation:
1. Bloated corpse
2. Blotchy corpse
3. Festering corpse
4. Cut up corpse
5. Gnawed corpse
6. Scattered corpse
7. Mutilated Corpse
8. Bleeding Corpse
9. Worm-infested corpse
10. Skeleton

Ten Perfections (*pāramī*):
1. Generosity (*dāna*)
2. Morality (*sīla*)
3. Renunciation (*nekkhama*)
4. Wisdom (*paññā*)
5. Effort (*viriya*)
6. Patience (*khanti*)
7. Truth (*sacca*)
8. Resolution (*adhiṭṭhāna*)
9. Loving-kindness (*mettā*)
10. Equanimity (*upekkhā*)

Ten powers of a Buddha (*bala*):
1. Knowing possibilities from impossibilities
2. Knowing the fruits of *karma*
3. Knowing the courses of action leading to all states of existence
4. Knowing all the worlds composed of various elements
5. Knowing the various dispositions of all beings
6. Knowing the level of development for the faculties of all beings
7. Knowing the levels of meditation and the defilements
8. Knowing previous existences
9. Possessing the Divine Eye that sees the births and deaths of all beings
10. Knowing that one's mental intoxicants have been destroyed

Ten Precepts:
1. Refrain from killing
2. Refrain from stealing

3. Refrain from engaging in immoral sex
4. Refrain from lying
5. Refrain from taking intoxicants
6. Refrain from adorning oneself
7. Refrain from attending shows
8. Refrain from eating after noon
9. Refrain from sleeping in a high, comfortable bed
10. Refrain from handling gold and silver

Twelvefold Chain of Dependent Co-Arising (*pratītya-samutpāda*):

1. Ignorance (*avidyā*)
2. Karmic Dispositions (*saṃskāra*)
3. Consciousness (*vijñāna*)
4. Name and Form (*nāma-rūpa*)
5. Six Sense Fields (*sad-āyatana*)
6. Contact (*sparśa*)
7. Feeling (*vedanā*)
8. Desire (*tṛṣṇā*)
9. Clinging (*upādāna*)
10. Becoming (*bhava*)
11. Conception (*jāti*)
12. Old Age and Death (*jarāmaraṇa*)

Twelve sense bases (*āyatana*):

1.	Eye	7.	Forms
2.	Ear	8.	Sound
3.	Nose	9.	Smells
4.	Tongue	10.	Tastes
5.	Body	11.	Tangibles
6.	Mind	12.	Mental objects

Thirteen ascetic practices (*dhutaṅga*):

1. Wearing robes made from refuse-rags
2. Wearing only the three monastic robes
3. Subsisting only on alms given on alms-rounds
4. Seeking alms from each dwelling without skipping any
5. Eating in one session only
6. Eating food from only one alms bowl
7. Refusing extra food
8. Dwelling in the forest
9. Dwelling at the root of a tree
10. Dwelling in the open air without covering

11. Dwelling in cremation grounds
12. Accepting any mat on which to sit or sleep
13. Resting by sitting without lying down

Sixteen thought moments of cognition (*ciitavīthi*):

1. Undisturbed flow of latent stream of consciousness (*bhavanga*)
2. Sense-impression disturbs *bhavanga*
3. Steady flow of *bhavanga* is arrested
4. Becoming conscious of sense-impression as it enters through one of the five sense doors
5. One of the five sense-consciousnesses (or mind-doors) is activated
6. The sense-impression is received as a real object
7. The mind investigates the sense-impression and tries to understand it
8. The mind determines and assigns the sense-impression within one's field of knowledge
9. The mind actively dwells on the sense-impression and forms an attitude toward it (*javana*)
10. Active consciousness (*javana*) continues
11. Active consciousness continues
12. Active consciousness continues
13. Active consciousness continues
14. Active consciousness continues
15. Active consciousness continues
16. Sense-impression is held and registered in sub-conscious mind

Eighteen elements (*dhātu*):

1.	Eye	7.	Forms	13.	Eye-consciousness
2.	Ear	8.	Sound	14.	Ear-consciousness
3.	Nose	9.	Smells	15.	Nose-consciousness
4.	Tongue	10.	Tastes	16.	Tongue-consciousness
5.	Body	11.	Tangibles	17.	Body-consciousness
6.	Mind	12.	Mental objects	18.	Mind-consciousness

Glossary

Abhidharma – The "Higher Teaching" attributed to the Buddha. Numerous Mainstream Buddhist schools developed their own *Abhidharma* texts that featured philosophical and psychological examinations of the nature of existence, the functioning of *karma*, and the processes associated with mental cognition.

***anātman* (P: *anattā*)** – The Buddhist teaching of "No-Self," or the rejection of any eternal, unchanging core substance (like a "Self" or a "soul") to one's individuality.

aniconic – The term used to describe symbolic representations of the Buddha without using a humanlike or anthropomorphic form. For example, the depiction of the Buddha in terms of a footprint or a *stūpa* reflect aniconic images.

***arhat* (P: *arahant*)** – An individual who has attained nirvāṇa while in this world. This figure was denigrated by Mahāyāna texts as inferior to a Buddha.

aṭṭhakathā – Written commentaries on the Pāli Canon preserved by the Sri Lankan Theravāda community. Ancient commentarial traditions in an old form of Sinhala were emended and translated into Pāli by the monk Buddhaghosa in the fifth century CE.

***bhikṣu* (P: *bhikkhu*)** – An ordained alms-recipient or monk who lives off gifts of food and other requisites while pursuing the moral discipline and knowledge that lead to liberation. Such monks were often also interested in earning merit and involved in the economic affairs of monasteries.

***bhikṣuṇī* (P: *bhikkhunī*)** – An ordained female alms-recipient or nun who follows a similar path of renunciation and study as Buddhist monks, but who is subordinated by "eight special conditions" or rules that place the nuns under the control and supervision of monks.

Bodhi Tree – The "Tree of Awakening" under which the Buddha sat when he attained his Awakening. Subsequently, the Bodhi Tree has become a relic as an object used by the Buddha and a symbol for his Awakening.

bodhicitta – "Awakening Mind" or "Thought of Enlightenment" that is initially generated in the mind of one who takes up the *bodhisattva* path to become a Buddha.

bodhisattva – A future Buddha or a being who has made a vow to become a Buddha and show others the path to liberation. Bodhisattvas represent exemplary models for religious striving and figures of devotion.

Brahmā – The "creator-god" believed by Hindus to have created the universe. In Buddhism, Brahmā was reinterpreted as a divine devotee of the Buddha.

Brahmin – Term used to refer to the priestly class at the top of the ancient Indian social hierarchy. Brahmins were charged with preserving and chanting sacred *mantra*s and with performing sacrifices and other rituals to sustain the social and cosmic orders.

buddhavacana – The "Word of the Buddha," which refers to the authoritative teachings attributed to the Buddha and held by Buddhists to exist in various *sūtra*s or scriptures.

canon – A collection of authoritative texts, which in Buddhism are normally associated with the Word of the Buddha. South Asian Buddhism witnessed the development of several different canons linked to different monastic orders or geographical regions.

***cetasika*s** – Mental states or phenomena such as feeling, perception, energy, greed, etc. that arise and are associated with consciousness according to Pāli *Abhidhamma* texts.

citta – Consciousness in the form of discrete moments of mental activity that may be conditioned by *karma*, productive of subsequent karmic effects, or neither in the case of morally neutral acts or Awakened actors who have extinguished the roots of *karma*.

dāna – Acts of giving that comprise one of the major forms of Buddhist practice. Such giving, whether directed toward the Saṅgha or toward other beings in need, allows people to develop virtue and earn merit.

dasa sil mātā – "Ten Precept Mothers," or female renunciants in Theravāda Buddhist cultures such as Sri Lanka. These women adopt the appearance and lifestyle of Buddhist nuns but lack the formal ordination to become *bhikkhunī*s.

dhāraṇī – Verses containing strings of words that are identified as magical utterances and that contain the teaching of the Buddha in condensed form. *Dhāraṇī*s were commonly employed in Mahāyāna and Vajrayāna contexts.

dharmas **(*P: dhammas*)** – The collection of physical and mental factors held by most Mainstream schools to be the momentary and mutually conditioned qualities that constitute the basic experience and reality of *saṃsāra*. The analysis of these irreducible factors of existence appears in the *Abhidharma* literature.

dharmakāya – The "truth body" of the Buddha or the "body of the doctrine," which could be identified with the Buddha himself. As the most abstract manifestation of the Buddha, it was variously conceived—ranging from the teachings or qualities of a Buddha to an overarching universal reality identified with truth itself.

dukkha – The Pāli term for suffering, dissatisfaction, or discomfort that is held to be inevitable for sentient beings who exist in the cycle of birth and death.

Great Cosmic Mountain – Mount Meru, or the mythic mountain in the center of this world-realm as depicted in ancient Indian Buddhist cosmology.

Jātaka – Stories of the Buddha's previous existences in human, animal, and divine forms. These stories made up popular Buddhist narratives, many of which were collected into a canonical text or other popular narrative compilations.

lama – A lay or monastic teacher associated with Buddhist traditions located in or derived from Tibet. *Lamas* are typically revered figures that show the path to liberation and sometimes have administrative responsibilities over monasteries, schools, or states.

Madhyamaka – The Middle Way School of Mahāyāna Buddhist thought. Associated with the author Nāgārjuna, it emphasized the emptiness of all conditioned phenomena and the ultimate non-distinction between *saṃsāra* and *nirvāṇa*.

Mahar – A Dalit or "untouchable" caste based in Maharashtra, India that has converted in large numbers to Buddhism since 1956, following the example of Dr. Bhimrao Ambedkar, a Mahar political leader.

Mahāsāṃghika – An early Mainstream Buddhist school that asserted *arhats* were imperfect and that the Buddha was transcendent and merely appeared to conform to the ways of human existence in the world.

Mahāvihāra – An ancient Sri Lankan monastic order that asserted its links to the senior monks who rehearsed the Dharma at the First Council of Rājagṛha. Known for maintaining conservative Theravāda teachings, this order wrote down the Pāli Tipiṭaka starting around 20 BCE.

maṇḍala – Geometric designs of cosmic worlds normally associated with one or another Buddha or Buddhist deity and employed for meditative practices, often in Buddhist Tantra.

mantra – Sacred chants that are uttered to effect desired results in the performance of rituals. These chants were typically believed to possess power that is inherent in the sounds that make up the *mantra*, and they are found in a wide variety of ancient Indian religions.

mātṛkā – "Matrices" or summary lists used to classify and memorize the Buddha's teachings. Such lists likely formed the sources out of which later Abhidharma texts were composed.

merit – The future good results of morally positive actions performed by Buddhists who are aware of the potential effects of their deeds. Merit can be earned by doing good *karma*, but it is routinely shared with others to deflect the selfish desire to earn merit for oneself alone.

mudrā – A physical gesture, often made with the hands, representing an act performed by a Buddha. These gestures became important artistic conventions and were ritually reenacted by Tantric Buddhists. A *mudrā* could also be a Tantric "seal" that confirms and deepens one's practice.

mūla – A term used to denote a fraternity of monks within the Sri Lankan Saṅgha during the medieval period. A *mūla* represented a more circumscribed group than the broader category of *nikāya*.

nikāya – The term used to refer to the different scriptural collections of sermons attributed to the Buddha. The same term also functioned to denote a particular monastic order within Mainstream Buddhist communities.

nirvāṇa – The condition of liberation wherein one extinguishes all the roots of rebirth by bringing all traces of ignorance and desire to an end. Described paradoxically as an indescribable state beyond all mundane thoughts and feelings, *nirvāṇa* is said to be identifiable with the world-transcending experience of a Buddha.

***pāramitā* (P: *pārami*)** – "Perfection" or a moral virtue that is cultivated to the highest degree imaginable by one who seeks to become a Buddha. Usually found in a list of six or ten moral virtues to be perfected by *bodhisattva*s.

pāribhogika-dhātu – Relics of objects once used by the Buddha or an *arhat*, which may include the Bodhi Tree and an alms bowl. Such objects used by an Awakened One are seen to be worthy of veneration.

parinirvāṇa – The final passing away of a Buddha where all mental and physical activity reaches complete cessation. Upon reaching this moment, a Buddha theoretically transcends the world of *saṃsāra* and is not reborn in the world.

pirivena – The generic name for a center of monastic learning in Sri Lanka, where monks are trained primarily in Buddhist thought and literature.

pramāṇa – A valid means of knowledge or cognition, often the subject of philosophical debate in ancient South Asia.

Prātimokṣa – The section of the *Vinaya* literature that deals with the individual code of conduct for a monk or a nun. Varying to some degree from one monastic order to another, the *Prātimokṣa* prescribes rules and punishments for those who violate them.

pratītya-samutpāda – Dependent co-arising, or the theory discovered and taught by the Buddha wherein everything that comes to be due to causes and conditions must also come to an end when its causes and conditions cease. This theory that identifies twelve links from ignorance through old age and death illustrates both the impermanence and interdependence of the factors of existence.

pudgala – An abstract entity or "person," neither equivalent to the Five Aggregates nor wholly separate from them, that transmigrates and carries the Five Aggregates from one lifetime to the next. The Mainstream Pudgalavāda School maintained the real existence of the "person" across lifetimes over against the denunciations of other Buddhist schools.

pūjā – A devotional offering of flowers, food, incense, etc. given to the Buddha in the form of his relics or image. Usually such offerings are understood as ways to earn merit.

Rana – An aristocratic, hereditary dynasty of prime ministers that ruled Nepal from 1846 to 1953 and restricted the practice of Buddhism.

sādhana – A set of meditative and liturgical practices directed toward a particular deity or deities in Tantric Buddhism.

saṃsāra – The nearly endless cycle of birth and death recognized by many communities in ancient India. The repetition of births and deaths is understood by Buddhists to be tiresome and subject to dissatisfaction.

Saṅgha – The assembly of monks and nuns who follow the monastic discipline attributed to the Buddha. This body of Buddhist renunciants is widely seen as the third member of the "Three Jewels" of Buddhism.

sarīra-dhātu – Bodily relics of the Buddha or an *arhat* who has similarly attained Awakening. Such relics may be comprised of bones or ash that is collected and enshrined for veneration.

Sarvāstivāda – A Mainstream Buddhist school that produced a large collection of Abhidharma texts and maintained that the factors of existence (*dharma*s) survive over three periods of time: future, present, and past.

***śāsana* (P: *sāsana*)** – The "Dispensation" of the Buddha, or the texts and the monastic institutions held to have been established by the Buddha for the purpose of teaching the Dharma.

Sautrāntika – The Buddhist school that split from the Sarvāstivāda. Unlike the latter community, the Sautrāntika focused solely on the Sūtra Piṭaka texts and claimed that *dharma*s have merely an instantaneous existence before passing away.

siddha – A "perfected one" who represents the ideal spiritual path in Buddhist Tantra. *Siddha*s typically resided outside of monastic settings and employed socially transgressive practices to attain their Awakening more rapidly in the current life.

skandhas – The five aggregates or heaps of material and mental factors comprising individual existence in *saṃsāra*. These are said to include physical form, feelings, perceptions, dispositions, and consciousness.

śramaṇa – Ascetic recluses that renounced the ordinary life of married householders to seek the knowledge leading to liberation from *saṃsāra*. The early Buddhists were just one community of *śramaṇa*s among others in ancient India.

***sthavira* (P: *thera*)** – The term used to designate an elder-monk in the Buddhist tradition. This designation appears to have been claimed by certain Mainstream Buddhist schools to claim an association with the Buddha's original disciples who met at the First Council of Rājagṛha.

stūpa – A shrine thought to house a deposit of a bodily relic or relics from the Buddha or another Awakened disciple. In South Asia, *stūpa*s were often constructed as large dome-like monuments made out of brick that became popular sites of worship early on in the tradition.

śūnyatā – The notion of "emptiness," which denotes the lack of inherent, independent existence in all so-called entities or things, which arise and fall away due to conditions.

sūtra – The term for a Buddhist scripture that carried the authority of being a text attributed directly to the Buddha and transmitted into writing by one or more of his disciples.

tantra – A class of texts—variously categorized but purportedly from the Buddha—that are associated with the esoteric ritual and meditative practices of Vajrayāna Buddhism. The word Tantra also denotes systems of religious practice linked with these texts and dealing with the appropriation of power as an overlord or a deity.

Tathāgata – The "Thus-Gone-One" or, alternatively, "Thus-Come-One." An epithet for a Buddha, it signifies one who has traversed the path leading to Awakening and liberation from repeated births and deaths.

tathāgatagarbha – The "Womb of Buddhahood," or an early Mahāyāna notion identified with the intrinsic purity of consciousness and an innate potential for attaining Buddhahood.

trikāya – The "Three Bodies" of a Buddha, which according to Mahāyāna thought consist of the truth body that is omnipresent, the enjoyment body that resides in celestial paradises, and the apparition body that appears on earth in conformity with what is expected of human existence.

Tripiṭaka (P: Tipiṭaka) – The "Three Baskets" or the traditional, threefold division of the word of the Buddha into his teachings on monastic discipline, his discursive sermons, and technical reflections on the higher teachings of the Buddha.

upāsaka/upāsikā – Terms denoting male and female lay devotees of the Three Jewels of Buddhism. At times these terms signified laypersons that adopted stricter forms of Buddhist practice short of monastic ordination to cultivate Buddhist virtues.

upasampadā – The formal higher ordination ceremony that is used to confer the status of a fully ordained monk or nun in the Saṅgha. This ceremony may only be offered to an individual at or after age twenty, and it requires at least five fully ordained monks or nuns to administer it to a male or female candidate, respectively.

vajrācārya – "Vajra-masters" or Tantric Buddhist ritual specialists who perform the esoteric rights of Tantric Buddhism. In Nepal, it refers to a high-caste group among Newar Buddhists.

Vibhajyavāda – The name adopted by Mainstream Buddhists who rejected the Sarvāstivāda tenet of the existence of *dharma*s at all times. Linked with the Sthaviravāda community, they included monks who belonged to the Dharmaguptaka, Theravāda, and other schools.

vihāra – A sizable dwelling or monastic residence wherein Buddhist monks or nuns lived on a fairly permanent basis.

Vinaya – The collection of monastic disciplinary codes attributed to the Buddha for the sake of regulating the conduct of monks and nuns.

Yogācāra – The Mahāyāna School of philosophy that analyzed the nature of the mind and stressed the need to purify consciousness to remove the false conceptualization of experience in terms of a dichotomous subject and object.

Bibliography

Abe, S.K. (1995) "Inside the Wonder House: Buddhist Art and the West," in D.S. Lopez, Jr. (ed.) *Curators of the Buddha: The Study of Buddhism under Colonialism*, 63–106, Chicago, IL: University of Chicago Press.

Abeysekara, A. (2002) *Colors of the Robe: Religion, Identity, and Difference*, Columbia, SC: University of South Carolina Press.

Adikaram, E.W. (1994) *Early History of Buddhism in Ceylon: Or "State of Buddhism in Ceylon as Revealed by the Pāli Commentaries of the 5th Century A.D."*, reprint, Dehiwala, Sri Lanka: Buddhist Cultural Centre.

Adikari, A. (2006) *The Classical Education of the Community of MahaSaṅgha in Sri Lanka*, Colombo, Sri Lanka: Godage International Publishers.

Ahir, D.C. (1995) "100 Years of Buddhism in Modern India (1891–1991)," in D.C. Ahir (ed.) *A Panorama of Indian Buddhism: Selections from the Maha Bodhi Journal (1892–1992)*, 595–600, Delhi: Sri Satguru Publications.

Anacker, S. (1984) *Seven Works of Vasubandhu: The Buddhist Psychological Doctor*, Delhi: Motilal Banarsidass.

Aris, M. (1979) *Bhutan: The Early History of a Himalayan Kingdom*, Warminster, UK: Aris & Phillips.

Arnold, D. (2005) *Buddhists, Brahmins, and Belief: Epistemology in South Asian Philosophy of Religion*, New York: Columbia University Press.

Avedon, J.F. (1984) *In Exile from the Land of Snows*, New York: Alfred A. Knopf.

Bailey, G. and Mabbett, I. (2003) *The Sociology of Early Buddhism*, Cambridge: Cambridge University Press.

Bareau, A. (1955) *Les sectes bouddhiques du petit véhicule*, Paris: École Française Extreme-Orient.

Bareau, A. (1989) "Hinayana Buddhism," in J.M. Kitagawa and M.D. Cummings (eds.) *Buddhism and Asian History*, 195–214, New York: Macmillan.

Bartholomeusz, T.J. (1994) *Women Under the Bō Tree: Buddhist Nuns in Sri Lanka*, Cambridge: Cambridge University Press.

Bechert, H. (2004) "Buddha, Life of the," in R.E. Buswell, Jr. (ed.) *Encyclopedia of Buddhism*, 82–8, New York: Macmillan.

Beltz, J. (2005) *Mahar, Buddhist and Dalit: Religious Conversion and Socio-Political Emancipation*, New Delhi: Manohar.

Berkwitz, S.C. (2004) *Buddhist History in the Vernacular: The Power of the Past in Late Medieval Sri Lanka*, Leiden: Brill.

Berkwitz, S.C. (2006) "Buddhism in Sri Lanka: Practice, Protest, and Preservation," in S.C. Berkwitz (ed.) *Buddhism in World Cultures: Comparative Perspectives*, 45–72, Santa Barbara, CA: ABC-CLIO.

Berkwitz, S.C. (trans.) (2007) *The History of the Buddha's Relic Shrine: A Translation of the* Sinhala Thūpavaṃsa, New York: Oxford University Press.

Berkwitz, S.C. (2008) "Resisting the Global in Buddhist Nationalism: Venerable Soma's Discourse of Decline and Reform." *Journal of Asian Studies* 67: 73–106.

Bhadra, B. (2001) *Higher Ordination and Bhikkhuni Order in Sri Lanka*, Dehiwala, Sri Lanka: Sridevi Printers.

Blackburn, A.M. (2001) *Buddhist Learning and Textual Practice in Eighteenth-Century Lankan Monastic Culture*, Princeton, NJ: Princeton University Press.

Blackstone, K. (1998) *Women in the Footsteps of the Buddha: Struggle for Liberation in the Therīgāthā*, Richmond, UK: Curzon Press.

Bodhi, B. (1984) *The Noble Eightfold Path: Way to the End of Suffering*, Kandy, Sri Lanka: Buddhist Publication Society.

Bodhi, B. (ed.) (1993) *A Comprehensive Manual of Abhidhamma: The Abhidhammattha Sangaha of Ācariya Anuruddha*, Kandy, Sri Lanka: Buddhist Publication Society.

Bodhi, B. (2005) *In the Buddha's Words: An Anthology of Discourses from the Pāli Canon*, Boston, MA: Wisdom Publications.

Bond, G.D. (1988) *The Buddhist Revival in Sri Lanka: Religious Tradition, Reinterpretation and Response*, Columbia, SC: University of South Carolina Press.

Bond, G.D. (2004) *Buddhism at Work: Community Development, Social Empowerment and the Sarvodaya Movement*, Bloomfield, CT: Kumarian Press.

Boucher, D. (2008) *Bodhisattvas of the Forest and the Formation of the Mahāyāna: A Study and Translation of the* Rāṣṭrapālaparipṛcchā-sūtra, Honolulu, HI: University of Hawai'i Press.

Bronkhorst, J. (2007) *Greater Magadha: Studies in the Culture of Early India*, Leiden: Brill.

Brown, R.L. (2004) "Buddha Images," R.E. Buswell, Jr. (ed.) *Encyclopedia of Buddhism*, 79–82, New York: Macmillan.

Chakravarti, U. (1987) *The Social Dimensions of Early Buddhism*, Delhi: Oxford University Press.

Champakalakshmi, R. (1998) "Buddhism in Tamil Nadu: Patterns of Patronage," in R.S. Murthy and M.S. Nagarajan (eds.) *Buddhism in Tamil Nadu: Collected Papers*, 69–96, Chennai, India: Institute of Asian Studies.

Chaudhuri, S. (1982) *Contemporary Buddhism in Bangladesh*, Calcutta: Atisha Memorial Publishing Society.

Chaudhuri, S. (1983) *Analytical Study of the Abhidharmakośa*, 2nd edn., Calcutta: Firma KLM.

Clayton, B.R. (2006) *Moral Theory in Śāntideva's* Śikṣāsamuccaya*: Cultivating the Fruits of Virtue,* London: Routledge.

Cleary, T. (trans.) (1987) *Entry into the Realm of Reality, the Text: A Translation of the* Gandavyuha, *the final book of the* Avatamsaka Sutra, Boston, MA: Shambhala.

Collins, S. (1982) *Selfless Persons: Imagery and Thought in* Theravāda *Buddhism*, Cambridge: Cambridge University Press.

Collins, S. (1992) "On the Very Idea of the Pali Canon," *Journal of the Pali Text Society* 35: 89–126.

Coningham, R. (2001) "The Archaeology of Buddhism," in T. Insoll (ed.) *Archaeology and World Religion*, 61–95, London: Routledge.
Conze, E. (1967) *Buddhist Thought in India: Three Phases of Buddhist Philosophy*, Ann Arbor, MI: University of Michigan Press.
Conze, E. (1968) *Thirty Years of Buddhist Studies: Selected Essays by Edward Conze*, Columbia, SC: University of South Carolina Press.
Conze, E. (trans.) (1994) *The Perfection of Wisdom in Eight Thousand Lines & Its Verse Summary*, Delhi: Sri Satguru Publications.
Coomaraswamy, A.K. (1927) "The Origin of the Buddha Image," *The Art Bulletin*, 9: 287–329.
Cox, C. (2004a) "From Category to Ontology: The Changing Role of Dharma in Sarvāstivāda Abhidharma," *Journal of Indian Philosophy* 32: 543–97.
Cox, C. (2004b) "Mainstream Buddhist Schools," in R.E. Buswell, Jr. (ed.) *Encyclopedia of Buddhism*, 501–7, New York: Macmillan.
Crosby, K. and Skilton, A. (trans.) (1998) *Śāntideva: The Bodhicaryāvatāra*, Oxford: Oxford University Press.
Davids, T.W.R. and Oldenberg, H. (trans.) (1990) *Vinaya Texts: Part I*, Delhi: Motlilal Banarsidass.
Davidson, R.M. (2002) *Indian Esoteric Buddhism: A Social History of the Tantric Movement*, New York: Columbia University Press.
Davidson, R.M. (2004) "Vajrayāna," in R.E. Buswell, Jr. (ed.) *Encyclopedia of Buddhism*, 875–7, New York: Macmillan.
De Silva, C.R. (1998) "The Plurality of Buddhist Fundamentalism: An Inquiry into Views among Buddhist Monks in Sri Lanka," in T.J. Bartholomeusz and C.R. de Silva (eds.) *Buddhist Fundamentalism and Minority Identities in Sri Lanka*, 53–73, Albany, NY: State University of New York Press.
De Silva, L. (1980) *Paritta: A Historical and Religious Study of the Buddhist Ceremony for Peace and Prosperity in Sri Lanka*, Colombo, Sri Lanka: National Museums of Sri Lanka.
DeCaroli, R. (2004) *Haunting the Buddha: Indian Popular Religions and the Formation of Buddhism*, Oxford: Oxford University Press.
Deegalle, M. (2004) "Politics of the Jathika Hela Urumaya Monks: Buddhism and Ethnicity in Contemporary Sri Lanka." *Contemporary Buddhism* 5: 83–103.
Dehejia, V. (1987) "The Persistence of Buddhism in Tamil Nadu," *Mārg* 39: 53–74.
Desikan, V.N.S. (1998) "Buddhist Art and Architecture in Tamil Nadu," in R.S. Murthy and M.S. Nagarajan (eds.) *Buddhism in Tamil Nadu: Collected Papers*, 149–56, Chennai, India: Institute of Asian Studies.
DeVotta, N. (2007) *Sinhalese Buddhist Nationalist Ideology: Implications for Politics and Conflict Resolution in Sri Lanka*, Policy Studies 40, Washington, DC: East–West Center Washington.
DeVotta, N. and Stone, J. (2008) "Jathika Hela Urumaya and Ethno-Religious Politics in Sri Lanka." *Public Affairs* 81: 31–51.
Dhammajoti, B.K.L. (2002) *Sarvāstivāda Abhidharma*, Colombo, Sri Lanka: Centre for Buddhist Studies.
Dhirasekera, J. (1982) *Buddhist Monastic Discipline: A Study of its Origin and Development in Relation to the Sutta and Vinaya Pitakas*, Colombo, Sri Lanka: Ministry of Higher Education.

Doyle, T.N. (2003) "'Liberate the Mahabodhi Temple!': Socially Engaged Buddhism, Dalit Style," in S. Heine and C.S. Prebish (eds.) *Buddhism in the Modern World: Adaptations of an Ancient Tradition*, 249–80, Oxford: Oxford University Press.

Drewes, D. (2007) "Revisiting the Phrase '*sa pṛthivīpradeśaś caityabhūto bhavet*' and the Mahāyāna Cult of the Book," *Indo-Iranian Journal* 50: 101–43.

Dundas, P. (1992) *The Jains*, London: Routledge.

Dunne, J. (2004) *Foundations of Dharmakīrti's Philosophy*, Boston, MA: Wisdom Publications.

Dunne, J. (2005) "Buddhism, Schools of: Mahāyāna Philosophical Schools of Buddhism," in L. Jones (ed.) *Encyclopedia of Religion*, 2nd edn., 1203–13, Detroit: Macmillan Reference.

Dunne, J. (2006) "Realizing the Unreal: Dharmakīrti's Theory of Yogic Perception," *Journal of Indian Philosophy* 34: 497–519.

English, E. (2002) *Vajrayoginī: Her Visualizations, Rituals, and Forms: A Study of the Cult of Vajrayoginī in India*, Boston, MA: Wisdom Publications.

Enomoto, F. (2000) "'Mūlasarvāstivādin' and 'Sarvāstivādin'," in C. Chojnacki, J.-U. Hartmann, and V.M. Tschannerl (eds.) *Vividharatnakaraṇḍaka: Festgabe für Adelheid Mette*, 239–50, Swisttal-Odendorf, Germany: Indica et Tibetica Verlag.

Garfield, J. (1995) *The Fundamental Wisdom of the Middle Way: Nāgārjuna's* Mūlamadhyamakakārikā, New York: Oxford University Press.

Garfield, J. (2002) *Empty Words: Buddhist Philosophy and Cross-Cultural Interpretation*, New York: Oxford University Press.

Geiger, W. (trans.) (2001) *The Mahāvaṃsa or the Great Chronicle of Ceylon*, Oxford: Pali Text Society.

Gellner, D.N. (1992) *Monk, Householder, and Tantric Priest: Newar Buddhism and its Hierarchy of Ritual*, Cambridge: Cambridge University Press.

Gellner, D.N. (2005) "The Emergence of Conversion in a Hindu–Buddhist Polytropy: The Kathmandu Valley, Nepal, c. 1600–1995," *Comparative Studies in Society and History* 47: 755–80.

Gethin, R. (1992) *The Buddhist Path of Awakening: A Study of the Bodhi Pakkhiyā Dhammā*, Leiden: Brill.

Gethin, R. (1998) *The Foundations of Buddhism*, Oxford: Oxford University Press.

Gethin, R. (2004) "He Who Sees Dhamma Sees Dhammas: Dhamma in Early Buddhism," *Journal of Indian Philosophy* 32: 513–42.

Gokhale, B.G. (1980) "Early Buddhism and the Brahmanas," in A.K. Narain (ed.) *Studies in the History of Buddhism*, 67–80, Delhi: B.R. Publishing Company.

Gokhale, B.G. (1999) "Theravada Buddhism and Modernization: Anagarika Dharmapala and B.R. Ambedkar," *Journal of Asian and African Studies* 34: 33–45.

Gombrich, R. (1990) "How the Mahāyāna Began," in T. Skorupski (ed.) *The Buddhist Forum, Volume I: Seminar Papers 1987–1988*, 21–30, London: School of Oriental and African Studies.

Gombrich, R. (2006) *How Buddhism Began: The Conditioned Genesis of the Early Teachings*, London: Routledge.

Gombrich, R. and Obeyesekere, G. (1988) *Buddhism Transformed: Religious Change in Sri Lanka*, Princeton, NJ: Princeton University Press.

Gómez, Luis O. (1996) *The Land of Bliss: The Paradise of the Buddha of Measureless Light*, Honolulu, HI: University of Hawai'i Press.

Goswami, B. (trans.) (2001) *Lalitavistara*, Kolkata, India: The Asiatic Society.

Gray, D.B. (2005) "Disclosing the Empty Secret: Textuality and Embodiment in the Cakrasamvara Tantra," *Numen* 52: 417–44.

Gray, D.B. (2007) *The Cakrasamvara Tantra (The Discourse of Śrī Heruka): A Study and Annotated Translation*, New York: American Institute of Buddhist Studies.

Griffiths, P.J. (1994) "Indian Buddhist Meditation," in Y. Takeuchi (ed.) *Buddhist Spirituality: Indian, Southeast Asian, Tibetan, and Early Chinese*, 34–66, New York: Crossroad.

Gunawardana, R.A.L.H. (1979) *Robe and Plough: Monasticism and Economic Interest in Early Medieval Sri Lanka*, Tucson, AZ: University of Arizona Press.

Guruge, A. (ed.) (1991) *Return to Righteousness: A Collection of Speeches, Essays and Letters of the Anagarika Dharmapala*, Battaramulla, Sri Lanka: Department of Cultural Affairs.

Gyatso, S. (2003) "Of Monks and Monasteries," in D. Bernstorff and H. von Welck (eds.) *Exile as Challenge: The Tibetan Diaspora*, 213–43, New Delhi: Orient Longman.

Hallisey, C. (1991) "Councils as Ideas and Events in the Theravāda," *The Buddhist Forum* 2: 133–148.

Hallisey, C. (1995) "Roads Taken and Not Taken in Theravāda Buddhism," in D.S. Lopez, Jr. (ed.) *Curators of the Buddha: The Study of Buddhism Under Colonialism*, 31–61, Chicago, IL: University of Chicago Press.

Hallisey, C. (2003) "Works and Persons in Sinhala Literary Culture," in S. Pollock (ed.) *Literary Cultures in History: Reconstructions from South Asia*, 689–746, Berkeley, CA: University of California Press.

Harris, E.J. (1999) "The Female in Buddhism," in K.L. Tsomo (ed.) *Buddhist Women Across Cultures: Realizations*, 49–65, Albany, NY: State University of New York Press.

Harris, E.J. (2006) *Theravāda Buddhism and the British Encounter: Religious, Missionary and Colonial Experience in Nineteenth-Century Sri Lanka*, London: Routledge.

Harrison, P. (1982) "Sanskrit Fragments of a Lokottaravādin Tradition," in L.A. Hercus et al. (eds.) *Indological and Buddhist Studies: Volume in Honour of Professor J.W. de Jong on his Sixtieth Birthday*, 211–34, Canberra: Faculty of Asian Studies.

Harrison, P. (1992) "Is the *Dharma-kāya* the Real 'Phantom Body' of the Buddha?" *Journal of the International Association of Buddhist Studies* 15: 44–94.

Harrison, P. (1995) "Searching for the Origins of the Mahāyāna: What Are We Looking For?" *The Eastern Buddhist* 18: 48–69.

Harrison, P. (2003) "Mediums and Messages: Reflections on the Production of Mahāyāna Sūtras," *The Eastern Buddhist* 35: 115–51.

Harrison, P. (2007) "The Case of the Vanishing Poet: New Light on Śāntideva and the *Śikṣā-samuccaya*," in K. Klaus and J.-U. Hartmann (eds.) *Indica et Tibetica: Festschrift für Michael Hahn zum 65. Geburtstag von Freunden und Schülern überreicht*, 215–48,Vienna: Arbeitskreis für Tibetische und Buddhistische Studien.

Hazra, K.L. (1995) *The Rise and Decline of Buddhism in India*, New Delhi: Munshiram Manoharlal.

von Hinüber, O. (1995) "Buddhist Law According to the Theravāda-Vinaya: A Survey of Theory and Practice," *Journal of the International Association of Buddhist Studies* 18: 7–45.

Hirakawa, A. (1990) *A History of Indian Buddhism: From Śākyamuni to Early Mahāyāna*, (trans. and ed. Paul Groner), Honolulu, HI: University of Hawai'i Press.

Holt, J.C. (1983) *Discipline: The Canonical Buddhism of the* Vinayapiṭaka, Delhi: Motilal Banarsidass.

Holt, J.C. (1991) Buddha in the Crown: Avalokiteśvara in the Buddhist Traditions of Sri Lanka, Oxford: Oxford University Press.

Huntington, S.L. (1990) "Early Buddhist Art and the Theory of Aniconism," *Art Journal* 49: 401–8.

Hurvitz, L. (trans.) (1976) *Scripture of the Lotus Blossom of the Fine Dharma (The Lotus Sūtra): Translated from the Chinese of Kumārajīva*, New York: Columbia University Press.

Ilangasinha, H.B.M. (1992) *Buddhism in Medieval Sri Lanka*, Delhi: Sri Satguru Publications.

Jackson, R.R. (trans.) (2004) *Tantric Treasures: Three Collections of Mystical Verse from Buddhist India*, New York: Oxford University Press.

Jaini, P.S. (1958) "On the Theory of Two Vasubandhus," *Bulletin of the School of Oriental and African Studies*, 21: 48–53.

Jaini, P.S. (1959) "The Sautrāntika Theory of *Bīja*," *Bulletin of the School of Oriental and African Studies*, 22: 236–49.

Jaini, P.S. (1980) "The Disappearance of Buddhism and the Survival of Jainism: A Study in Contrast," in A.K. Narain (ed.) *Studies in History of Buddhism*, 81–91, Delhi: B.R. Publishing.

Jayawickrama, N.A. (ed. and trans.) (1986) *The Inception of the Discipline and the Vinaya Nidāna* (reprint 1962), London: Pali Text Society.

Jayawickrama, N.A. (trans.) (1990) *The Story of Gotama Buddha: The Nidāna-kathā of the Jātakaṭṭhakathā*, Oxford: Pali Text Society.

Jones, J.J. (trans.) (1949–1956) *The Mahāvastu*, 3 vols., London: Luzac & Company.

Kantowsky, D. (1980) *Sarvodaya: The Other Development*, New Delhi: Vikas.

Kapstein, M.T. (2005) "Buddhism, schools of: Tantric Ritual Schools of Buddhism [Further Considerations]," in L. Jones (ed.), *Encyclopedia of Religion*, 2nd edn., 1221–2, Detroit: Macmillan.

Karlsson, K. (2006) "The Formation of Early Buddhist Visual Culture," *Material Culture* 2: 68–95.

Karunatillake, W.S. (1979) " The Religiousness of Buddhists in Sri Lanka Through Belief and Practice," in J.R. Carter (ed.), *Religiousness in Sri Lanka*, 1–34, Colombo, Sri Lanka: Marga Institute.

Kashyap, B.J. (1954) *The Abhidhamma Philosophy: Or The Psycho-Ethical Philosophy of Early Buddhism*, Nalanda (Patna), India: Buddha-Vihara.

Kawamura, L. (2004) "Bodisattva(s)," in R.E. Buswell, Jr. (ed.) *Encyclopedia of Buddhism*, 58–60, New York: Macmillan.

King, R. (1994) "Early Yogācāra and its Relationship with the Madhyamaka School," *Philosophy East and West* 44: 659–83.

King, R. (1999) *Indian Philosophy: An Introduction to Hindu and Buddhist Thought*, Washington, DC: Georgetown University Press.

Kloppenborg, R. (1977) "Theravāda Buddhism in Nepal." *Kailash* 5: 301–22.

Kloppenborg, R. (1995) "Female Stereotypes in Early Buddhism: The Women of the Therīgāthā," in R. Kloppenborg and W.J. Hanegraaff (eds.) *Female Stereotypes in Religious Traditions*, 151–69, Leiden: E.J. Brill.

Kochumuttom, T.A. (1989) *A Buddhist Doctrine of Experience: A New Translation and Interpretation of the Works of Vasubandhu the Yogācārin*, Delhi: Motilal Banarsidass.

Kowalewski, M. (1994) "Religion in Bhutan II: The Formation of a World-View," in M. Aris and M. Hutt (eds.) *Bhutan: Aspects of Culture and Development*, 123–35, Gartmore, UK: Kiscadale.

Lamotte, E. (1988) *History of Indian Buddhism; From the Origins to the Śaka Era*, (trans. S. Webb-Boin), Louvain-la-Neuve, Belgium: Institut Orientliste de l'Université Catholique de Louvain.

Lang, K. (2004) "Madhyamaka School," in R.E. Buswell, Jr. (ed.) *Encyclopedia of Buddhism*, 479–85, New York: Macmillan.

Larson, G.J. (1995) *India's Agony over Religion*, Albany, NY: State University of New York Press.

Law, B.C. (1923) *The Life and Work of Buddhaghosa*, Calcutta: Thacker, Spink, & Co.

Leve, L.G. (2002) "Subjects, Selves, and the Politics of Personhood in Theravada Buddhism in Nepal," *Journal of Asian Studies* 61: 833–60.

LeVine, S. (2000) "At the Cutting Edge: Theravāda Nuns in the Kathmandu Valley," in K.L. Tsomo (ed.) *Innovative Buddhist Women: Swimming Against the Stream*, 13–29, Richmond, UK: Curzon.

LeVine, S. and Gellner, D.N. (2005) *Rebuilding Buddhism: The Theravada Movement in Twentieth-Century Nepal*, Cambridge, MA: Harvard University Press.

Lewis, T.T. (2000) *Popular Buddhist Texts from Nepal: Narratives and Rituals of Newar Buddhism*, Albany, NY: State University of New York Press.

van Lohuizen-de Leeuw, J.E. (1979) "New Evidence with Regard to the Origins of the Buddha Image," in H. Härtel (ed.) *South Asian Archaeology 1979*, 377–400, Berlin: Dietrich Reimer Verlag.

Lopez, Jr., D.S. (1998) *Prisoners of Shangri-La: Tibetan Buddhism and the West*, Chicago, IL: University of Chicago Press.

Malalasekera, G.P. (1994) *The Pāli Literature of Ceylon*, Kandy, Sri Lanka: Buddhist Publication Society.

Malalgoda, K. (1976) *Buddhism in Sinhalese Society, 1750–1900: A Study of Religious Revival and Change*, Berkeley, CA: University of California Press.

McMahan, D. (1998) "Orality, Writing, and Authority in South Asian Buddhism: Visionary Literature and the Struggle for Legitimacy in the Mahāyāna," *History of Religions* 37: 249–74.

McMahan, D. (2004) "Modernity and the Early Discourse of Scientific Buddhism," *Journal of the American Academy of Religion* 72: 897–933.

Moran, P. (2004) *Buddhism Observed: Travelers, Exiles and Tibetan Dharma in Kathmandu*, London: RoutledgeCurzon.

Morris, R. (ed.) (1961) *Aṅguttara Nikāya, Part I*, rev. A. Warder, 2nd edn., Oxford: Pali Text Society.

Moynihan, M. (2003) "Tibetan Refugees in Nepal," in D. Bernstorff and H. von Welck (eds.) *Exile as Challenge: The Tibetan Diaspora*, 312–21, New Delhi: Orient Longman.

Mrozik, S. (2007) *Virtuous Bodies: The Physical Dimensions of Morality in Buddhist Ethics*, New York: Oxford University Press.

Mus, P. (1978) *Barabudur: Esquisse d'une Histoire du Bouddhisme Fondeé sur la Critique Archéologique des Textes*, New York: Arno Press.

Nagao, G. (2005) "Vasubandhu," in L. Jones (ed.), *Encyclopedia of Religion*, 2nd edn., 9525–8, Detroit: Macmillan.

Ñāṇamoli, B. (trans.) (1991) *The Path of Purification (Visuddhimagga)* (reprint 1956), Kandy, Sri Lanka: Buddhist Publication Society.

Ñāṇamoli, B. (1992) *The Life of the Buddha: According to the Pali Canon*, 3rd edn., Kandy, Sri Lanka: Buddhist Publication Society.

Ñāṇamoli, B. and Bodhi, B. (trans.) (1995) *The Middle Length Discourses of the Buddha: A New Translation of the Majjhima Nikāya*, Boston, MA: Wisdom Publications.

Nattier, J. (2000) "The Realm of Akṣobhya: A Missing Piece in the History of Pure Land Buddhism," *Journal of the International Association of Buddhist Studies* 23: 71–102.

Nattier, J. (2003) *A Few Good Men: The Bodhisattva Path according to* The Inquiry of Ugra (Ugraparipṛcchā), Honolulu, HI: University of Hawai'i Press.

Obeyesekere, G. (1972) "Religious Symbolism and Political Change in Ceylon," in B.L. Smith (ed.) *The Two Wheels of Dhamma; Essays on the Theravada Tradition in India and Ceylon*, 58–78, Chambersburg, PA: American Academy of Religion.

Oldenberg, H. (ed.) (1997) *The Vinaya Piṭakaṃ*, vol. I, Oxford: Pali Text Society.

Olivelle, P. (1992) *Saṃnyāsa Upaniṣads: Hindu Scripture on Asceticism and Renunciation*, New York: Oxford University Press.

Olivelle, P. (trans.) (1996) *Upaniṣads*, Oxford: Oxford University Press.

Olivelle, P. (trans.) (2008) *Life of the Buddha by Aśvaghoṣa*, New York: New York University Press and JJC Foundation.

Olschak, B.C. (1979) *Ancient Bhutan: A Study on Early Buddhism in the Himālayas*, Zürich: Swiss Foundation for Alpine Research.

Osto, D. (2009) "The Supreme Array Scripture: A New Interpretation of the Title '*Gaṇḍavyūha-sūtra*'." *Journal of Indian Philosophy*, 37: 273–90.

Panabokke, G. (1993) *History of the Buddhist Saṅgha in India and Sri Lanka*, Colombo, Sri Lanka: Postgraduate Institute of Pali and Buddhist Studies.

Paranavitana, S. (1960) "Civilisation of the Polonnaru Period (Continued): Religion, Literature and Art," in H.C. Ray (ed.) *University of Ceylon History of Ceylon*, Vol. I, Part II, 563–612, Colombo, Sri Lanka: Ceylon University Press.

Paranavitana, S. (1970) *Inscriptions of Ceylon, Volume I: Early Brāhmī Inscriptions*, Colombo, Ceylon: Department of Archaeology.

Paul, D.Y. (1985) *Women in Buddhism: Images of the Feminine in the Mahāyāna Tradition*, 2nd edn., Berkeley, CA: University of California Press.

Pereira, J. and Tiso, F. (1987) "The Life of Vasubandhu according to Recent Research," *East and West* 37: 451–4.

Piyadassi, T. (1974) *The Buddha's Ancient Path*, Kandy, Sri Lanka: Buddhist Publication Society.

Pollock, S. (2006) *The Language of the Gods in the World of Men: Sanskrit, Culture, and Power in Premodern India*, Berkeley, CA: University of California Press.

Potter, K.H. (1996) "A Few Early Abhidharma Categories," in K.H. Potter (ed.) *Encyclopedia of Indian Philosophies, Volume VII: Abhidharma Buddhism to 150 A.D.*, 121–33, Delhi: Motilal Banarsidass.

Potter, K.H. (ed.) (1999) *Encyclopedia of Indian Philosophies, Volume VIII: Buddhist Philosophy from 100 to 350 A.D.*, Delhi: Motilal Banarsidass.

Poussin, L.L.V. (1988) *Abhidharmakośabhāṣyam of Vasubandhu*, (trans. L.M. Pruden), Berkeley, CA: Asian Humanities Press.

Prebish, C.S. (1974) "A Review of Scholarship on the Buddhist Councils," *Journal of Asian Studies* 33: 239–54.

Prebish, C.S. (1975) *Buddhist Monastic Discipline: The Sanskrit Prātimokṣa Sūtras of the Mahāsāṃghika and Mūlasarvāstivādins*, University Park, PA: Pennsylvania State University Press.

Priestley, L.C.D.C. (1999) *Pudgalavāda Buddhism: The Reality of the Indeterminate Self*, Toronto: University of Toronto, Centre for South Asian Studies.

Queen, C.S. (1996) "Dr. Ambedkar and the Hermeneutics of Buddhist Liberation," in C.S. Queen and S.B. King (eds.) *Engaged Buddhism: Buddhist Liberation Movements in Asia*, 45–71, Albany, NJ: State University of New York Press.

Quintanilla, S.R. (2007) *History of Early Stone Sculpture at Mathura, ca. 150* BCE *– 100* CE, Leiden: Brill.

Rāhula, W. (1974) *The Heritage of the Bhikkhu: a Short History of the Bhikkhu in Educational, Cultural, Social, and Political Life*, (trans. K.P.G. Wijayasurendra), New York: Grove Press.

Rāhula, W. (1993) *History of Buddhism in Ceylon: The Anuradhapura Period, 3rd Century BC – 10th Century AC*, reprint (1956), Dehiwala, Sri Lanka: Buddhist Cultural Centre.

Ram, R. (1978) *A History of Buddhism in Nepal: A.D. 704–1396*, Delhi: Motilal Banarsidass.

Ray, R.A. (1994) *Buddhist Saints in India: A Study in Buddhist Values and Orientations*, New York: Oxford University Press.

Reynolds, F. and Hallisey, C. (2005) "Buddha," in L. Jones (ed.) *Encyclopedia of Religion*, Vol. 2, 1059–71, 2nd edn., Detroit: Macmillan.

Robinson, R., Johnson, W., and Thanissaro, B. (2005) *The Buddhist Religion: A Historical Introduction,* 5th edn., Belmont, CA: Wadsworth/Thomson Learning.

Ruegg, D. S. (1981) *The Literature of the Madhyamaka School of Philosophy in India*, Wiesbaden, Germany: Otto Harrassowitz.

Said, E.W. (1979) *Orientalism*, New York: Vintage Books.

Salgado, N. (2000) "Unity and Diversity Among Buddhist Nuns in Sri Lanka," in K.L. Tsomo (ed.) *Innovative Buddhist Women: Swimming Against the Stream,* 30–41, Richmond, UK: Curzon.

Salomon, R. (1999) *Ancient Buddhist Scrolls from Gandhāra: The British Library Kharoṣṭhī Fragments*, Seattle, WA: University of Washington Press.

Salomon, R. (2006) "Recent Discoveries of Early Buddhist Manuscripts: And Their Implications for the History of Buddhist Texts and Canons," in P. Olivelle (ed.)

Between the Empires: Society in India 300 BCE *to 400* CE, 349–82, New York: Oxford University Press.
Scharfe, H. (2002) *Education in Ancient India*, Leiden: Brill.
Schober, J. (1997) "Trajectories in Buddhist Sacred Biography," in J. Schober (ed.) *Sacred Biography in the Buddhist Traditions of South and Southeast Asia*, 1–15, Honolulu, HI: University of Hawai'i Press.
Schopen, G. (1997) *Bones, Stones, and Buddhist Monks: Collected Papers on the Archaeology, Epigraphy, and Texts of Monastic Buddhism in India*, Honolulu, HI: University of Hawai'i Press.
Schopen, G. (2004a) *Buddhist Monks and Business Matters: Still More Papers on Monastic Buddhism in India*, Honolulu, HI: University of Hawai'i Press.
Schopen, G. (2004b) "Vinaya," in R.E. Buswell, Jr. (ed.) *Encyclopedia of Buddhism*, 885–9, New York: Macmillan.
Schopen, G. (2005) *Figments and Fragments of Mahāyāna Buddhism in India: More Collected Papers*, Honolulu, HI: University of Hawai'i Press.
Seneviratne, H.L. (1999) *The Work of Kings: The New Buddhism in Sri Lanka*, Chicago, IL: University of Chicago Press.
Seth, V. (1992) *Study of Biographies of the Buddha: Based on Pāli and Sanskrit Sources*, New Delhi: Akay Book Corporation.
Skilling, P. (1993) "Theravādin Literature in Tibetan Translation," *Journal of the Pali Text Society* 19: 69–201.
Skilling, P. (2000) "Vasubandhu and the *Vyākhyāyukti* Literature," *Journal of the International Association of Buddhist Studies* 23: 297–350.
Skilton, A. (1994) *A Concise History of Buddhism*, Birmingham, UK: Windhorse Publications.
Skilton, A. (2004) "Sanskrit, Buddhist Literature in," in R.E. Buswell, Jr. (ed.) *Encyclopedia of Buddhism*, 745–9, New York: Macmillan.
Slusser, M.S. (1982) *Nepal Mandala: A Cultural Study of the Kathmandu Valley*, vol. 1, Princeton, NJ: Princeton University Press.
Smith, B.K. (1994) *Classifying the Universe: The Ancient Indian* Varṇa *System and the Origins of Caste*. New York: Oxford University Press.
Snellgrove, D.L. (1959) *The Hevajra Tantra: A Critical Study*, part I, London: Oxford University Press.
Snellgrove, D.L. (1987) *Indo-Tibetan Buddhism: Indian Buddhists & Their Tibetan Successors*, vol. I, Boston, MA: Shambhala.
Soma, G. (2002) *Dēśaya Surakina Ran Asipata*, Colombo, Sri Lanka: Dayawansa Jayakody.
Sorata, W. (ed.) (1950) *Daḷadā Sirita*, Colombo, Sri Lanka: M.D. Gunasena.
Sorata, W. (ed.) (1966) *Amṛtāvaha naṁ vū Butsaraṇa*, Galkisse, Sri Lanka: Abhaya Prakāśayō.
Sponberg, A. (1992) "Attitudes toward Women and the Feminine in Early Buddhism," in J.I. Cabezón (ed.) *Buddhism, Sexuality, and Gender*, 3–36, Albany, NY: State University of New York Press.
Steinkellner, E. (1994) "Buddhist Logic: The Search for Certainty," in T. Yoshinori (ed.) *Buddhist Spirituality: Indian, Southeast Asian, Tibetan, and Early Chinese*, 213–17, New York: Crossroad.

Steinkellner, E. (2005) "Dharmakīrti," in L. Jones (ed.) *Encyclopedia of Religion*, 2nd edn., 2336–7, Detroit: Macmillan.

Strathern, A. (2007) *Kingship and Conversion in Sixteenth-Century Sri Lanka: Portuguese Imperialism in a Buddhist Land*, Cambridge: Cambridge University Press.

Thapar, R. (2002) *Early India: From the Origins to AD 1300*, Berkeley, CA: University of California Press.

Tillemans, T.J.F. (1999) *Scripture, Logic, Language: Essays on Dharmakīrti and his Tibetan Successors*, Boston, MA: Wisdom Publications.

Trainor, K. (1997) *Relics, Ritual and Representation in Buddhism: Rematerializing the Sri Lankan Theravāda Tradition*, Cambridge: Cambridge University Press.

Tuladhar-Douglas, W. (2006) *Remaking Buddhism for Medieval Nepal: The Fifteenth-Century Reformation of Newar Buddhism*, London: Routledge.

Wallace, V.A. (2001) *The Inner Kālacakratantra: A Buddhist Tantra View of the Individual*, New York: Oxford University Press.

Wallace, V.A. (2005) "A Generation of Power Through Ritual Protection and Transformation of Identity in Indian Tantric Buddhism," *Journal of Ritual Studies* 19: 115–28.

Wallis, G. (2001) "The Buddha's Remains: *Mantra* in the *Mañjuśrīmūlakalpa*," *Journal of the International Association of Buddhist Studies* 24: 89–125.

Walser, J. (2005) *Nāgārjuna in Context: Mahāyāna Buddhism and Early Indian Culture*, New York: Columbia University Press.

Walshe, M. (trans.) (1995) *The Long Discourses of the Buddha: A Translation of the Dīgha Nikāya*, Boston, MA: Wisdom Publications.

Warder, A.K. (1956) "On the Relationships between Early Buddhism and Other Contemporary Systems," *Bulletin of the School of Oriental and African Studies, University of London*, 18: 43–63.

Warder, A.K. (1991) *Indian Buddhism*, 2nd revised edn., Delhi: Motilal Banarsidass.

Wayman, A. (1977) *Yoga of the Guhyasamājatantra: The Arcane Lore of Forty Verses, A Buddhist Tantra Commentary*, Delhi: Motilal Banarsidass.

Wayman, A. (1997) *Untying the Knots in Buddhism: Selected Essays*, Delhi: Motilal Banarsidass.

White, D.G. (1996) *The Alchemical Body: Siddha Traditions in Medieval India*, Chicago, IL: University of Chicago Press.

White, D.G. (2003) *Kiss of the Yoginī: "Tantric Sex" in its South Asian Contexts*, Chicago, IL: University of Chicago Press.

Wijayaratna, M. (1990) *Buddhist Monastic Life: According to the Texts of the Theravāda Tradition*; (trans. C. Grangier and S. Collins), Cambridge: Cambridge University Press.

Willeman, C., Dessein, B. and Cox, C. (1998) *Sarvāstivāda Buddhist Scholasticism*, Leiden: Brill.

Williams, P. (1989) *Mahāyāna Buddhism: The Doctrinal Foundations*, London: Routledge.

Williams, P. with Tribe, A. (2000) *Buddhist Thought: A Complete Introduction to the Indian Tradition*, London: Routledge.

Wilson, L. (1996) *Charming Cadavers: Horrific Figurations of the Feminine in Indian Buddhist Hagiographic Literature*, Chicago, IL: University of Chicago Press.

Xing, G (2005) *The Concept of the Buddha: Its Evolution from Early Buddhism to the* Trikāya *Theory*, London: Routledge.

Index